183- pious evangelicals [Her] had decreased religionists in rush for wealth in CA

Yale Historical Publications

Shasta City

0   25   50 miles
0 20 40 60 80 kilometers

NEVADA

CALIFORNIA

Pacific
Ocean

Sacramento R.

Rich Bar

Feather R.

SIERRA

Downieville

CENTRAL

Rough
and Ready

Nevada City

Marysville

Yuba

Grass
Valley

American R.

N. Fork American R.

Rubicon R.

NEVADA

Lake
Tahoe

MINES

CENTRAL

Coloma
(Sutter's Mill)

S. Fork American R.

Placerville

Healdsburg

Sacramento

Consumnes R.

Petaluma

Mokelumne R.

Mokelumne Hill

SOUTHERN

Berkeley

Stockton

Columbia

Contra Costa

Sonora

Tuolumne

San Francisco

Oakland

VALLEY

Stanislaus R.

Alvarado

Tuolumne R.

San Jose

Merced R.

MINES

Santa Cruz

San Joaquin R.

Patricia H. Neumann

California's Mining Frontier, 1848–1869

Religion and Society in Frontier California

Laurie F. Maffly-Kipp

Yale University Press   New Haven & London

Published under the direction of the Department of History of Yale University with assistance from the income of the Frederick John Kingsbury Memorial Fund.

Set in Cheltenham type by Marathon Typography Services, Durham, North Carolina. Printed in the United States of America by Edwards Brothers, Inc., Ann Arbor, Michigan.

Library of Congress Cataloging-in-Publication Data

Maffly-Kipp, Laurie F., 1960–
   Religion and society in frontier California / Laurie F. Maffly-Kipp.
) p.   cm. — (Yale historical publications)
   Includes bibliographical references and index.
   ISBN 0-300-05377-0 (alk. paper)
   1. California—Church history.   2. California—Religion.
   3. California—History—1850–1950.   I. Title.   II. Series:
Yale historical publications (Unnumbered)
BR555.C2M34   1994
277.94'081—dc20   93-24808
                                            CIP

A catalogue record for this book is available from the British Library.

The paper in this book meets the guidelines for permanence and durability of the Committee on Production Guidelines for Book Longevity of the Council on Library Resources.

10   9   8   7   6   5   4   3   2   1

To Peter and Wesley,
and to the memory of my brother,
Robert Leroy Maffly

Contents

Acknowledgments   ix

Introduction   1

1   Republican Virtues and Western Dreams   13

2   A Gilded Opportunity   38

3   Taming the Physical Landscape   63

4   Mapping the Moral Landscape   86

5   The Moral World of the California Miner   110

6   The "Wondrous Efficacy" of Womanhood   148

7   A Marketplace of Morals   181

Abbreviations   187

Notes   189

Select Bibliography   219

Index   235

Acknowledgments

Like many westerners, I became interested in the history of my native region only after leaving it. And like some migrants, I now find myself in the position of interpreting western history and culture for those in other places, as well as arguing for their relevance to other aspects of American history. In telling this story, I wish to thank the many people who already knew how important this topic was without being told (or trusted that I would make it clear) and who generously assisted my work at every stage.

Many friends, colleagues, and organizations shared in the creation of this book. Financial support was provided by the John F. Enders Fellowship Fund at Yale University; the Association of American Colleges; the Copeland Fellowship Program and the religion department of Amherst College; the Institute for the Study of American Evangelicals; and Junior Faculty Development and University Research Council Grants from the University of North Carolina at Chapel Hill. The religious studies department of the University of North Carolina at Chapel Hill contributed many of the nuts and bolts of research: paper, hard disks, software, and moral support.

Librarians in many places also helped this project at crucial moments by locating important primary materials. Special thanks go to Oscar Burdick, the inimitable archivist at the Graduate Theological Union in Berkeley, and to George Miles at the Beinecke Rare Book and Manuscript Library at Yale. Librarians at the Pacific School of Religion, the Bancroft Library, San Francisco Theological Seminary, the Presbyterian Historical Society, Yale Divinity School, and the Huntington Library also proved to be gracious and knowledgeable about rare sources.

I am especially grateful for the mentors and teachers who have helped to guide my thinking. David Brion Davis, a marvelous adviser, consistently pushed me past easy conclusions to examine four or five sides of every question. Jon Butler, Howard Lamar, and Harry Stout also encouraged me to look

ix

beyond New England ministers and to expand the limits of what is normally considered American religious history. David Wills, a longtime friend and teacher whose probing mind misses absolutely nothing, contributed his own special blend of incisive criticism and wholehearted support.

Many other colleagues and interested friends read or discussed portions of the project as it slowly took shape, including Tony Fels, Gil Greggs, Yvette Huginnie, Judith Hunter, Susan Johnson, Margaret Kellow, Regina Kunzel, Alec Solomita, and Mark Valeri. A small but energetic number read and commented on the entire manuscript: to Bart Ehrman, Peter Kaufman, Malcolm Rohrbough, and Grant Wacker, and the students in my graduate seminar in the fall of 1992, I give special thanks. Jennifer Wojcikowski provided research assistance for the preparation of the manuscript, and Patricia Neumann offered her cartographic expertise and artistry for the creation of the map. I am also grateful for the support of Chuck Grench and Lorraine Alexson at Yale University Press.

Finally, to those I come home to, I owe more than I can name. I give thanks to my parents for placing a very high value on education and for knowing that this is a real job. Wesley Robert, an energetic little boy whose birth intersected with this project midstream, surprised me with gifts of joy and humor and thereby kept this "second child" in its place. This book is dedicated to him and to my husband, Peter, who has cooked, cleaned, and changed addresses and jobs and diapers, believing all along that this project was, like everything else, a shared endeavor.

Introduction

A "forty-niner" returning to California ten or twenty years after the gold rush would have found little that looked familiar. Bayard Taylor did just that. A world traveler who wrote extensively about his journeys, Taylor revisited the state "ten years and ten days" after first landing there in August 1849. He expected to find San Francisco as he had left it: "a large encampment of tents and canvas houses," a "bleak and barren" series of sand-hills, home to some five thousand restless, striving inhabitants. Instead, in August 1859, he gazed upon a bewildering array of church spires, "fantastic" engine houses, and factories. A series of devastating fires had erased most evidence of earlier years: the wooden shacks and cloth enclosures that barely separated men from the elements had been replaced by brick and stone structures. What must have seemed oddest to Taylor was that parts of San Francisco Bay had been filled in to create more room for the city— filled simply by burying the abandoned ships that had brought argonauts seeking their fortunes. Instead of the familiar squalor, Taylor saw "well-built streets . . . completely covering the former anchorage for smaller vessels." He was stunned by the transformation that had taken place in a relatively brief span of time. "Without the evidence of my own experience," he remarked, "I should have found it impossible to believe that I looked upon the product of ten years."[1]

Taylor could do little but muse on the passing of this earlier era, a transitory period that soon gave way to permanency, to utility, to solidity. In this respect, he resembled other observers of his day. Josiah Royce, reared in the mining town of Grass Valley, breathed a sigh of relief at the moral progress that followed the apparent chaos of the 1850s; San Francisco's growth as an urban center convinced him that this was where "the great battle was to be fought and the victory won for the cause of lasting progress in California."[2]

Historians have since followed suit, covering over the vessels of adventurers with their own interpretations of the gold rush of 1849 as a passing

1

moment on the way toward a less ethically ambiguous age. From the outset, the rush to El Dorado evoked a search for meaning from both participants and observers. For religious leaders of all persuasions, it connoted something negative; and for middle-class Anglo-Protestants and their scholarly descendants in particular, it represented the opposite of the social order, clear moral boundaries, and the maintenance of tradition that evangelical religion prized. Gold rush California has consequently been depicted as a society without religion—a "prehistory," before communal stability paved the way for familiar religious patterns.

Yet, ironically, the reputed immorality of the California gold rush rendered it one of the most morally significant events in nineteenth-century American life. Clerical participants and observers speculated endlessly about its deleterious effects. One minister quipped unhappily that the California settler "left his religion on the plains." The Reverend Daniel Woods, an immigrant miner-turned-preacher, invoked a supernatural explanation: "As each one steps his foot on shore, he seems to have entered a magic circle, in which he is under the influence of new impulses." Horace Bushnell, a celebrated New England theologian who visited the state in the mid-1850s, was captivated by California's wealth and beauty, but winced at its spiritual desolation. For Bushnell and others like him, California in the 1850s represented both the ultimate hope and the greatest tragedy of human endeavor, an American Eden scarred by the self-inflicted wounds of mortal weakness. San Francisco, the urban center of the young state, came under particular scrutiny as an "instant city," an immoral metropolis built on the fast fortunes of gold seekers, gamblers, land speculators, and railroad magnates. It was a place destined, as another New England clergyman put it, to become "the great hell of the continent."[3]

The energy with which clerical leaders attacked the chaotic effects of the gold rush suggests that the event had struck a deep spiritual nerve. Yet, even though one might have expected such alarmist rhetoric from the Protestant clergy, who were in the business of alerting citizens to their ethical obligations, echoes of the same concern resounded elsewhere. In less histrionic fashion, the influx into El Dorado also evoked a search for meaning and moral order from the most ordinary participants. Lorena L. Hays, an emigrant from Pike County, Illinois, was one of many men and women in California who commented extensively on the moral character of society. People were "reckless and wild" in their striving for gold, she noted in her diary, yet money seemed to be used "prodigally and lavishly on all occasions, some in the promotion of Christianity, and morality."[4] Others, less concerned about religious institutions, raised questions about the fate of a society that had been thrown together quickly by a common impulse to "get rich and get out."

In this book, I endeavor to tell at least three interconnecting stories. The first concerns the attempt by Protestant evangelicals to transplant their religious institutions, beliefs, and practices to California in the 1850s and 1860s. Domestic or "home" mission societies, collectively constituting one of the most broad-based and enduring of the evangelical benevolent enterprises to emerge from the ferment of the Second Great Awakening, were the primary vehicle of this western crusade. Founded locally in the early years of the century and organized nationally by the 1830s, these societies included northern Protestants from across the evangelical spectrum—Baptist, Methodist, Congregationalist-Presbyterian (united in benevolent enterprises under the Plan of Union of 1801), as well as denominational societies within the Episcopalian and Old School Presbyterian folds. Through the work of these societies, thousands of eastern evangelicals channeled funds and voluntary labor into the establishment of Christian communities on the western frontier. Initially, these societies were fueled by the revivals of the 1820s and 1830s, but their organizations outlived the fervor that spawned them. Indeed, the movement represented not merely a manifestation of evangelical zeal, but also its systematization. As Perry Miller has noted, the home mission movement was not simply one among many antebellum reform movements; it was a mechanism for the institutionalization of revivalism and a vehicle for the transmission of evangelical culture well into the nineteenth century and beyond.[5]

Although home mission societies were established throughout the western states, those in California offer a particularly important lens through which to examine their efforts in the American West. By the 1840s, California, poised on the Pacific and facing the untapped markets of East Asia, served as the linchpin for the continuing Protestant dream of the westward progress of Christian civilization. The western territories were considered both promising and fearful, vast expanses where the millennial destiny of the republic would be decided. The economic and social dislocations surrounding the gold rush and the early growth of the state added to California's reputation as a moral wilderness that required a Protestant errand.

As missionaries moved westward, they took with them eastern perceptions of time, space, community, and providential progress. Just as Protestants had planted the seeds of evangelical piety in the agricultural frontiers of Iowa and Minnesota, so they expected to revitalize the forty-niners amassing on the West Coast. The strange new world that missionaries found in California, however, eluded many of their strategies of sacralization. They frequently were confounded by the physical and spiritual disorder of a society with one overriding aim: to strike it rich. Surrounded by gambling parlors, saloons, brothels, and bear-wrestling contests—all of which uninterruptedly cele-

brated material consumption and pleasure—religious leaders despaired that
they would ever prompt Christian observance, much less true morality. Ministers reserved particular venom for the many evangelical church members
who, leaving their homes and families on the East Coast, seemed also to have
forgotten their obligations to God and their own souls. At the same time,
clergy encountered increasing resistance from their eastern-based mission
boards, which failed to comprehend the distinctive challenges of evangelizing El Dorado.

The second story involves the dramatic collision on the Pacific Coast of
some of the most cherished values of Euro-American antebellum culture, values that extended far beyond the missionary societies. An optimistic and
wholehearted commitment to progress, an abiding concern with individual
self-discipline and moral character, and a dedication to community and the
gendered division of labor that made society possible all typified the outlook
of Protestant Americans on the eve of the gold rush. Yet so did a popular thirst
for wealth fostered by a growing ideological commitment to the spirit of free
enterprise. Both of these sets of values, ironically, were embodied in the rush
of prospectors and missionaries to northern California: each group was in
search of the dream that promised, in turn, economic or spiritual salvation.
The resulting clash of moral purposes, the suddenly irreconcilable claims of
wealth and Christian piety, struck at the heart of what many had assumed to
be a providential coincidence in the young republic.

The consequent social chaos, in turn, splintered other cherished values.
Prompting the largest emigration in United States history up to that time, the
lure of El Dorado separated families, tore communities apart, caused enormous losses of life owing to diseases and accidents, and witnessed family
savings augmented (though more often diminished) in a short period. Many
of these features, of course, characterized frontier expansion throughout the
nineteenth century. The timing and scale of the migration to El Dorado, however, eclipsed the steadier settlement of other frontiers, as some 350,000 aspi-
rants from around the globe arrived to try their luck in the gold fields, "make
their piles," and head home. Morality seemed to fall by the wayside as familiar forms of society and behavior were left behind.

Despite the fears of their ministers, Euro-American immigrants to the
region did display patterns of religiosity—but not necessarily the piety desired
by the clergy. Popular religious beliefs and practices took many different
forms, but they were most often linked to a moral interpretation of the mining
economy itself as a realm in which luck and chance figured prominently. In
this setting, the Protestant-inspired ideals of ascetic self-discipline held out
no sure promise of reward. Even those immigrants who desired the discipline

and order extended by evangelical Protestantism had difficulty accommodating its comforts to a world with few families, homes, or practical rewards for the life-style offered by ministers. A dizzying array of alternative religious conceptions competed with evangelicalism in this marketplace of morals. Spiritual persuasions from Universalism to Mormonism to Buddhism flourished among the diverse population of the state, further complicating the ability of ministers to establish a Protestant sway, either on the landscape or in the hearts and minds of settlers.

For all Euro-American Protestants, religious questions invariably were connected to gender issues, and specifically, to the religious functions of women in society. Therefore, the disproportionate number of men in the state—in mining camps often as high as 92 percent of the population—greatly affected the piety of settlers. Ministers compensated for the dearth of women by reminding men constantly of their obligations to females at home, by promoting the institution of marriage, and by recreating a domestic environment in their own homes for their parishioners to share. Yet in so emphasizing the importance of women and home to a socially stable community, ministers ironically discouraged men from settling; instead, men merely longed all the more for a return to familiar surroundings and religious patterns. At the same time, women encountered their own problems in trying to adjust to an overwhelmingly male environment. Some found an unusually large and varied number of opportunities. Others found only hard work and social condemnation. The few evangelical women in California, hailed by men as saints and saviors, found their traditional religious roles impossible to fulfill without the help of family networks and domestic help—those very features of eastern life that made possible the idealization of "true womanhood."

Finally, this is also a story of the creation of a new type of society in the American West that exhibited new patterns of religious adherence. Mining culture, with its transiency, social mobility, and commitment to speculative ventures, did not provide a welcoming climate for the transplantation of evangelical culture. The "Protestantization" of California was, by nearly any measure, a dismal failure. As can be seen in table 1, in 1860 California had not blossomed into a fully christianized community, despite the efforts of evangelical ministers. In comparison with New York and Ohio, two eastern states with thriving Protestant institutional infrastructures, California still resembled a spiritual wasteland: New York had one church for every 734 of its citizens, and Ohio boasted a national high of one for every 449. California, in contrast, had one church for every 1,297 people. Even if only the Euro-American population in the state (the focal concern of the home missionaries) were counted, there was no more than one church for every 1,103 inhabitants. Reli-

6   **Introduction**

Table 1   Comparison of Number of Churches and Ministers by State in 1860

Number of Churches	New York	Ohio	Iowa	California
Baptist	765	489	112	22
Congregational	231	142	71	10
Methodist	1,683	2,341	344	118
Presbyterian	715	631	111	22
Roman Catholic	360	222	70	86
Total churches	5,287	5,210	949	293
Total ministers	5,235	2,927	1,208	348
Total population	3.8 mil	2.3 mil.	674,913	379,994

gious leaders in Iowa, another frontier region that was settled and evangelized at roughly the same time as California, had managed to construct a church for every 711 settlers. Something quite distinctive had taken place on the Pacific Coast, and the state remained distinctive thereafter. By 1906, Protestants constituted only 14 percent of the California population.[6]

Given the arbitrary ways historians traditionally have carved out their academic niches, this study is necessarily cross-disciplinary. American religious historians have shown little interest in the West as an area of study other than to reflect upon its more bizarre elements. Aside from William Warren Sweet's groundbreaking work on frontier religion and Louis B. Wright's study of the development of eastern cultural forms in the West, the scope of religious belief and activity in the western states has only recently come to light.[7] One reason for the dearth of scholarship is that, following Sweet and Wright, scholars have seen eastern patterns of religiosity as normative for religious developments in other regions. Rather than seeing the West as a distinctive area contributing unique but related pieces to a broader picture of American religion, many scholars have continued to believe the reports of missionaries and observers that pioneers were irreligious (or worse) because they did not behave in familiar ways. In this respect, scholarly ghettoization has been a self-fulfilling prophecy: religion in the West has remained the well-kept secret of local archivists and regional and denominational historians.[8] California alone has fared slightly better, although scholars have been disproportionately fascinated by the state's uniqueness. In examining its religious exceptionalism, they have found precisely what they were looking for—difference.[9]

Important questions remain unanswered by the excellent studies that are available. How did the development of Protestantism in California fit into the larger currents of American religious history? How does its study reshape our understanding of American religion as a whole? It is too easily forgotten that the majority of the Americans who immigrated to California in the 1850s were natives of regions east of the Mississippi (predominantly the Northeast and the Midwest) and were not pioneers by birth. Thus, most had been reared, at least to some extent, on eastern notions of Protestant piety and culture. Even many of the people migrating from western Pennsylvania, Ohio, Indiana, and Illinois were but one generation removed from the Northeast; some had been brought West by their parents as small children. Studying the responses of evangelical immigrants to the Pacific Coast and the fate of eastern models of religiosity there can reveal as much about eastern religious beliefs as it does about western society. Far from providing a story of regional culture, the study of evangelicalism in California forms part of the larger history of American ideals and aspirations.

I am indebted to the work of a generation of scholars who have asked new and provocative questions about the history of the American frontier. The economic, political, and social development of western settlements, as well as the interactions of men and women, Euro-Americans, American Indians, Hispanics, Asian-Americans, African-Americans, and other ethnic groups in the West, have been significant areas of recent scholarly attention. The study of religion, however, has lagged behind. At least one reason for this delay is that, in general, the religious history of the West is still dependent on a static model of culture: in discussing religious beliefs, practices, and institutions, scholars often use agricultural metaphors of "transplantation," of "division," and of "growth," as if religion were a seed that the hardy pioneer packed away in his saddlebag, pulled out on the frontier, replanted in rocky soil, and watched for signs of growth. According to this notion, religious success is typically measured by how well the seedling develops, and inquiry centers around a narrow range of concerns: Did westerners reject traditional religious patterns? or did they recreate them?

The transmission of eastern cultural patterns to western settlements involved a far more complicated process. The "seed" of eastern culture, in this case evangelical religion, was itself an internally conflicting set of ideas and practices, loosely held together by patriotic zeal, revivalist enthusiasm, and governmental boosterism. Designed to grow in a specific climate, it took on a very different shape when planted on the nation's first gold mining frontier, despite the best efforts of ministers and other religious leaders to form it in the image of its eastern counterpart. The history of Protestant developments in the West, therefore, is necessarily the story of a dialectic between aspirations (differing even between members of the religious community) and social circumstances, as they worked constantly to reshape one another. Just as religious ideology defined the social world of California evangelicals by providing them with the categories by which to understand their new experiences, so the exigencies of their material circumstances shaped and restructured their worldviews.

As abstract as this process may sound, a historical understanding of its practice requires simply that a different set of questions be asked. My analysis, in this respect, is also informed by scholarship in the anthropology and sociology of religion, which allows for a more critical approach to the study of religious beliefs, practices, and cultures than those methods traditionally employed by historians. Especially useful has been the notion that religion itself is not simply a matter of intellectual assertions or institutional expressions, but instead is concerned with one's basic orientation to the world, comprising concepts of time, space, causality, and ultimate purpose.[10] This understanding is most useful for assessing the moral worlds of lay immigrants to California, persons who were not particularly committed to the task of articulating and promoting a normative set of religious practices. Rather than asking, then, whether these people believed and acted as they were instructed by evangelical missionaries, it is far more fruitful to analyze what forms, if any, their religious faith took, and why. In turn, we can assess the lay understanding of religion in light of the missionary enterprise and see how the two interacted.

Participants in the California gold rush were an extremely self-conscious group of men and women. They knew that this movement was historically unique, and consequently many of them kept marvelous records of their experiences to pass along to their children and grandchildren. The proliferation of written sources is both a dream and a nightmare for the historian, who marvels at the many vivid accounts yet shrinks at their sheer number. I have necessarily been selective in my own use of sources. This story is therefore only one among the many worth telling about gold rush cultures. Much work remains in order to uncover the narratives of African-Americans, Asian-Americans, and Latin Americans within this highly diverse society.

My focus is primarily on the ministers of the four largest northern denominations that were organizationally committed to the task of evangelism—of converting people to the Christian faith. Distinctive in their reliance on revivalism as a means of prompting a conversion experience and unmatched in their institutional zealousness in both domestic and foreign work, these groups blazed a trail across the American frontier. Southern missionaries also came to California, but never in the numbers of their northern brethren and without the same consciousness about the importance of spreading both Christian and republican values westward. By the 1850s, southern evangelicals had concentrated much of their attention on the domestic mission at home: the conversion and control of the slaves. My use of the term *missionary* is also fluid and inclusive. Since the majority of Baptist, Congregational, and Presbyterian ministers in California were commissioned officially by eastern societies, the designation is generally an appropriate one. Even those ministers who came West on their own, however, either considered themselves emissaries of eastern religious values or came into contact with agencies and boards sponsored by eastern benevolence. They were all, in a generic sense, missionaries; thus, unless otherwise noted, I have used the designation interchangeably with *minister*.

The Methodists present the greatest challenge to the usefulness of these categories. With respect to missionary activity, Methodists were demonstrably more successful than the missionaries of any other denomination. The reason is not hard to discern: the Methodist church itself was structured precisely for the purpose of evangelization; the entire organization was, in the truest sense, a missionary society. Since Methodists did not require a separate agency to conduct home missions, a "mission movement" did not function for them as it did for other denominations. Their ecclesiological distinctiveness, however, was outweighed by their intellectual and social commonalities with other missionaries. In their newspapers and sermons, Methodists discussed California and its significance in much the same way that Baptists or Presbyterians did. At times, to be sure, they concentrated more intensely on the internal drama of the sanctified life, but when they turned to social issues they tended to be at one with other evangelicals. Therefore, the narrative will point to moments when Methodist views seemed distinctive, but otherwise the Methodists are considered here alongside their evangelical brethren.

Yet these Protestant leaders can tell us only part of the story. Although they certainly were not the only Californians interested in questions of morality, they were the most literate and articulate, and they often were paid (although not much), organized, and educated to think in these terms. Thus, in this book I also attend to other renderings of western experience. There was never *one* moral experience of early California, even among Protestants. In voices that vividly illustrate the aggressive popularization of antebellum Christianity, ordinary people in California talked about spiritual issues in ways that often differed markedly from those of the missionaries.[11] I have attempted to tell both the story of the fate of a particular religious tradition in the state and suggest the wide variety of spiritual and cultural options available to Euro-American immigrants.

Trying to describe the gold rush as a single entity presents a host of difficulties. I have chosen to discuss the period between 1848 and 1869 as a continuous whole, pointing in passing to changes over time that affected religious patterns. Scholars better versed in the economic intricacies of mining have identified several subdivisions within this period, as certain kinds of technologies and organizations of labor replaced their predecessors. There is no doubt that these changes had enormous social and cultural consequences, which spelled dramatic alterations in patterns of work and leisure. Additionally, California society was much more settled in 1869 than it had been in 1849: there were more women and children, more homes, more churches, and more permanent settlements. Yet for ministers and for many lay settlers, these changes were quantitative, not qualitative. California remained a place apart, with spatial, temporal, and religious configurations that differed markedly from those of other regions. This distinctiveness shaped the spiritual and moral experiences of Californians, and thus I highlight this sense of difference at the risk of obscuring incremental changes.

Speaking of the California frontier as a whole also obscures the many different societies that flourished within the state's borders. As early as 1850, urban and cosmopolitan San Francisco was quite a different world from both the agricultural communities of the valleys and the mining camps in the foothills of the Sierra Nevada. Yet because the population was so mobile, it is next to impossible to identify certain individuals with specific environments. Most California residents, ministers included, had ample exposure to all of these forms of society, and they moved between them interchangeably. This cultural mobility and exposure to disparate societies are precisely what made frontier California exceptional. Moreover, the mining economy had tremendous effects throughout the state, even on those settlers who did not themselves extract minerals from the mother lode. Therefore, while it is important to be aware of the different social experiences encompassed by this region, I consider all its societies as a single entity.

Because the study of the American West is so politically charged, it is appropriate and important to explain one's word choices, inasmuch as they reveal a great deal about one's scholarly assumptions. The nomenclature used here for white, native-born Protestant Americans is employed with a consciousness as to its inadequacy. I have chosen to use the terms *Euro-American, Anglo-American,* and *Anglo-Protestant* fairly interchangeably. The reader will doubtless become aware that such terminology, in light of the cultural diversity of native-born settlers coming to California, is not a precise description of national heritage; instead, these phrases refer to those Americans who identified themselves with denominations of English background, that is, those descending either from Puritanism or Anglicanism; or, at times, depending on the context, they refer more broadly to native English speakers. Similarly, my references to *frontier* California signify the first two decades of rapid Euro-American settlement, the period that Kevin Starr has called "provincial" California, with a recognition that the history of the region stretches back considerably further than this designation suggests.

A full understanding of Euro-Protestantism on the California frontier begins in the East, with an analysis of the religious ideology that undergirded the movement westward. The first chapter of this study focuses on the motives behind the founding of home mission boards in the 1820s and traces the growth of a religious concern for the development of the American West. In chapter 2, I discuss eastern religious responses to the gold rush itself and the concern for acquisition, community, and moral character that it provoked. In chapters 3 and 4, I assess the missionary attempt to recreate evangelical culture in gold rush California, including efforts to sacralize both the physical landscape and the interior, moral terrain of Euro-American immigrants. In chapter 5, I shift to the religious worlds of California miners and suggest additional reasons for how and why the cause of evangelicalism failed at the popular level. Finally, in chapter 6, I discuss the significance of gender for a culture in which notions of piety and sanctity were inextricably intertwined with that of "evangelical womanhood," but which lacked a strong female presence.

Chapter 1

Republican Virtues
and Western Dreams

Facing west from California's shores,
Inquiring, tireless, seeking what is yet unfound,
I, a child, very old, over waves, towards the house of maternity,
the land of migrations, look afar,
Look off the shores of my Western Sea, the circle almost circled.
—Walt Whitman, "Facing West from California's Shores"

In 1841, the Reverend Steven Chapin of Maine addressed the American Baptist Home Missionary Society (ABHMS) at its annual meeting in Baltimore. His remarks concerned the significance of the United States in God's providential plan. The first proof he offered for the importance of America was its geographical position: strategically located across the Atlantic from Europe, it was far removed from the "centers of despotism"—ensuring its survival as a democratic republic. If this was not enough to sway his approving audience, Chapin offered a second proof in the character and extent of the national domain. Because no country could become powerful without room for expansion, America's bounty was surely a sign that God had a great work in store for the country. "Now why should God have assigned us a country so extensive, so fertile, and occupying the most favorable position for inter-communication with every other quarter of the globe," Chapin reasoned, "unless it be his design to make us eminently instrumental in accomplishing his purposes of mercy."[1] In Chapin's understanding, providential destiny and American geography were integrally related and mutually reinforcing. Although he did not foresee the mechanism God would use to achieve the great ends he envisioned, the vastness of the North American

13

continent and its location were sufficient proof of divine intention to convince him of the necessity for missionary work in western territories.

Chapin's vision was hardly idiosyncratic. Between 1796 and 1845, thousands of home mission societies, located primarily in the northeastern states, embraced the notion that the settlement of vast territories to the west played a crucial role in the divine plan of salvation. If properly educated in an evangelical faith and bolstered by American political institutions, communities in these newly developed regions would provide the ideal setting for the final stage of sacred history. The Reverend M. J. Hickock, a Presbyterian minister from Rochester, New York, echoed Chapin's sense of America's providential election: "Our country is a perfect anomaly in the history of this earth's settlement. Its discovery and position . . . mark it out as destined to accomplish a great and blessed work in the world."[2]

From the founding of local missionary societies in New York, Connecticut, and Massachusetts in the 1790s, the home mission movement grew exponentially after the turn of the century. The acquisition of new western territories quickly expanded both the geographical and conceptual scope of operations. In keeping with a growing nationalist sentiment after the War of 1812 and the desire of religious leaders to avoid a duplication of resources, evangelical laborers began to consolidate the work of the many local missionary agencies. In 1826, representatives of thirteen states and four denominations (with primary support from Presbyterians and Congregationalists) founded the American Home Missionary Society (AHMS); by 1833, the society sponsored over six hundred missionaries to the West.[3] The Baptists formed the ABHMS in 1832. Northern Methodists, Episcopalians, and eventually the Old School Presbyterians (after their break with the New School in 1837) also established home mission boards but preferred to work within a denominational context. Despite differences over polity, all of these groups saw themselves waging a common battle for the social and political stability of western communities, as well as for the souls of Euro-American settlers.[4]

During the first half of the nineteenth century the tactics and strategies of the home mission movement evolved as well. The Connecticut Missionary Society, founded in 1798, provided a model for subsequent evangelical labors. One of the earliest and most aggressive of the state missionary agencies to sponsor clerical tours of the West, the organization inaugurated its work by sending ministers on six- to eight-week tours of "New Connecticut," the Western Reserve (now Ohio), which belonged originally to the state. Publicized in the pages of the *Connecticut Evangelical Magazine,* these short-term laborers served the dual purpose of surveying prospects for settlement and assessing the spiritual needs of the population. As the frontier became increasingly inaccessible and further removed from eastern centers, agencies extended the length of the tours and eventually changed strategy by commissioning ministers to settle permanently in rural communities and preach the gospel, establish churches, and hold revivals.[5]

Initially an effort of a small group of fervent religious leaders, the movement caught fire during the revival seasons of the Second Great Awakening. Concentrating most of their efforts on recent immigrants to the canal towns and agricultural communities of western New York in the 1820s and 1830s and following on the heels of successful itinerants like Charles Grandison Finney, missionary societies established an effective strategy for evangelism all along the northern frontier. Local home mission groups, working in conjunction with their East Coast sponsors, initiated revivals that targeted "unchurched" Christians, people who by dint of circumstance or recent immigration were separated from a church community. Advocates believed that once the revival had converted (or more accurately, "restored") Christians to the faith, the reborn would be compelled by the grace of God to work for social and moral improvement in their towns. Individual salvation would necessarily lead to an interest in social reform, thereby ensuring the religious well-being of the entire community.[6] In this manner, popular religious zeal could be enlisted in the crusade for christianization. The success of such activities was demonstrated by the blossoming of scores of voluntary reform societies, ranging from women's rescue associations to anti-Masonic organizations. Home mission proponents, in turn, construed these developments as a sign of divine favor.

At the level of strategy, what held together this interdenominational coalition was the essentially pragmatic character of the home mission cause. By the 1830s, evangelical Congregationalists and Presbyterians downplayed doctrinal and theological distinctions and increasingly followed the standard set by Charles Finney's "New Measures," revivalist guidelines that underscored the role of human will and experience in shaping religious belief. These changes thereby brought the former Calvinists more closely into line with Methodist and Baptist techniques and allowed for religious events that were accessible to people from the widest possible variety of Protestant churches.[7]

But if an intentional blurring of ecclesiastical distinctions facilitated interdenominational unity in frontier communities, it was the rhetoric of sacred American destiny that catalyzed the crusade for domestic missions in the eastern states. Linking the Euro-American movement through space with an appeal to a common past and millennial future, and uniting geography with history, home mission strategists promised that the christianization of western territories would eventually free evangelicals altogether from the confinements of time and space. By the 1840s—the heydey of speculation about the inherent meaning of westward movement—this evangelical ideology was fully developed and functioning as a rhetorical strategy to attract financial support and counter both secular nationalistic and southern understandings of America's manifest destiny, the political rhetoric that attempted to justify the forceful acquisition of all continental territories. While the evangelical formulation was new in many particulars, it was also distinctly American. Not unlike the early Puritans, many nineteenth-century evangelicals located their hopes for human redemption in the promises of a region unsettled and largely unexplored by Euro-Americans. And like their religious forbears, these missionaries only later discovered some of the internal contradictions and problems inherent in their dreams of a promised land.

Some problems stemmed from the sheer emotional and psychological force of the evangelical rhetoric itself. Just as denominations once again competed for members after the enthusiasms of the communal revivals had abated, so the stirring calls to action sounded by home mission proponents inevitably gave way to the necessities of community building. Yet the mundane present was initially overshadowed by a rhetoric of past achievements and future glory. A close examination of the self-understanding of the crusade, its sense of history and purpose, and an analysis of its definition of Christian community reveal a sprawling and internally conflicting ideology held together by vague notions of American destiny. For all of its rhetorical virtues and purported pragmatism, the missionary worldview contained within itself the seeds of discord over the precise means of implementing the grand vision of providential destiny that was its guiding force.

Reflecting on the ethos of the early 1840s, a contributor to the *New Englander* in 1844 summed up the growing attention paid to the development of western territories: "'Westward the star of empire takes its way,' was the leading idea of the day and the one that more than any other thing gave direction to men's plans and enterprises."[8] A belief in continental destiny—the notion that the United States had a natural right to occupy and develop the North American continent from coast to coast—had been a key ingredient in an unfolding American nationalism well before Thomas Jefferson dispatched Meriwether Lewis and William Clark on the first scientific exploration of the Far West.[9] It was not until the 1840s, however, that the western territories fully captured the imaginations, and the concerns, of the American public.[10]

Scholarly analyses of the debates over westward movement in the 1840s characteristically have focused on the understanding of manifest destiny as a monolithic and coherent set of ideas.[11] Yet most northern evangelicals, as

Daniel Walker Howe has demonstrated, were guided by an ideology of westward movement that differed sharply from the policies espoused by Jackson and his Democratic successors. Evangelicals tended to align themselves with the political and social assumptions of the Whig party, with its emphasis on the organic unity of society, leadership by an educated elite, and communal duties rather than individual rights. By the 1840s evangelicals, shocked by the overt violence of the "trail of tears," openly rejected the policies of forced Indian removal and aggressive military expansionism favored by the Democrats.[12] Instead, they adopted a political style that stressed persuasion, education, and the civilizing process as keys to the construction of a moral society. Only by muting social conflict and giving conscious direction to the expansion of the nation, religious leaders insisted, could America escape the fate of classical republics—a precipitous decline into moral chaos.[13] As a contributor to the New York–based Baptist *Home Mission Record* put it, neglecting the growth of the country would cause future generations to "record the history of our nation's decline and fall, as we are forced to read the same sad memoirs of republican greatness, that once made the Roman name a praise in all the earth, and the land of Greece, the pride and song of all the world."[14]

Central to the evangelical goal of building an organic community was the idea of America's covenantal relation to God. Simply put, evangelicals may have seen all nations as equal under God, but some were more equal than others. America had been chosen by God to fill a special role in providential history. In his discourse before the ABHMS, Chapin stressed the special position held by America in God's soteriological scheme. Although he acknowledged that "the conversion of one nation to Christianity, independently considered, is as desirable as that of another of the same population," he argued that the results were far more significant in the case of America: "The wise and the good in other parts of Christendom . . . would turn their eyes to the American Church, in the belief that she is destined to be the chief instrument in bringing every anti-christian nation under the power of the cross."[15] Similarly, the editors of the AHMS-sponsored *Home Missionary* stressed America's role as a "savior nation" in the world, reasoning that just as the salvation of certain individuals—St. Paul or Martin Luther, for example—has had a greater impact on historical progress than other experiences of salvation, so it is with nations. America's conversion, because of its freedoms, religious unity, superior language ("which contains more that the nations of the earth need to know"), and enterprising citizens, would have greater import for the unfolding of world history.[16]

The dominant archetype for the evangelical understanding of the American covenant was the Puritan covenantal community. Like the foreign mission movement, home mission activities in the East were controlled primarily by New Englanders, particularly Massachusetts Congregationalists, who, as William Hutchison observes, "spoke and wrote as heirs of the Puritans."[17] The Reverend Samuel W. Fisher, speaking before the gathering assembled to commemorate the twentieth anniversary of the AHMS, called upon his audience to imagine the heroes of colonial New England: "Bradford, and Winslow, and Davenport, and Winthrop, and Cotton, and their glorious compeers, appealing to you to save this land—this brightest jewel in the coronal of nations—from flaming in the forehead of the prince of darkness."[18] Fisher and others understood their mission across the continent as the logical extension of the settlement at Massachusetts Bay. American history began not with the founding of the Republic but with the Reformation and the ensuing migration of Puritans to America. God had given to the New World the most "unconquerable spirits" of the Old World; the coincidence of the Reformation and American colonization was, as one observer pointed out, no coincidence at all: "This continent was hidden from the keen eye of civilized man for thousands of years, till those great events that mark a new era in human progress, had all taken place."[19]

Given their emphasis on the role of America in God's divine plan, and their corresponding nostalgia for an era in which community structure was perceived to be morally coherent, it is not surprising that the proponents of missions stressed the continuities between their goals in the West and the religious heritage of Puritanism. More was at stake than just the fate of remote settlements. They argued, along with Fisher, that stopping the progress of missionary activity would also destroy the accomplishments of the past two centuries. "Shall an experiment begun under an extraordinary concurrence of providential circumstances, which never existed before, and may never exist again, miserably fail? Fail it most assuredly will, unless that part of the country which is overshadowing all the rest, is pervaded by the spirit of the Gospel. The waves of an ungodly and most heterogeneous population will sweep away every landmark which the blood and toil and wisdom of ages has set up."[20] Frontier communities, by definition new settlements, could not themselves be blamed for falling away from the paths of righteousness; home mission advocates instead challenged easterners to support their efforts as a sign of spiritual fidelity. "Shall that which has cost many years of hard toil be thrown away?" asked B. B. Edwards of Andover, Massachusetts.[21] Evangelicals envisioned themselves extending the Puritan community across the continent, fighting the forces of infidelity and atheism that threatened to destroy the glorious destiny of America.

Not all mission advocates, it should be noted, gave such weight to the importance of the Puritan heritage. Such sentiments were most common among ministers in New England, a region with a sharp self-consciousness about its own history.[22] Congregational ministers, as well as others trained at centers of missionary activity such as Yale and Andover, emphasized the significance of the Puritan tradition to the exclusion of more recent American history. Other proponents of missions rendered history in somewhat different terms, giving more weight to the influence of the American political system and revolutionary heritage in the progress of providence. The "coincidence" of the founding of the Union with the opening of western territories was proof of divine favor, noted M. J. Hickock: "After the Revolution, and the firm establishment of our Republican government and free institutions, God opened to American enterprise the broad valley of the Mississippi, one of the richest and fairest regions on this globe."[23]

In his Thanksgiving sermon of 1855, the Reverend Charles Wadsworth, an Old School Presbyterian and an active promoter of home missions who later served in California, preached about "America's Mission in the World." Ecclesiastically removed from the intense proselytizing of his brethren to the north, Wadsworth nonetheless articulated many of the themes of American election and the duty to God's providential plan that evangelicals shared. He likened America to a "great spring lever, or wheel," a part of the divine historical machinery that would serve as an instrument of religious salvation in the world. As proof of its sacred status, Wadsworth compared the United States with the "antagonistic" condition of the European nations. Clearly, he concluded, ours is the only country with the necessary combination of "real liberty" and "true Christianity" to act as God's agent in history.[24]

Unlike Wadsworth's New England counterparts, who located their understanding of America's chosenness in its Puritan beginnings, the Philadelphian stressed the political genius of the Republic. For Wadsworth, the proof of America's special calling was to be found in its revolutionary heritage and the genius of the Constitution, as well as in the nation's subsequent political and social progress. This formulation led him into a circular argument for the obligations bestowed on America by virtue of its superiority: national progress is proof of a divine call, but this call also leads to further national progress. Ultimately, for Wadsworth as for New Englanders, God's sovereignty took causal priority over, and was indeed responsible for, the growth of America's stature in the world. Americans were indebted to God and were obligated by that relation, Wadsworth concluded, because "our own national prosperity and our own national existence" depended upon our carrying out the evangelization of the rest of the world.[25] Covenant, expressed as Puritan community or constitutional government, was still the controlling theme of missionary ideology. Evangelicals saw themselves as participants in a cosmic drama that preceded the founding of the United States and would continue until the millennium arrived.

As strategic rhetoric, the dual images of Puritan organic community and constitutional democracy worked side by side as evidence of the scope of divine history. As paradigms for community building that logically extended to settlements in the West, however, the two models were inherently contradictory. Although evangelicals modified and made more "democratic" the Puritan model of an established church—a hierarchical social order with God as the absolute sovereign and a loyalty to communal notions of order that subsumed individual rights—their authoritarian tendencies nonetheless undergirded their social theory. Conversely, the "revolutionary heritage" so praised by other home mission advocates stressed individual liberty, relative freedom of conscience in religious matters, and a democratic order that rejected concepts of hierarchy. Clearly, a community could not adhere, in practice, to both social ideals.[26]

How did evangelicals resolve the apparent conflict between these two models of community? As Harry Stout shows, these ideas, somewhat ironically, coexisted with little practical difficulty. In his analysis of the "rhetorical worlds" of the Federalist clergy, Stout points to two competing understandings of America in the early nineteenth century. Although the clergy shared a certain set of assumptions with the Founding Fathers that stemmed from a common classical education and were based on an elitist understanding of history and society, the Federalist perception of reality "at its most formative level" was shaped by an inherited Puritan world untarnished by the previous century. In Stout's estimation, this reality embraced the understanding of a good society as defined by the "peculiar" national covenant between God and God's sovereignly chosen people. According to this rhetorical strategy, Federalists preached sermons on national occasions that envisioned America as Puritan New England writ large. Although such a characterization contradicted the main outlines of the Constitution and a democratic government, Stout concludes that it continued to define reality for many Americans well into the nineteenth century.[27]

Similarly, home mission theorists, a generation removed from the Federalist clergy, only nominally acknowledged republican values and attributes as true models for community building. Suspicious of laws that restrained individual behavior instead of promoting public virtue, evangelicals held democratic values in an ambivalent tension with their primary commitment to the growth of an organic, covenantal Christian community. To the elitist heirs of this Federalist heritage, democracy was a necessary evil that had to be counterbalanced by the "saving power" of the Gospel.

Although they were somewhat less suspicious of unrestrained individualism, even Methodists and Baptists acknowledged that the forces of human sinfulness required the constraints of the Christian community. Despite their aversion to an established church, these denominations shared the distinctive evangelical emphasis on self-discipline.[28] Chapin pointedly suggested that one important reason for saving souls was the peculiar temptations resulting from the freedoms of the American political and economic systems. In a country where the "means of worldly enjoyment are abundant," where citizens enjoy equality of rights, where there are few distinctions of wealth and poverty, such freedoms can make for an "ambitious and worldly people." Chapin did not criticize these values overtly but suggested that they were always suspect: "They must exist among us in all their strength, for their annihilation would, in truth, be the annihilation of our whole political fabric."[29] Yet in the end, as another mission advocate asserted, only the cross of Christ could render these temptations harmless: "No lasting empire can be built upon wickedness. Self-interest will not hold people together. It is a solvent, not a cement. Jesus Christ is the rock around which these shifting sands must gather."[30]

Despite its special destiny, the American Republic was not, for evangelicals, the kingdom of God. Democracy could, in fact, obscure the primary moral objective of binding God's chosen community together. All the more reason, home mission proponents reasoned, for supporting Christian work in the West: to temper the dangers of democracy. The AHMS even suggested that if Americans would not submit willingly to the benevolent rule of evangelicals, sterner measures could be taken: "Something more is needed than a good constitution and equal laws," one spokesperson insisted. "Laws are but cobwebs, without public virtue. . . . There are but two great methods of governing men—by *moral motives* or by *physical force.* If our patriots will not sustain and spread the Gospel that provides the former, they must put the musket and the sword into the hand of the latter.[31]

The ambivalence of missionary social theory was also connected to more sweeping changes that were taking place in the ideology of Protestant social reform and in theological discourse at midcentury. The social theories of Puritanism and Republicanism were premised upon divergent conceptions of human sinfulness and the possibility of redemption. With regard to the settlement of the West, the pragmatic concerns that distinguished these ideologies were: left to their own devices and given a situation with few social constraints, how would Christians naturally behave? Was individual religious belief a strong enough force to keep society from disintegrating? From the standpoint of Puritan social theory, the human being, saved or not, was still inherently sinful. Original sin was a powerful force in shaping perceptions of a moral community: because of the inability of the individual *not* to sin, strong institutional and communal restraints were necessary to preserve social order. In keeping with this Calvinist understanding of human nature, Congregationalists and Presbyterians had traditionally supported the need not only to plant the seeds of faith in western communities, but also to institutionalize the educational systems and civic institutions that would make it possible for Christians to control their tendency to sin.[32]

Still, by the early nineteenth century, these traditional doctrines increasingly were being softened by the growing appeal of a more liberal and optimistic view of human nature. At Yale, Nathaniel William Taylor, the teacher of a generation of home missionaries, struggled to enlarge the scope of human responsibility by arguing that humans were not bound to sin but instead had the "power to the contrary," the ability to choose to act morally.[33] This changing theology also affected the evangelical understanding of social reform by rejecting the determinism of earlier benevolent causes and by unleashing the forces of "romantic perfectionism" that looked to the "liberated individual" for remedies to social problems. Social change, in this new ideology, became a moral crusade rather than a product of legislation; rather than reigning in human nature, as the Puritans had urged, reformers waged a perfectionist campaign that appealed to the rational capabilities of the individual conscience.[34] Still in flux, caught between a commitment to the communal covenant and quickly changing notions of human ability, the statements of home mission proponents demonstrated a deep-seated ambivalence about individual moral potential. The resulting theological vagueness allowed Congregationalists and Presbyterians to act in common cause with Methodists and Baptists in the movement, despite their many differences. Wary of the theocratic social model, the latter denominations nonetheless placed great emphasis on the role of the gathered Christian community in tempering individual weaknesses. As evangelical Congregationalists and Presbyterians, then, moved ever closer to functional Arminianism and a principled attachment to religious voluntarism, they met Baptists and Methodists at the crossroads of the revivalist system.

Yet while the curious mix of social theories found in the literature of the home mission movement resulted partly from its ecumenical nature, the ambiguities of the ideology also reached deep within the denominations themselves. The dispute between Taylor and Leonard Woods at Andover in the 1830s demonstrated one such conflict: although Yale and Andover together sent more young missionaries to the West than any other seminaries and both Taylor and Woods were active members of the AHMS, the two men could never agree on the true understanding of human nature that supported these activities.[35]

As academic discourse, such theological disputes may have shaped careers, but they did not adversely affect the lives of eastern evangelicals. The exigencies of the missionary movement, however, lent such disputes pragmatic implications largely unfelt—and certainly misunderstood—by theorists. In other words, intellectual ambiguities became problematic only in practice—in the lives and work of home missionaries, thousands of miles from their source.

The contradictions of home mission theory were also apparent in evangelical understandings of the nature of individual character necessary to establish a Christian community. One of the greatest fears that evangelicals shared about western settlements centered on the cultural and ethnic heterogeneity of the population. Indeed, fear of heterogeneity was arguably the reason that evangelicals of various denominations could cooperate as well as they did. Unlike the small, relatively homogeneous New England towns from which most home mission advocates came, many frontier settlements attracted widely divergent groups of immigrants, making a shared sense of communal purpose difficult to create.

In a sense, evangelization became both the goal and the method for the homogenization of the American population. Conversion was, of course, an end in itself for the carrying out of God's purposes. Yet as the AHMS warned, the country should also be evangelized because homogeneity was an important feature of a cohesive community: "Now it is evident," one promoter insisted, "that this foreign population *must be evangelized, or they will give us trouble*. The religion which they bring with them is unfriendly to ours, and to all our civil institutions."[36]

Although the danger of this diversity was clear, the rhetoric of the mission movement once again offered contradictory theories for combating it, theories that focused on the potential malleability of individual character. Revivalist strategy, seated in the romantic understanding of Christian perfectionism that was gaining acceptance by the 1840s, was premised on a fairly egalitarian conception of conversion as the birth of a "new being in Christ." History, tradition, and culture were, in the evangelical worldview, garments shed in the process of "putting on Christ." Theoretically, anyone—Catholic, infidel, or Mormon—could become a good Christian; piety was determined not by one's descent, but by one's consent to live life by a particular set of guidelines.[37] In a revivalistic framework, this emphasis on religious experience as the cornerstone of faith had democratic and egalitarian implications that meshed easily with certain strands of republican thought.[38] The experience of rebirth also motivated social reform efforts premised on lay voluntary activity, spawning organizations that rejected elitist notions of religious authority.

The evangelical belief in the democratic nature of revivalism resulted in the prevalent assumption that immigrants moving into the western territories were not only diverse but were tractable in character. In the West, the lack of an established church and strong local government could be seen, ironically, as virtues that distinguished home missions from foreign efforts: "Here are none of the impediments of an adverse government, and an alien nation suspicious of your missionaries as foreign emissaries," noted one Baptist.[39] A writer for the AHMS expressed this point more dramatically: "Here are minds collected from the four winds. They are held together by no fixed principles, no homogeneous preferences, and by no long-established usages." Most evangelicals conveniently overlooked the fact that many migrants brought with them their own strong convictions and cultural mores; they instead viewed the presumed moral rootlessness of settlers as the perfect opportunity to impress evangelical values upon the population. Although he was a bit hazy about the precise contours of these new communities, the writer continued, "How much does such a population need to be followed up by men of strong minds, of sound judgment, of established principle, and of ardent piety."[40]

The heterogeneous western population thus was depicted as morally and spiritually pliant; at the same time, evangelicals were impressed by the "intense energy" that characterized newer settlements. Populated primarily by young men seeking economic opportunities, western communities seemed alive with movement, action, and dynamism.[41] Osgood C. Wheeler, a Baptist reporting on the prospects for missionary work in the Far West, rhapsodized about the diverse settlements he had visited: "The effect which this compression of vital energy must exert in intensifying the life and increasing the vigor of the community is apparent. Imagine the power, physical, mental, and moral, of four men compressed into one, and the colossal intellect and giant frame thus formed would illustrate this people in the comparison with other communities. A nation of men, in the prime of life, in the full strength of manhood's perfected powers! . . . It is only rational to anticipate for the future of the Pacific States a life of intense energy, such as has never yet been exhibited in the progress of the human family."[42] In what was almost a foreshadowing of a later era's attraction to eugenics, home mission theorists looked to western settlements as the perfect planned communities that they could shape as they wished. The West was an area of pure potential, commented the Reverend N. S. S. Beman of Troy, New York, after a trip through the Mississippi valley: "Here is spread out before us an embryo world, and that world is to be peopled by a race of giants; but whether they will be giant-angels or giant-demons, must depend on the beneficence of Eastern churches and the grace of God."[43]

Yet the parameters of acceptable cultural difference, for most evangelicals, were fairly strict. Even as Presbyterian Albert Barnes praised the vast energy of the western mind for its heterogeneity because "there meet and mingle . . . all the elements of power which characterized different portions of the world," theorists simultaneously lauded the superior culture of Anglo-Protestantism.[44] As Reginald Horsman has pointed out, by the middle of the nineteenth century, Protestant Americans tended to see themselves not only as chosen, but as sharing in an impeccable Anglo-Saxon ancestry. Reinforced by the literary and historic movements of romantic nationalism, this sense of Anglo-Saxon superiority was premised on the notion that the hybrid nature of the English race had imbued it with its innate, vital force. Many Protestants, embracing the British legacy, viewed American expansion as evidence of this racial superiority.[45] The genius of America's heritage uniquely equipped its natives for the task of social regeneration, explained Charles Wadsworth: "The American character holds, in combination, all the available peculiarities of every nation under heaven, while the original Anglo-Saxon is the controlling element of the mass, and will be."[46]

Neither Wadsworth nor other theorists pondered what would happen if a western community were settled by immigrants who were not predominantly Anglo-Saxon; they assumed that in any event the superior social and political institutions of the Anglo-Saxon heritage would be universally acknowledged as the best possible foundation for community existence. In the end, the fusion of American heterogeneity with Anglo-Saxon institutions would make for a "new and nobler style in the development of manhood."[47] They also predicted that immigration to western territories would come primarily from northern European countries. Used in imprecise ways by Americans, the term *Anglo-Saxon* generally connoted groups from Protestant Europe.[48] More specifically, it served negatively to exclude Hispanic, Asian, and African cultures, along with a variety of Europeans that Anglo-Protestants found particularly offensive. Like Barnes, most evangelicals envisioned the future "western mind" as the precise opposite of the "slothful" inhabitants of southern Europe, the Middle East, and East Asia: "Whatever else it may be, it is to be unlike the intellect of the sluggish Turk in his Seraglio; of the effeminate Italian in his own land; of those who repose on soft couches in Persia; of those who seek a gradual approximation to annihilation in the countries where Buddhism prevails."[49] Heterogeneity was a virtue, provided it was tempered and refined by the superior virtues of Anglo-Saxon culture.

As good Whigs, most evangelicals did not read into this racialism the same rationalization for the aggressive use of force espoused by the Democratic party. Nonetheless, home mission literature was filled with the elitist notion that evangelicals, as the natural inheritors of this Anglo-Saxon heritage, were the proper midwives for the creation of western character. The Reverend E. P. Barrows, professor of Sacred Literature at Western Reserve College in Ohio, surmised that

> there is no nation in the world that possesses greater energy of character or mightier resources than the United States. As the Saxon is the predominating element in our language, so is it also in our national character. The history of England from the landing of Hengist and Horsa on her shores to the present hour is an illustration, on a stupendous scale, of the energy of the Saxon race. To this race we belong. It was because our fathers were Englishmen, and felt the blood of Englishmen coursing through their veins that they took up arms, in their poverty and weakness, against the oppression of England. . . . And the same vigor of character which carried them through the war of the revolution is now manifesting itself in all the departments of civil and social life.[50]

This notion of benevolent rule by a chosen cultural class—tempered somewhat by the inexact terms used to define that class—ran counter to more egalitarian understandings of the universal accessibility of evangelical beliefs and to the democratic tendencies that these understandings implied. Home mission theorists vacillated between an older understanding of social reform as moral stewardship, in which only people of a certain character and background could take part and in which history and tradition played a large role in shaping moral character, and the relatively egalitarian notions of Christian perfectionism that were gaining ground by the 1840s.[51]

Belief in the innate superiority of American character and the American religious heritage, then, were the foundation on which the ideology of the home mission movement rested. But mission advocates also looked forward, stressing the millennial importance of the westward progress of civilization and Christianity. Evangelicals based their predictions on biblical prophecies, outlining the process through which God would bring about the final unfolding of history through the labor of domestic missions. The Reverend Absalom Peters, the featured speaker at the annual meeting of the Massachusetts Home Missionary Society in 1846, predicted that "There is coming a millennium. . . . This world is to enjoy the reign of universal piety for a thousand prophetic years. . . . Such are the prospects of the missionary work when it shall be finished."[52] In keeping with Walt Whitman's poetic evocation of the westward course of empire, the eventual mingling of all peoples, and the closing of the cycles of history, home mission theorists interpreted the missionary goal as eschatological, catalyzing a series of events that would remove America from the boundaries of time and space.[53]

Geographical characteristics of the West itself confirmed and heightened millennial expectations. Barnes, in an address devoted to "The Characteristics of the Western Mind," pointed to the sheer size of western topography as an indication of its spiritual potential. "Everything, too, in the natural scenery is on a scale so vast and grand," he noted, "the majestic rivers, the boundless prairies, the deep forest, the very immensity almost of the rich domain which is spread out there as to make man vast in his schemes, gigantic in his purposes, large in his aspirations, boundless in his ambition."[54] For Barnes and others captivated by its grandeur, western land was innately redemptive, making all things new. In this belief, evangelicals shared in the widespread American perception of the West as an untamed wilderness, an Eden before the fall, or a primordial garden waiting to be cultivated.[55] For many antebellum Americans, the frontier was a region without history, a land that had not suffered the ravages of human use and abuse, but had instead remained in a state of innocence. That this depiction overlooked the presence of indigenous peoples and earlier migrations was beside the point for northern Protestants, who historically had conceived of American history as beginning with their own arrival.[56] Western lands, by providing a continually renewable source of land and job opportunities for the young nation, symbolized the boundlessness of American hopes for the progress of the republic.[57]

This nostalgia for a return to a state of innocence did not, however, reflect a merely reactionary or regressive historical posture. Scholars of antebellum reform have tended to overstate the degree to which evangelicals longingly looked backward for their models of community. Despite their reverence for the deeds and traditions of their American forebears and a firmly rooted historical consciousness, home mission advocates were not consumed by nostalgia for a bygone era.[58] Indeed, they more frequently expressed a deep-seated conviction that America was a country of progress and forward movement and that Protestantism would lead the nation speedily toward its destiny. "What an eventful day is approaching!" declared a contributor to the *Home Mission Record.* "How widely will future history differ from the past—and how solemn the prospect!"[59] "We are sometimes charged with exaggerating the future greatness of our country," explained Samuel Fisher somewhat defensively, "with indulging Utopian imaginations of her glory and vastness—with declaiming too much what we are to be, rather than dwelling upon what we are." To Fisher, America's present was self-evident, and it was not a matter of choice to meet the future enthusiastically, for "every hour reveals something vast, starting ahead of our anticipations."[60] Home missions were part of the innovative process that would unify the entire globe, as one AHMS editor explained: "When the bearings of our work are justly considered, the distinction between Home and Foreign missions disappears. The enterprise of evangelizing this land becomes, in effect, and on a grand scale, a MISSION TO ALL MANKIND."[61] Like many antebellum reformers, mission leaders employed the techniques of the present to bring about the society of the future, based in large measure on their interpretation of the past. Their ideology represented a hybrid of hopes and fears, at once regressive and progressive. As one Baptist leader aptly phrased it, "We *must be progressive,* but let us be conservative of all that is good."[62]

Antebellum evangelicals hailed American technological and social progress as signs of religious progress.[63] The AHMS was particularly mindful of the untapped socioeconomic potential of western lands. In describing the pressing need for evangelization, *Home Missionary* editors invariably stressed the latent promise of the given area, commenting on the size of a given territory, its projected population, and its agricultural and mercantile possibilities. On a yearly basis, the journal provided statistics that related the growing population of the western states, and writers delighted in reporting any increase. In contrast to the modern-day reverence for untrammeled open space, evangelicals clearly equated progress with the "filling" of the continent. "Nearly all social improvements spring from the reciprocal influence of large and condensed numbers, and diffused intelligence," stated AHMS editors. By 1940, they predicted, the projected population of the United States would reach 275,200,000 people.[64] Another mission advocate estimated that, although the industrial and spiritual development of the country would take time, within the century the population would likely triple: "It may require a period of two hundred years fully to people the North American plain; but, within the present century, before the year 1900, within the lifetime of persons now living, it will contain seventy-five millions, being nearly three times the present number of the whole nation."[65]

Evangelicals seldom questioned the desirability of such a high rate of immigration. As J. W. Scott suggested, the growing population would continue to improve existing technology and the national infrastructure, in turn encouraging even more immigrants to come: "So far is this influx from lessening the inducements to future immigration, that every million of new comers creates

new comforts for the common use of the millions who follow."[66] Technological, demographic, and religious progress were all inextricably joined in the
march of the divine plan.

The use of statistics and alarming visual metaphors also dramatized the
urgency of the missionary task. In one hundred years, Scott stressed, "sixteen
times as many souls must pass their probation on our soil—will be exposed
to eternal peril—and will require a proportional amount of effort for their salvation."[67] If sheer numbers were not enough to warn evangelicals of the
growing necessity for missions, promoters displayed an arsenal of catastrophic scenarios:

> Day by day, we see the waters rise higher, but never ebb. The
> flood covers the eastern plains; it beats against the breast of the
> hills; it swells above the mountain tops, and pours in a thousand
> Niagaras over into the great open bosom of the West. We see it
> rolling on, northward, and southward, and westward, sweeping
> away the forests from states and territories yet unnamed, until, at
> length, the turbulent waters repose on the bed of a vanquished
> continent! Every wave of this ocean is a tribe of men; every drop
> is a human soul—instinct with life—born in sin—to be
> converted and saved, or to live in rebellion and be lost. How will
> those thronging generations crowd after each other, over the
> verge of life, into the eternal world! . . . These are no mere *possi-*
> *bilities;* they are approaching *history.* These millions are coming;
> they will be here before we are prepared to receive them. . . .
> This generation must *make haste,* and have the Gospel ready to
> take hold of them and mould them, as soon as they are born.[68]

These dire predictions provided a counterpoint to the giddy optimism of
most missionary rhetoric. A looming fear of failure, and an obsession with
the "thronging generations" that separated missionaries from their goal of
world evangelization, tempered evangelical zeal. In their most pessimistic
moments, Protestants expressed uneasiness about the rapidity of settlement
and the mysterious nature of the determinative power that the West was to
exercise. "The reflecting Christian," commented B. B. Edwards, "as he sur-
veys the condition of our country, will be the subject of various and conflicting emotions. . . . While we seem to hear encouraging voices, there are other
sounds which whisper that there is little hope."[69]

These undercurrents of doubt reflected another recurring theme in American thought, one that viewed the West as a fearful chaos. Even before the
Puritan colonization, the American wilderness had acquired significance in

the European mind as a dark and sinister symbol, a "cursed wasteland." The Federalist Timothy Dwight worried that as the pioneer moved westward, into the heart of the wilderness, he became "less and less a civilized man."[70] In his view, the building of settlements on the frontier attained the symbolic status of a moral battle against the forces of darkness; westward expansion became a morality play with the wilderness as the villain.[71]

The expansion of the nation itself also prompted a fair measure of ambivalence, reflecting long-standing debates in American politics over the virtues of a large republic. "We sometimes exultingly say that our territory extends from sea to sea," mused Edwards: "But in passing from East to West, shall we not find the poor remnants of once powerful tribes, far away from the graves of their fathers, and now congregated together as if to come more surely within the grasp of the Shylocks around them? We speak of thirteen feeble Colonies grown into twenty-eight sovereign states, extending across the temperate zone and embracing the products of almost every clime. But may not all this be inherent weakness, presaging, that the country, like Rome, will fall by its own weight?"[72] Hearkening back to an earlier anti-Federalist tradition that emphasized the importance of a small, manageable republic as the key to national security and prosperity, some home mission advocates feared the consequences of swift expansion and the inherent weakness of large dispersed territories.[73] Quick growth held not only the potential for impeding proper social planning and consequently the inculcation of sound morality, but prosperity in itself magnified the potential for evil. Taking as his example the downfall of classical republics that had attained wealth too quickly and echoing the sentiments of James Madison, Lyman Beecher warned, "The greater our prosperity the shorter its duration, and the more tremendous our downfall, unless the moral power of the Gospel shall be exerted to arrest those causes which have destroyed other nations."[74]

These competing interpretations of future events—exhilarating yet foreboding, optimistic but riddled with doubt—characterized the hopes and fears of home mission advocates contemplating the grand work to be done. Their sentiments were not so much contradictory as they were different aspects of the same condition: as evangelicals marched bravely toward their divine destiny, the obligations that God had placed upon them to evangelize the country were at once burdensome and challenging. And while job insecurities gave vent to a range of honest emotion regarding the task at hand, home mission advocates also discovered that both encouragement and fear proved to be effective rhetorical strategies to shepherd their flocks. The two were often used in the same breath. "Now is the day of our salvation. . . . Already the stream of our destiny has acquired such momentum that little less than the strength of that hand which turned back the sun upon the dial plate of Ahaz, can either check it or change it," proclaimed the Reverend David Brierly of Salem, Massachusetts, in an address before the ABHMS. But as if to prevent his listeners from becoming too complacent about their own destiny, he quickly added, "If we act now, if we act promptly and vigorously, we may be successful; if we delay half a century longer, no earthly shell or power can save us. We are rapidly approaching the maelstrom which threatens to engulf us."[75] One's perspective depended entirely on whether one was contemplating the glorious future ahead, or was turning to examine the bogeyman in pursuit.

It is instructive, in light of the liberal use of images of disaster, to analyze more closely the nature of perceived threats to evangelical efforts. Scholars traditionally have characterized the home mission crusade as a reactionary movement established specifically to battle the forces of evil—be they embodied in foreigners, southerners, or infidels—that were thought to be taking over western communities. Ray Allen Billington has pointed to two dominant motives in domestic missionary work: the natural desire of religious activists to perpetuate the ideals, traditions, and civilization of the East, and a desire to save the nation from the threat of Roman Catholicism.[76] While Billington rightly highlights the multifaceted nature of evangelical concern, Roman Catholicism, according to most antebellum mission theorists, was only a minor aspect of the threat represented by the open-ended nature of western communal existence. More often it was difficult to discern the precise character of the enemy. A close reading of missionary sources indicates that evangelicals were far from united about what forms subversion might take and were therefore not unified in their battles in western communities.

The spread of Roman Catholicism in the West was certainly the most loudly proclaimed threat to American morals and "true religion" in the antebellum era. As Catholic immigrants entered the Mississippi valley and the upper Midwest, they were followed by Catholic relief organizations and educational efforts such as the German Catholic Leopold Association and the Association for the Propagation of the Faith. These institutions aroused considerable fear among nativists and Protestant evangelicals, who saw them as weapons in the larger Protestant-Catholic struggle for the religious and cultural fidelity of the American people.[77] Lyman Beecher, perhaps the most famous evangelical anti-Catholic activist, pictured the battle as part of the ongoing cosmic conflict "for purposes of superstition, or evangelical light; of despotism, or liberty."[78] Hysteria had mounted in the late 1830s to the point where nativists imagined that a papal plot was afoot to populate the West in order to gain political control of the area, at which time Catholics would rise in armed revolt and establish "popery and despotism" in America.[79]

The connections between the home mission movement and nativist activism are, however, more tenuous than this description would suggest, for they fail to take into account the remarkable ability of evangelicals to turn necessity into virtue. Beecher notwithstanding, by the mid-1840s mission advocates were just as likely to hail the Catholic presence as to revile it. Even during a period when Protestants had considerable objective evidence to reinforce their alarm, the editors of the *Home Missionary* remained sanguine. By 1847, more than two hundred thousand Irish immigrants were arriving in the United States each year. Additionally, the cession of southwestern territory after the Mexican war spurred further speculation among nativists that large numbers of Catholics in the West would move the nation one step closer to papal subjugation.[80] Yet AHMS editors chose not to tie these events to papal plots or Jesuit conspiracies, but rather to God's divine plan to populate the nation: "While the Papists were coming at a much slower rate, most Christian minds had a dread of their immigration, and a fear that they were sent hither to enslave us. And now that they are coming by the thousands, and in a way to show more distinctly the hand of God in their coming, fear and prejudice seem to have died away. The public mind seems to have received the idea that there is a benevolent purpose in it, and that we are called upon to welcome the exiles, and bless them with the light and privileges of the Gospel."[81]

Far from picturing Catholic immigrants as conspirators to be reviled, the AHMS editorial board connected this mass migration to their own ongoing population projections for the country. Propitiously, the Irish had been brought by God to assist in the millennial purpose of strengthening the United States. The West, in this framework, had been left sparsely populated precisely for this moment, and home mission proponents could only marvel at the efficiency of Providence: "It is a mysterious feature in the divine plan, that has kept in reserve, in our West, so much of the best land in the world, for the exigencies of this era, and for the purpose for which this emigration is now taking place."[82]

By the late 1840s, then, home mission advocates were far from united in their opposition to Catholic immigration. Publicists like Beecher continued to use anti-Catholic rhetoric, particularly in the urban Northeast, as a fund-raising technique for the cause, and missionaries visiting the East from their mission posts knew that they could gain financial support by invoking the specter of Catholic educational and religious competition. Many evangelical leaders, however, increasingly viewed Catholics not as monsters to be prevented from breaking down the doors, but as sinners and oppressed slaves in need of conversion and liberation.[83] Charles Wadsworth, critical of the anti-Catholic hysteria that some of his colleagues intentionally provoked, bluntly stated that such rhetoric was "a phantom, conjured up by religious demagogues, a kind of man of straw to set up on a platform." He rejected as ridiculous the notion that "this Anglo-American people are ever to go back in any considerable mass to the drivelling mummeries of Popish superstition."[84]

Unnamed fears increasingly eclipsed papal conspiracy theories. Evangelicals, with their affinity for notions of moral, political, and technological progress and forward momentum, were frightened by the mere existence of so much open space, territory that could best be likened to primordial chaos. As they saw it, the laws of progress would necessitate the filling of this land with some form of habitation, some sense of order, and the task for missionaries was to ensure that the communal order was properly Christian. Without forward progress, the only alternative was not inertia but decline, a degeneration into savagery and barbarism.

Horace Bushnell, an avid promoter of domestic missionary activity, gave perhaps the most thorough explanation of this "moral vacuum" theory. In "Barbarism the First Danger," he compared the present moment of American settlement in 1847 to the "emigrant age of Israel," a time when social declension loomed as a possibility. The New England theologian reasoned that Americans, like the Israelites, were standing on the precipice of chaos, and a fatal plunge could be prevented only by the rapid christianization of western populations.[85]

Bushnell attributed the danger of decline to increased immigration and cultural dispersion. Unlike evangelicals who extolled the virtues of a heterogeneous and inherently vigorous hybrid population in western territories, the liberal theologian feared the inevitable disruption of community ties and widespread relocation; he understood the core of religious nurture to lie not in the conversion experience, but in the slow process of cultural and spiritual education that settled societies alone could provide. A society cannot carry its roots with it, Bushnell insisted: "Transplanted to a new field, the emigrant race lose, of necessity, a considerable portion of that vital force which is the organic and conserving power of society."[86] Even if the first generation retained its cultivation and intellectual capabilities, the second and third generations would be stunted by the inferior educational opportunities in a newly established community.

For Bushnell, the greatest threat to community came from a heterogeneity of population that hindered a new society's need to coalesce. Even in the Puritan migration, he pointed out, where a common religious purpose provided a strong sense of community loyalty, settlement was followed by a period of decline, exemplified by the Salem witchcraft trials. America, as a result of its heterogeneity, still had a "raw, unfinished aspect" to it; the nation was mired in a state of transition brought about by continual migrations. The western states had begun their growth with some distinct advantages, Bushnell noted: better and more available markets, a well-established government, moral and cultural connections with the East, and a common American history. Unlike the Puritans, who forsook a history to come to the new world, westerners retained that intangible sense of belonging to a past: the westerner "looks out from his hut of logs on the western border, and feels the warmth of a distinct nationality glowing round him, like the clear warm light of day itself."[87]

In Bushnell's analysis, this lapse into barbarism was a greater, more fundamental danger to the future of the nation than Catholicism. Barbarism left a moral vacuum into which Catholicism, as well as many other "isms," was likely to fall. Rather than blaming the conspiring Jesuits, Bushnell concluded that if Protestant Americans neglected this moral vacuum, the consequences would be entirely their own fault: "Romanism can do any thing in this country which we will help it to do, and we ought not to complain if it does no more."

Mormonism was the most striking example, to Bushnell, of this tendency for nature to fill a vacuum. Referring to the growth of the Mormon community in Nauvoo, Illinois, Bushnell marveled: "Who could have thought it possible that a wretched and silly delusion, like that of the Mormons, could gather in its thousands of disciples in this enlightened age, build a populous city, and erect a temple, rivalling in grandeur, even that of the false prophet at Mecca?"[88] Bushnell went farther than most mission proponents in calling for ecumenical cooperation as the only effective means of christianizing the West; few would have agreed that "we must be willing to stretch our forbearance and charity even to Romanists themselves, when we clearly find the spirit of Jesus in their life."[89] But his sentiments provide further demonstration of a growing willingness to accommodate Catholics as allies in the face of greater threats to civilization.

Slavery provided a ready example that proved Bushnell's theory. Many western settlers were southerners, and they supported an institution that imperiled the well-being of civilized society if left unchecked by proper Christian influence. Slavery, for Bushnell as for most northern evangelicals, represented a relic of barbarism, a condition against nature that exemplified the worst aspects of community life.[90] Mission proponents characterized the South as the archetype of moral decay, a "bowie-knife style of civilization" responsible for all remnants of violence and disorder in American society, including the war with Mexico. Its dissipated state served as a warning of the clear dangers of society without Christian nurture.[91]

The moral vacuum theory, as well as the anti-Catholicism of home mission ideology, is closely related to what David Brion Davis has identified as a pervasive fear of internal subversion in the antebellum period. Between 1825 and 1850, as the fears of foreign invasion became remote for most Americans, the suspicion of subversion from within increased and surfaced in a number of reactionary movements such as anti-Catholicism, anti-Masonry, and anti-Mormonism. Davis asserts that these movements arose from a fundamental conflict between the Jacksonian desire to ensure individual liberties and the opposing desire to preserve common links with traditions, fundamental loyalties, and a sense of social unity. In a shifting social environment, these countermovements served to unite the American public against a common enemy, clarify "national values," and supply unity and meaning for people's common experience.[92]

The ideology of home missions served some of the same purposes. Fears of the possibility of failure, conspiracy, and the natural processes of decay and decline permeated the literature of the movement. Evangelicals believed that through a process of cultural homogenization through education, conversion, and persuasion, the worst evils of western life could be avoided. Although millennial aspirations were of paramount importance to these theorists, they were also well aware, from their endless demographic projections, that the time would soon arrive when the population center of the nation would shift out of the hands of the East and into these newly formed communities. As one advocate put it, "If we will not labor for them [the immigrants] from a higher motive, we must do it in self-defence."[93]

The nebulous nature of the western "enemies of civilization" underscores the point that the one common concern among home mission advocates was the preservation of eastern culture. This was the fundamental cause around which all northern evangelicals could rally. If a lack of social order invariably led to national decline and decay, the seemingly chaotic and individualistic nature of frontier communities also posed a direct threat to the well-being of eastern communities. Beecher spoke most forcefully to this often tacit fear: "And let no man at the East quiet himself, and dream of liberty, whatever may become of the West. Our alliance of blood, and political institutions, and common interests, is such, that we cannot stand aloof in the hour of her calamity, should it ever come. Her destiny is our destiny; and the day that her gallant ship goes down, our little boat sinks in the vortex!"[94]

It is therefore somewhat ironic that home mission theorists promoted the benevolent notion that only eastern morality and civilization could save the

West from anarchy and ruin because regional destinies were so clearly inter-twined. The naturally innocent West, like Rousseau's Emile or Horace Bush-nell's Christian child, could just as easily be corrupted as educated; it held as much potential for evil as it did for good.[95] Only the superior virtues of evan-gelical culture could salvage the inherent potential of these new territories. The West, indeed, held the promise of eventually saving the East from its own downfall, but first the West had to be saved from itself. A home missionary in Wisconsin nobly reported that "with the West I have united my destiny. . . . I have consecrated myself to the moral cultivation of that natural Eden . . . [so that] we may see a continuation of the magnificent, moral scenery of New England, extending from the Penobscot to the Columbia River."[96] In their more candid moments, other evangelicals admitted that they had little choice. The destinies of East and West were inextricably linked.

By the late 1840s, evangelicals were proud of their benevolent empire, the interdenominational unity that seemed to signal the imminent arrival of a truly evangelical republic. Home mission activists felt particular satisfaction as they surveyed the steady growth of western activity: "No sectarian jealousies disturb the harmony of either allied or rival denominations," boasted the *Home Missionary,* "and the gossip and the clamor ecclesiastical of the East, grows very faint and ineffectual ere it has crossed the liberal breadth of the North American Continent."[97] But this growing sense of evangelical common purpose was also deceptive in that it masked the underlying tensions and overt contradictions of missionary theory. These tensions evinced diverging theolog-ical assumptions and corresponding models of Christian social reform, an ambivalence toward the West itself as a symbol of America's future, and a vari-ety of techniques for coping with the headlong rush of technological and spir-itual progress in the early nineteenth century.

On the positive side, these contradictions served an important rhetorical function, uniting and combining as they did a wide variety of cherished beliefs and values. They made the home mission effort accessible to a wide constituency, which was precisely the purpose of circulating addresses and articles in missionary journals. Evangelicals had a strong sense of their ideal moral community—an organic settlement held together by the bonds of Christian love, guided by the edicts of divine Providence and the skills of a benevolent, Anglo-Saxon elite committed to republican government as the political form that God's covenant had provided. Eastern evangelicals, through the rhetoric of the home mission movement, could embrace the cre-ative tensions of the theory while holding in mind the final goal of moral coherence.

But moral coherence was, at best, a product of regional self-interest, the dream of a western community defined by the ideals of eastern visionaries. Unlike John Winthrop's "city on a hill," the western dream inverted the allegory of the Israelite exile. Whereas the Puritan migration preserved a remnant of religious virtue in the face of corruption back home, mission theorists hoped to transplant eastern morality fully intact to western soil, thus preserving the virtue of the nation as a whole. Protestant leaders saw their ideals as universal, not regional; this, ironically, was the claim that missionary success in the West was called upon to validate.

Increasingly, as the Second Great Awakening lost energy in eastern communities, evangelicals found in the West a blank slate upon which to etch their own dreams and fears about the future of the Republic.[98] Missionary work in the "Old Northwest," and in other suitably agricultural areas such as Iowa and later, Oregon, never presented a great challenge to evangelical theory, because it followed a recognizable pattern: settlement by stable family groups organized into small towns and farms and generally Protestant and northern in origin.[99] But the early difficulties encountered by Timothy Flint and Samuel Giddings, two home missionaries who traveled to Missouri in 1816 and were appalled by the "moral chaos" and prejudice against Yankees that they encountered there, foreshadowed the challenges to come on the Pacific Coast.[100] California, a frontier filled with individuals from all over the globe—mostly men without families and without immediate prospects for settling, engaged in the morally questionable profession of seeking instant wealth from the rivers and hills—would present a direct challenge to the ability of home missionary theory to adapt to the realities of western existence.

Chapter 2

A Gilded Opportunity

For gold, they say, is brighter than the day,
 And when it's mine,
 I'm bound to shine,
 And drive dull care away.
—*Mrs. Mary Dunn,* "Gold"

While missionary concern with western settlement generally intensified in the 1840s, interest in California as a field for domestic missions grew slowly. Remote, relatively untouched by Euro-American settlement, and not yet recognized as a promising area for agricultural development, the Pacific Coast was not the obvious choice for evangelical attentions. In 1845, the region contained a sparsely settled collection of small inland ranches and coastal hamlets that served as mercantile centers. Several hundred Mexicans occupied the small town of San Francisco. The Spanish missions, in disarray since the Mexican occupation of 1823, had been abandoned during the secularization of the 1830s, and the few Indians and Catholic missionaries still in residence were a shadowy reminder of the earlier days of Spanish conquest. By 1846, more migrants had settled in a single county of the territory of Wisconsin than had ventured west of the Rocky Mountains. Despite the mad rush for gold after 1849 and the Mormon migration to Utah, the 1850 census reveals that the increase in population in any one Mississippi valley state over the previous decade remained considerably larger than the total population west of the Rockies. As late as 1846, roughly seven hundred Anglo-Americans resided in California.[1] Trained to think in terms of a region's potential to sustain and support large numbers of settlers, evangelicals only gradually recognized the importance of the Pacific Coast.

Moreover, home mission societies conceived of the West in mental categories that rendered California temporarily irrelevant. Evangelical theorists
organized their efforts in terms of a spatial movement westward, with a line
of Christian culture moving gradually toward the Pacific Ocean. By the mid-
1840s, home missionaries had helped to settle the Old Northwest and were
following immigrants into the newly opened regions of Iowa and Wisconsin.
In 1845, the AHMS boasted 649 missionaries serving in twenty-three states and
territories, as well as Canada and Texas. Of this number, over half ministered
to settlers in the largely agricultural districts of Ohio, Indiana, Illinois, Michigan, Missouri, Wisconsin, and Iowa, with another handful scattered in the
southern border states and the final third occupying fields within New England.[2] The Methodists had moved somewhat farther afield, supporting a single missionary outpost in Oregon as early as the 1830s.[3]

But evangelical interest in California increased rapidly after 1845. To understand the full religious import of the gold rush for the home mission movement, it is necessary first to set it in the context of waxing political and social
attention to the Pacific Rim and then to analyze the strategic concerns of eastern evangelicals in 1848. Seen in the light of expanding eschatological expectations, the uncovering of the mother lode could only be interpreted as a sign
of providential favor. Yet the glad tidings of newfound prosperity also catalyzed new evangelical worries and revitalized long-standing concerns about
the swiftness of American expansion, the meaning of wealth, and the appropriate limits of liberal individualism and acquisitiveness.

Protestant missionaries in the antebellum era did not break new ground in
their discovery of California. As was the case in the Western Reserve, the Old
Northwest, and Oregon, missionary interest followed—and saw its task as
integrally related to—American economic and political developments. As
early as 1810, fur trade routes linked Boston, by way of Cape Horn, with California. After 1826, as British merchants eased their monopoly on the hide and
tallow trade in the Pacific, Yankee mercantilists seized the opportunity and
established economic ties with both California and Hawaii, convenient stops
along the Pacific route northward from South America. For American merchants, the Pacific Coast functioned both as an exploitable and accessible
private resource, and also as a link to trade in the rest of the Pacific basin.
New England entrepreneurs like Thomas Oliver Larkin, armed with generous
Mexican land grants or diplomatic posts, settled in the region, married into
Mexican families, and established their own small empires on the Pacific.
Businessmen on the Atlantic also took advantage of California's natural
resources: tanneries in Boston and New York purchased California hides and

later sold the finished products back to Pacific settlers at more than double their cost, earning far more profit than eastern sales garnered. Fur traders in the continental interior soon discovered that a trail linking St. Louis, Santa Fe, and California provided a needed point of access for their own merchandise.[4]

Even as California fulfilled the economic dreams of Euro-American entrepreneurs, its development opened American enterprise to the wider world of the Pacific maritime trade. If eighteenth-century Americans pictured their world perched on the rim of the Atlantic with lines of communication and commerce circumscribed by trade routes between the American Continent, Africa, and Europe, their nineteenth-century counterparts gazed out upon a global landscape, one that encompassed oceans on both sides of the continent. The founding of the ABCFM in 1810 was only one sign that Americans had begun to perceive the benefits of establishing Pacific ties.[5] As early as 1818–19, Senate Democratic leader Thomas Hart Benton published a series of articles outlining prospects for Asiatic trade on the Pacific.[6] By the early 1820s, Hawaii, "a piece of New England in mid-Pacific," linked Boston merchants to ports in Canton, the South Pacific, and California.[7] This shift of economic focus received executive sanction as Presidents Jackson, Tyler, and Polk worked to penetrate closed or restricted markets in East Asia.[8]

Travel literature of the 1840s articulated and popularized the growing American spotlight on California. It also perpetuated the notion of the Pacific region as both a fulfillment and extension of the American dream of manifest destiny. Richard Henry Dana, Jr., Alfred Robinson, Thomas Jefferson Farnham, Edwin Bryant, and others wrote widely read books based upon their travels in the region. Thomas Larkin, American consul to California, contributed letters to the New York *Sun* and *Herald* about his life in the area. In these accounts, California emerged as a country at once mysterious and familiar, distant but recognizably close at hand. Augmenting this body of literature was the propaganda of eastern presses that highlighted the economic and political potential of the region. The United States government printed ten thousand copies of Lt. Colonel John C. Fremont's report of his federally funded expedition, a document that emphasized California's geographical and agricultural importance to the nation.[9]

The declaration of war with Mexico in 1846 provided additional impetus for missionary activities in California. Evangelicals were by no means united in their sentiments toward the war effort.[10] Initial opposition to the use of military force ran highest in the northeastern states, where the peace and abolitionist movements were strongest.[11] Home mission societies, particularly those dominated by Congregationalists and New School Presbyterians, tended to agree with the Reverend Burdett Hart, minister of the Fair Haven

Congregational Church in Connecticut, that the war was a "national wrong," hailing a new "era of conquest" in which America had contradicted its own constitution and trampled the rights of others.[12] The evangelical *New Englander,* blaming the war on the "blood-thirsty" South and its desire to spread slavery across the continent, self-righteously condemned President Polk's policy of aggressive manifest destiny as immoral: "There is an atrocious system of foul wrong in this land, closely intertwined into the very life of a part of it, living and eating out the better soul of some of our people." Appealing to the moral strength of his fellow northerners, the editor added, "Has not the northern and better spirit of the United States put itself, blindfolded, into the hands of the South?"[13] Even the more Democratically inclined northern Methodists, while less vociferous in their objections, questioned the need for military force. The New England Conference passed two general resolutions against the war, and the New York *Christian Advocate and Journal* repeatedly challenged its justice.[14]

But moral indignation soon gave way to "respectful obedience" to the government. As the editor of the *American Whig Review* put it, starting the war had been wrongheaded, but once the country was engaged militarily, loyal Americans should support the cause.[15] Evangelical fears of the spread of the "slavocracy" were mitigated by a firm belief in the beneficial effects that Protestantism could have on Mexican territories. Although not minimizing the inherent sinfulness of the war itself and the American aggression that precipitated it, some evangelicals quickly seized upon its providential significance. They argued that the addition of new territories to the Republic, albeit by means deplorable in themselves, also demonstrated the inscrutability of God's intentions, wherein seemingly unchristian methods could be put to good purposes. "A wise providence," reasoned E. Royall Tyler, editor of the *New Englander,* "may allow men to pursue a course of measures so palpably and flagrantly wrong, that no good motive is possible in the actors; and yet the world may be brought into a better state by their agency, and all futurity . . . may rejoice in their deeds; or rather in the superintending and overruling power of God."[16] The *Home Missionary* went even further by declaring that, although the war was barbarous and evil, God often used such events to bring about the greatest good: "The Mexican War, we can now see, was one link in a chain of providences, for the universal establishment of the Messiah's empire on the earth."[17]

If popular interest in California pulled home missionaries to establish outposts on the Pacific, the simultaneous disintegration of revivalist fervor at home pushed leaders to look for crusades that would reinvigorate grassroot support for their cause. A variety of factors transformed the status of missions in the 1840s. As the promise of a regenerated Christian nation splintered into the "ultraisms" of Millerite adventism, Mormon heresy, communal utopianism, and political abolitionism, the more conservative mission advocates sought new means of regaining public interest. At the same time, the interdenominational cooperation of the Evangelical United Front fell prey to a growing denominational consciousness, which tended to undercut financial support for joint benevolent enterprises. Although, as George Marsden points out, groups like the New School Presbyterians retained considerable zeal for interdenominational efforts throughout the antebellum era, competing denominational obligations threatened to curtail the work of the AHMS. Methodists and Baptists, already engaged in home mission work under denominational auspices, did not feel the full strain of these tensions. Yet they, too, suffered from the more pervasive disintegration of the fervor of the Second Great Awakening.[18] Finally, all evangelical organizations experienced financial setbacks after the Panic of 1837 and the ensuing depression, which necessarily affected their ability to promote domestic missions.[19] These organizational factors compounded the deep-seated anxieties that evangelicals already felt about christianizing the nation. The flowering of temperance and antislavery societies, the religious tract distribution movement, and missionary organizations in the 1820s and 1830s had seemed the harbingers of a final, sustained attack on the bastions of infidelity in the young republic. When popular support for these organizations faded, Protestant leaders were left to wonder about the spiritual course of the nation and to seek new methods of highlighting the old cause.

Aside from countering the general worries raised by changed public opinion and organizational redefinition, evangelicals also sought a means to reverse the disastrous trend of recent missionary attempts in the Pacific Northwest. Particularly significant were the seemingly fruitless efforts of Jason Lee and Marcus Whitman. In 1843 Lee, a Methodist missionary to the Chinook Indians in the Willamette River Valley, was dismissed by the Methodist mission board in New York on the grounds that his mission had grown too secular. In his nearly ten years of labor in the territory, Lee had experimented with a number of tactics to promote Christian community. He visited the East in 1838 to solicit funds for his work, and brought back with him to Oregon fifty-one New England settlers in order to lay a "moral foundation" for Methodism on the West Coast. But in the end, his efforts were viewed as a failure by his missionary colleagues.[20] The New York *Christian Advocate,* reporting on the progress of denominational missionary efforts in 1845, expressed subdued disappointment in Lee's work when it stated that "the hope of great and permanent good did not correspond with what the Missionary Board had been led to entertain."[21]

Close on the heels of this disappointment came news of the massacre of Marcus and Narcissa Whitman, along with twelve other missionaries, at Waiilatpu in 1847. In outline, this second Protestant attempt to christianize the Northwest closely paralleled the attempts and failures of Lee. Whitman, a medical missionary commissioned by the American Board of Commissioners for Foreign Missions (ABCFM) in 1836, labored among the Cayuse Indians for more than a decade. But tensions among the Washington missionaries threatened the existence of the mission: in 1842, Whitman traveled east to convince the board not to close down the operation entirely. In 1843, he returned with a large group of Oregon pioneers, in another attempt to lay groundwork for a white settlement in the territory. Aided by the increased immigration to the region in the 1840s, Whitman administered medical treatment to many Euro-Americans, who in turn passed diseases along to the Cayuse. By 1847, mounting death tolls from these newly introduced illnesses, combined with a growing indigenous animosity toward the white missionaries, provoked the wrath of the Cayuse, who massacred Whitman and his co-workers. In the panic that followed, other missionaries in the area were forced to flee south under military escort. As a result, Washington remained closed to Christian labors until 1859.[22]

Looking for a means of salvaging domestic efforts on the Pacific Coast, evangelicals noted that California lacked obvious logistical pitfalls. Free publicity provided by eastern boosters and the United States government held out a greater promise for rapid Euro-American settlement. Equally important, the Indian populations in the region were thought to be docile and non-aggressive, an essential virtue that distinguished it from areas to the north.[23] Missionaries thus hoped to avoid the cultural problems of the Lee and Whitman debacles. California's abundant resources, so well publicized in the 1840s, provided a perfect selling point for the mission movement to the Protestant public. In a number of respects, argued mission advocates, the raw materials for a Christian civilization were already present there; with the proper moral guidance, California could set a spiritual example for the rest of the nation to follow. "What member of our glorious Union will then be able to compete with her in population, in resources, in refinement, in intelligence, and in wealth?" one Methodist queried.[24]

These less-than-spiritual concerns—potential economic gains, the effects of California missions on evangelical strategies as a whole, or commentary on the political turmoil of day—do not, of course, negate the importance of the evangelical eschatological vision. Religious imagery was not merely a cover for imperialistic intentions, nor was it simply a handy and potent public relations device for the cause of home missions. Protestant aims were complex; to varying degrees, all of these goals coexisted in the minds of religious leaders. Evangelicals lived in a world in which the spread of the Gospel, from their perspective, fortuitously coincided with the furthering of American domestic and foreign political interests. Surely, there were better or worse means for bringing about this advance; but the advance itself was assumed to be largely unproblematic.

By early 1848, then, the promise of California as a region of tremendous religious import was already clear. Bolstered by its political and economic value, informed by boosters who articulated its concrete attractions, and invigorated by an eschatological framework that bestowed upon it divine significance, evangelical home missionaries began to chart their courses. A committee of the ABHMS advised in early 1848 that a mission should immediately be established in the new Pacific territory, with the object of preaching the Gospel "to the inhabitants of that land who had for ages been oppressed with the rule of Roman Catholic priests." Accordingly, Osgood Church and Elizabeth Hamilton Wheeler set out from New York in December of that year.[25] The AHMS also acted quickly after the signing of the treaty with Mexico. The first substantive mention of the region in the *Home Missionary* outlined the acreage of the Mexican cession, commenting that it affords "materials for much reflection on the prospects of our Republic; and the nature and extent of the Home Missionary enterprise." John Waldo Douglas and Samuel Hopkins Willey, commissioned by the society in November 1848, joined the Wheelers on the steamer to Panama.[26] Methodists expressed a desire to establish a college in California as early as 1847; they followed upon the heels of itinerant ministers, who traveled to California along with other emigrants, preached in the region in early 1847, and organized class and Sunday School meetings in San Francisco, Monterey, and San Jose.[27]

The news of the California gold discoveries stunned the nation. Few people, in fact, readily believed the seemingly fanciful tales of sudden and abundant wealth. James Marshall discovered gold at Sutter's Mill on 24 January 1848. By late February, the news had reached San Francisco, along with a few samples of ore, but it was not until mid-June that inhabitants virtually abandoned the small town in the rush for the mother lode, a narrow strip of land stretching approximately 120 miles along the foothills of the Sierra Nevada. The Mississippi valley and Atlantic Coast states received word of the finding in late August and early September; once again, initial reports attracted little public notice. Finally, during the week of 23 November, nearly a year after Marshall's discovery, gold mania broke out along the eastern seaboard. Commercial ventures and emigrating expeditions quickly formed in Boston,

New York City, Philadelphia, Baltimore and New Orleans, and the race was on.[28]

Once the initial shock subsided, Americans quickly constructed new frameworks of meaning that encompassed the startling information. As might be expected, the lure of gold meant different things to different people. Excitement ran especially high in New York City, where investors expected to garner huge profits from the new territory. Many individual "argonauts" had more modest dreams, seeing a tidy sum of money as the final answer to financial debt, or the first step on the road to personal independence, or even as just enough capital to "feel confident of being well off," as the wife of one prospector explained.[29] Following on the heels of a lengthy period of chronic economic depression, the news of wealth to be gained mobilized a broad spectrum of adventurers.

The rumors of streets paved with gold, and of vast stores of wealth waiting to be excavated from the Sierra Nevada, surpassed even the enthusiastic imaginings of northern evangelicals. It also raised the curious dilemma of how one reacts when one's wildest dreams are not only fulfilled, but exceeded. Mission advocates, in keeping with their belief in providential guidance, interpreted the gold strike as a sign of divine favor. But the dizzying speed of the national stampede also raised considerable alarm about the ability of home mission societies to meet the sudden challenge. In an editorial of March 1849, the *Home Missionary* acknowledged that the effects of the rush would certainly be beneficial, allowing for the building up of an "organized state," "furnished at once with all the elements of civilization"; but the writer anxiously reminded readers that this hasty movement had not been anticipated: "Had this great migration been submitted to human judgment, we might have objected to it as ill advised and premature. . . . But we are allowed no choice as to the emergency, and scarcely any as to whether we will meet it."[30]

Even as the gold rush reinforced an eschatological sense of urgency for the conversion of the West Coast, the mobile and heterogeneous society to which it gave rise presented new and difficult challenges. The opening of the Pacific world, the nearly instantaneous peopling of the territory with men and women from around the globe, the existence of the gold itself—all of these aspects of life in El Dorado raised as many concerns as they answered. California defied most of the theories upon which the home mission movement traditionally had based its work. As a result, ministers in 1849 and the years that followed, guided mainly by their belief in the eternal value of the cause, had to improvise, to make up their strategies as they went along. One of the first missionaries to the state, writing from the ship that would take him to his new home, expressed the sense of confused urgency engendered by the rush: "From what I learn from conversation with passengers *en route* thither, I am more convinced than ever, that *now is the time*."[31] The fate of the civilized world seemed to hinge upon the success of evangelical efforts on the Pacific.

The gold rush also extended the Protestant debate about California's future from the journals of missionary societies to the pulpits of ministers all along the Atlantic Coast. In Sunday sermons, in services of dedication for departing immigrants, in funerals for aspiring argonauts, evangelical clergy embraced the task of imbuing the acquisition and unexpected wealth of El Dorado with meaning and purpose. In their efforts to make sense out of fortune, to turn necessity into virtue, several broad issues surfaced as the focus of religious concern: the role of California society and the gold rush in sacred history; and the ethical implications of gold mining. These issues had their roots in Protestant theories of westward movement and its spiritual import, but they also transformed previous conceptions of missionary purpose. The presence of gold heightened and reinforced the ideology of westward movement; at the same time, it pitted various facets of the evangelical synthesis against one another, upsetting the fragile coherence of the missionary enterprise.

The first focus of religious concern was the providential import of the discovery itself. How were Protestants to understand this hitting of the geological jackpot? Surely it was too marvelous to be attributed to chance. Its occurrence so soon after the signing of the treaty with Mexico boosted the confidence of clergy like Samuel Worcester, who maintained that "it must certainly be that God has a purpose—a great moral purpose in all this."[32] The Reverend W. W. Newell of New York, in a farewell service for three AHMS missionaries to the region, asserted that God had purposely waited until the Jesuits were "driven" from California to uncap "those mountains of gold."[33] George Shepard, a pastor in Bangor, Maine, agreed that the fortuitous timing demonstrated divine preference for Protestant control of the area. "Does it not seem as if Providence had been keeping these regions from the attention of the great nations," he rhetorically asked his congregation of departing miners, "until a thoroughly *Protestant* people could occupy them?"[34] Milton Badger, one of the corresponding secretaries for the AHMS, attributed even more specific and wide-ranging spiritual significance to the gold rush.

> For more than two centuries had that immense coast been
> under the dominion of the man of sin. And God, in his
> inscrutable counsels, kept the precious things of the ancient
> mountains hidden from the Indian, the Mexican, the Spaniard,
> from every eye, till Popery had shown to all people how

indisposed and how impotent it is to bless mankind with the arts of civilization or the hopes of immortality. But, when the set time comes for opening the land for Protestantism to enter in and build everywhere over it the institutions of the Gospel, he lets the gold glitter in the sunbeams, to astonish the nations and gather the people from afar.[35]

Surely, Badger and others assured their audiences, God had performed a miracle in the West; the multitudes were being gathered there for a specific purpose.

For New Englanders, the coincidence of events in California strengthened the analogy between the Puritan settlement of Massachusetts and the New England exodus to California. Just as God had reserved the "howling wilderness" of North America for the reformers of the corrupted European Church, so was the West Coast intended for "a people of the Pilgrim blood; he would not permit any other to be fully developed there."[36] Edward Beecher, son of the ardent home mission advocate, Lyman Beecher, also stressed the parallel between the Puritan and California settlements. In an address to the New England and California Trading and Mining Association, delivered at Tremont Temple in January 1849, the young theologian emphasized the obligations that the Pilgrim precedent imposed on western immigrants. Significantly, he assumed that New Englanders would be the arbiters of culture in the newly opened territory. "What more sublime, what more glorious, than the beginning of the life of New England?" he asked. "Those pilgrims who landed on the rock of Plymouth, brought with them those elements of life, the healing power of which, not only New England, but this nation, still feels. Nay, more; they have become principles of life for the world. Now, upon the shores of the Pacific, in the valleys and on the hills of California, an American community is to be founded; and to you, in part, is committed the great question of deciding what the future life of that community shall be."[37]

Besides supplanting Catholicism and establishing Protestantism in its place, some northern evangelicals insisted that God was using California gold to hinder the spread of slavery into the region. A contributor to the *New Englander* declared that the discovery of the precious metal was a providential means of settling the dispute over slavery, because it would bring so many northern immigrants into the territory to vote against the institution: "In her golden dust there was a motive power which was sure to bring northern enterprise to her shores."[38] Edward Beecher, a vocal opponent of slavery, reasoned that the current state of society in California also discouraged southerners from bringing in slaves. "Notice how the Providence of God is excluding the emigration of slaveholders from California. They could not hold their slaves in bondage for an hour; they would escape like a bird from the snare of the fowler."[39]

Many of these confident claims were hardly more than wishful thinking. Southerners flocked to the mother lode alongside their northern counterparts, and some brought slaves with them. In later years, despite the ban on slavery in the state constitution, the California courts upheld the right of slaveowners to transport their chattel into and out of the region. Yet the assertions, in and of themselves, demonstrated the ability of northeasterners to see in the West the fulfillment of eastern dreams. Referring to the gold regions, Samuel Worcester insisted that "GOD will be there—the God of New England's founders." And, most assuredly, he concluded, slavery would *not* be there.[40] In early 1849, after perhaps a half dozen Protestant ministers had reached the territory, Beecher envisioned California society as a pious Puritan utopia: "On every hill, and in every dale, as in New England, the church spire is seen to rise, the gospel is faithfully preached, the Spirit is poured out, in every family the Bible is read and revered, and diffuses its elevating and sanctifying power through all the relations of life."[41]

According to some proponents, the Puritan connections to the gold rush also enhanced the importance of California for the cause of worldwide evangelization. With eastern settlement in the region, El Dorado would be populated by "a *missionary people*—a people who speak the *missionary language*—a people, too, just now in the flush and prime of their *missionary age*."[42] The large influx of Chinese into the state in the early 1850s reinforced and intensified the image of California as a stepping-stone to East Asia. The Reverend A. D. Smith, in his dedication of five California missionaries in 1852, urged his listeners to "think, too, *where* this work is to be done. The fabric to be reared on the Pacific Coast, is to overlook Asia; it is to be an object of curiousity and wonder, an incitement and a model to all dwellers there." Smith reasoned that Chinese immigration demonstrated the willingness of pagan populations to learn from the Protestant example: "More than forty thousand natives of the Celestial empire are already in California; they have come to see how you build; many of them, we would fain hope, to be themselves living stones in the spiritual temple."[43] The *California Christian Advocate,* published in San Francisco, predicted that "the day is near at hand when the Gospel shall be preached to all the world, or at least to the representatives of the world, on Portsmouth Square, in this city."[44]

Although most clergy agreed that the discovery of gold was providential, the dizzying speed and heterogeneous character of the settlement prompted considerable concern. Previous frontiers on which home missionaries had labored were predominantly rural and agricultural, consisting of slowly developing, stable communities settled by family groups. In Ohio, in Illinois, and later in Iowa and Minnesota, this pattern of gradual, measured growth repeated itself, giving rise to regions which, economically and socially, resembled many areas of rural New England. The gold rush ensured that the settlement of California would differ drastically from this model: the West Coast swiftly filled with "argonauts", young men either single or traveling without families, gathered from places as far-flung as Australia and China. Thus the "civilizing" of the new El Dorado, as mission leaders recognized, necessitated not simply a spatial extension of old missionary techniques to the Far West; it required a cognitive leap in the way evangelicals perceived the frontier and its spiritual future.

Another important facet of California's exceptionalism was the speed with which a society, and seemingly an entire civilization, settled the area. The spectacle of a hundred thousand immigrants, rushing toward the mother lode from all parts of the globe, led to its reputation as a Minerva-like region: just as the young goddess of wisdom sprang full-grown from the head of the powerful Jupiter, so would California arise full-grown from the combined culture and refinement of its latest colonizers. Observers marveled at the energy and industry with which westerners erected stores, houses, and roads. "California is the birth of a nation in a day," noted P. G. Buchanan, a newcomer to the state, in the pages of the *California Christian Advocate*. "Yesterday it was not, to-day it is seated, an empire of strength and civilization. . . . It hardly seems proper to apply the term 'growth' to such a land. Its population, its cities, its very surface of production, seem rather to have been transplanted than to have grown into existence."[45] The Reverend George Shepard agreed that California would "leap into being almost full grown, possessing at once the literature and the arts of their Atlantic sisters, and ere long, we trust, their institutions of religion."[46]

Words seemed inadequate to express the wonder that observers felt toward the growth of the Pacific region; only mythical similes could articulate the sense of mystery surrounding the dizzying turn that events there suddenly had taken. Evangelicals just as quickly found ways of incorporating the myth of California into previously held notions of millennial destiny. The rapidity of settlement reinforced the conviction that a new spiritual order had arrived; a "planned community," an "instant" society that allowed for progress ostensibly untrammeled by the constraints of history and tradition, appealed to those evangelicals who recognized in it the unprecedented potential for control over moral and social growth. Edward Beecher marveled at this unique opportunity, wherein social planning could be conscious and deliberate. Previous home mission operations, he noted, had proceeded on a mid-western model in which a slow trickle of immigration gradually allowed religion and culture to prosper. But an "instant" community brought with it the capacity for controlled supervision of its spiritual character. Most significant, in Beecher's mind, was that California could thrive as a community of free citizens, "untrodden by the footsteps of a slave."[47] More generally, the region offered itself as the birthplace of a new kind of human community, well-planned, organized, and untainted by the errors of the past. It would serve as the social analogy to the evangelical "new man," an intentional correction of the mistakes of the East.

This utopian vision reverberated with decades of Whig-inspired social planning. Indeed, it seemed the logical culmination of a generation of bridge and road construction, of canals dug and factory towns mapped. It demonstrated the ubiquity of human control over the environment, of obstacles to progress overcome, even to the extent of liberating Protestants from the shackles of history itself.

Yet the accelerated pace of civilization effected by the gold rush, even as it symbolized new opportunities for evangelicals, also presented the possibility of history careening out of human control. Like a bright but willful child, California was a prodigy with the capacity to turn upon its teachers. These mixed messages were only reinforced by the confusing reports coming back from the mother lode. Religious observers, looking for signs of moral promise and progress, saw either certain victory or sure defeat. One unidentified missionary, who had traveled extensively through the state, exuberantly told readers of the *Home Missionary* how promising Christian labors appeared: "Wherever, in this region, the energetic living preacher goes, fortifying his doctrine with strong argument and directing it home to the hearts of his hearers by plain and forcible application, large congregations assemble. . . . No time can be more favorable than the present for missionary labor. The ears of the people are open to the truth; the very *ennui* of this toil after gold, reacts in favor of the truth. The field is exceedingly great, promising the richest fruit."[48] Other reporters spoke with far more pessimism. Samuel Willey described the questionable character of California immigrants, noting that although he had met a few gentlemen during his journey westward, "the many are adventurers, with no local attachments, ready for anything. Lowest in the list are a few gamblers, and one of *pugilistic* notoriety."[49]

The heterogeneity of the California migration also captured the attention of eastern evangelicals. The ideology of the westward movement traditionally contained within itself a profound ambivalence about the diversity of cultures that mingled on the frontier. What would hold together and ultimately shape these communities morally, reasoned mission advocates, was the persuasive superiority of Euro-Protestant culture. As long as society contained a "saving remnant" of the faithful, Christianity would be secured. Yet California, unlike previous frontiers, attracted immigrants from all over the world. It contained a population unlike anything evangelicals had ever imagined. Horace Bushnell, in describing the early characteristics of the state, cautioned that the extreme diversity of settlers—including "border ruffians" from Missouri, Chinese, and southerners—would adversely affect the ability of missionaries to christianize the region. "The composition, or the combined elements of the emigration," he emphasized, "are not favorable to the immediate coalescence of the new state, in terms of order and public virtue."[50]

Eastern parish ministers registered increasing alarm about the spiritual con- sequences of such cosmopolitanism. They were particularly concerned about its effects on their own congregants who were rushing off to the mines. A few embraced the notion that Yankee settlers would be shielded from sin by the force of their backgrounds. "The most thoughtless of all New England's sons there, would scarcely feel that he could afford to dispense with what is so closely connected with the scenes and experiences of his childhood, as are the house of God and the preaching of the everlasting gospel," wrote one observer hopefully.[51] But most clergy lapsed into reactionary rhetoric that equated intercultural contact with utter depravity. The Baptist S. L. Caldwell of Bangor, Maine, told an audience of immigrants that in the "mixed society" of the mother lode, "in the filthy and discolored streams that shall flow in there from all lands, you will need whatever will keep you true to your hered- itary character."[52] Elisha Lord Cleaveland carried his congregants to new heights of xenophobia with his rendering of California's pluralism: "Half a mil- lion may be poured in there within two years—collected too under circum- stances most unpropitious to all the intellectual, social and religious interests of a permanent community. . . . The filth and scum of society, gathered and poured in there to seethe and ferment in one putrid mass of unmitigated depravity, and poison the earth and air with the pestiferous malaria of their concentrated wickedness."[53]

Whether predicting victory or destruction, the heated rhetoric of eastern ministers was not merely a device to command the respect of their restless parishioners. It was instead an intensified and heightened version of the euphoric anxiety evangelicals had always felt toward the West. Whatever fears the clergy had about a negative outcome were counterbalanced by mil- lennial optimism. The intimations of a worldwide gathering—a pentecostal union where the Gospel would be preached to all nations "right here on Portsmouth Square"—illustrate the extent to which many evangelicals saw the gold rush as an eschatological portent. The sheer speed of immigration and the extent of wealth reported had, as it were, burst the seams of the predictable pattern of national expansion. Just as the First Great Awakening had heralded the beginnings of a national consciousness, the various events of the late 1840s catalyzed the creation of an international consciousness, with America firmly at its center.

Religiously, home mission supporters interpreted this historical eruption as the herald of a new conceptual and geographical phase of providential work. As one Methodist theorist articulated it, for the Israelites "the West" was the land of Canaan. Now the West was California, and the next and final historical step had to be to the "remains of the Old Eastern civilization." Couching his discussion in biblical terms, he concluded that "Ophir has been already reached, and soon the long journeying of restless humanity will come round again to the plain of Shinar, or the region in which commenced the original dispersion of the race."[54] Even more symbolic of the hopes evangelicals placed in the christianization of California was a map of the world that appeared on the front page of the Baptist *Home Mission Record* in March 1850. Entitled "the position of America between the Atlantic and Pacific Oceans," the map depicted the Pacific Coast at its center. Radiating from San Francisco were dotted lines connecting the city to the ports of Japan, China, Southeast Asia, and Australia and indicating the mileage to each country. From New York two more lines linked the East Coast to England and to China by way of Cape Horn. The implied message was that California provided an ideal point of missionary access to the Pacific basin, complementing and completing the work of eastern missionaries across the Atlantic. In the accompanying article, the author noted that his object was to "invite the more particular attention of the Christian community to the important interests of religion, which are, obviously, connected with the wonderful changes in the affairs of our country, growing out of the acquisition of California." Continuing his message, he quoted from the Seventeenth Annual Report of the ABHMS:

> The geographical position and commercial advantages of
> California are matters of far greater interest and importance than
> its gold and silver. . . . Heretofore it has been regarded as the
> extreme verge of civilization, a point that would ever be such
> and only such . . . [but] in the estimation of many discerning
> men of other nations, it is already regarded as the continent
> which must become the centre of civilization. With its
> mountains, plains and rivers, subjected to the triumph of arts
> and science, it will be rendered the great thoroughfare of
> nations—the great mart of commerce—the vast central focus

for the concentration of means of commercial and social intercourse among men.[55]

In seeing California's "discovery" as an integral part of the millennial
scheme, home mission advocates echoed the desires of other millennial
movements of the 1830s and 1840s. The flowering of a wide variety of adven-
tist and utopian groups, including the widely popular Millerites of the early
1840s, indicates the broad extent of antebellum American interest in spiritual
liberation from the confines of history. Perhaps the most useful analogue can
be found in another westering movement, the Mormons of the Salt Lake
basin. Jan Shipps, in an insightful study of the origins and development of
Mormonism in the nineteenth century, argues that from its inception, the religious movement of Joseph Smith, Jr., and his followers was premised upon a
conscious rejection of much of the Christian tradition. The Book of Mormon
"left the Saints with an enormous 1,400- to 1,800-year lacuna in their religious
history," rendering parallels between their experiences and the experiences
described in the Bible much more evident. Indeed, in their mass migration to
Utah, their establishment of a latter-day kingdom, and their adherence to
Levitical laws, Mormons understood themselves to be "living through" the
events of the Hebrew Scriptures in a new age; the Salt Lake community
became the restored Zion, a physical manifestation of the sacred that liberated Mormons from the perceived chaos of European history.[56]

Like the Mormons, Protestant evangelicals yearned for the millennium that
would free them from the cycles of historical rise and decay. They, too,
located God's promise in the development of North America and in the
redemptive powers of the West. Yet unlike the Latter-day Saints, evangelicals
did not require a historical disjunction in order to fulfill the divine plan.
"When the world has been vitally Christianized; then man will be *completely*
redeemed, and not till *then,*" stated Charles Wadsworth. The birth of the
Republic had initiated a new Christian era; the missionary move across the
Pacific was to complete and perfect the exodus begun during the Reformation and subsequent settlement in the New World. "We stand today in the
world in precisely the place of old Israel," Wadsworth continued. "We are the
chosen and peculiar people of the new dispensation. . . . The isles of the sea
wait for us; the world waits for us."[57]

As was also the case with the Mormons, this movement westward, conceptually transformed into an errand and a mission, was necessitated by and
premised upon the failure of the religious task at home. As the spiritual condition of the East looked increasingly bleak, the success of the missionary
movement in the West attained increased significance. In this regard, the California gold rush, holding forth the promise of a sudden and sure spiritual

redemption, raised the religious stakes considerably. It represented not a break with the Euro-American past, but hope for a restoration of its original glories. More was expected in California because more had been promised there. Even as mission booster Reynell Coates urged California's "noble pioneers" to fulfill the American destiny, the forebodings of eastern failures beat like an obbligato in his call to "send to the councils of the nation men untrammeled with the prejudices of her infancy—men whose eyes can sweep the horizon of her vastness, and grapple with the duties of her manhood."[58]

The settlement of El Dorado also demonstrated the deeply rooted ambivalence evangelicals harbored toward their own past. As we have seen previously, home mission advocates simultaneously revered and sought escape from history. The West, paradoxically, represented both: easterners worked to extend and perpetuate their own culture in a new space while continuing to hope that they would be saved from its failures. Historylessness, the primary myth of the Euro-American cultivation of the West, was in turn both a blessing and a curse, depending upon whether one chose to emphasize its cultural potential or its moral vacuity. The Reverend George Burgess, in his dedication sermon for William Ingraham Kip, the first Episcopal missionary to California, cautioned Kip about the dangers to clergy in the new region, emphasizing that "there is no past on which you can much lean."[59] Mainstream evangelical leaders such as Charles Brigham shared this sentiment. Brigham reminded his company of Massachusetts adventurers that "all the softening influences of civilized society will be wanting,—nor will it be, either, like journeying in a land of ancient ruins, where hallowing associations of the Past yet linger. There is nothing to hallow the wilderness in the absorbing motive which brings so many there."[60]

Aside from intensifying and highlighting long-standing ambiguities in the evangelical worldview, the gold rush also provoked substantial soul-searching over the meaning and purpose of wealth. Outside the specific parameters of the antislavery debate, the Protestant economic ethic generally was not a pressing issue for antebellum evangelicals. This is not to suggest that Christians agreed about the proper attitude one should take toward the earning of money; the immense and far-reaching changes brought about by the industrial revolution assured that evangelicals, along with most other Americans at midcentury, were not sure precisely what prosperity represented in religious terms. By and large, however, their answer to this confusion was silence. When pressed, they retreated to former lines of battle.

In a sermon delivered at North Church, Hartford, in early 1847, Horace Bushnell outlined the traditional Protestant understanding of the relation

between virtue and wealth. Preaching on 2 Chron. 32:30 ("And Hezekiah prospered in all his works"), Bushnell posited a direct correlation between an
upright character and financial prosperity. "Any community or city will prosper that will do its duty"; conversely, a state of prosperity "is one of the truest
evidences of character and public virtue." Indeed, virtuous industry was connected "by a fixed law of nature" with growth and success. Prosperity, he
readily admitted, had its own pitfalls, but like most antebellum Americans,
Bushnell insisted that the dangers of "wasting and decline" were far more
threatening. "If prosperity is dangerous, decline is well nigh fatal" because it
breeds a population without energy or hope for the future. Bushnell's devel-
opmental analysis left no room for collective stasis; like the westward movement itself, society was either proceeding toward further spiritual and financial virtue or was receding into a pit of poverty and moral despair.[61]

Bushnell also could not foresee a possible conflict between individual and
communal prosperity. In fact, it was precisely the balancing of personal and
social needs that would allow both spheres to flourish. "It must be our study,
not how we may cripple or thwart any rival interest, but how we may build up
our own." Wealth, after all, should be sought not as an end in itself but for the
greater glory of God. We must renounce all schemes that benefit ourselves at
the expense of others, he continued, reiterating classic Christian prohibitions
against usury and the quick accumulation of money. Honorable fortunes
were built slowly, on the basis of steadily applied industry: "The only sound
law of increase is the law of production." Christian virtue, guiding both the
individual and society as a whole, would necessarily hold in check the
excesses of the economic sphere. "We have only to be true to ourselves and
nourish the seeds of growth we possess, to be sure of all the progress we
desire." Indeed, Bushnell and other Protestant leaders expressed confidence
that those who accumulated wealth illegitimately would inevitably be pun-
ished, either by the excesses of their own greed or by the failure of their business ventures.[62]

Bushnell accurately noted that his understanding of the economic law of
nature was premised upon the existence of a society with common interests,
that is, the furtherance of Protestant Christian values. Because of his own proclivities for social organicism, Bushnell looked back to the Puritans for his
model of a society embodying the ideal relation between virtue and prosperity. Updating John Winthrop's tune without changing the key, Bushnell called
upon Hartford residents to foster public spirit: "We must feel that we have
one interest, and all ranks and classes must unite heartily in the pursuit of it."
Embedded in his evocation of Puritan society, moreover, was a measured
dose of cultural determinism. Naturally, the values of Protestant Americans

led most easily to prosperity. Bushnell argued that Americans prospered not merely because of hard work or frugality, but because it was their peculiar right to do so as God's chosen people. Other cultures, already mired in the bogs of immorality, could not be further dishonored by decay or thriftlessness, "hence it will do for Mexicans, Neapolitans and Chinese, not to prosper, but it will not do for us."[63] This was an inspirational message suitable only for the ears of New Englanders.

If this evangelical formulation of the benign influence of wealth contained a fragile—and perhaps only a theoretical—equilibrium of personal and communal interest and of striving without grasping, it was a balancing act performed for the audience of the aspiring middle classes. As Daniel T. Rogers points out, the midcentury paean in praise of work appealed mainly to middling, largely Protestant, property-owning classes, including farmers, merchants, professionals, independent artisans, and nascent industrialists. For the remainder of the population, from factory workers to unskilled laborers, the burgeoning industrialization of the antebellum era "upset the certainty that hard work would bring economic success."[64] Rather than providing spiritual and financial stability, the surge of expansion produced anxiety and insecurity about the goals of life and the moral obligations of the individual. Religious leaders, like other apostles of self-help, witnessed a growing discrepancy between their cheerful admonitions to work diligently and the grim realities of wage labor and urban life. Like Bushnell, Protestant advisers fell back on traditional ethical models, if only because they were at a loss to provide new remedies for growing social unease over the emergence of a market economy.[65]

Not until the 1880s and 1890s did Protestant leaders fully grapple with the social changes wrought by industrialization and urbanization.[66] But the gold rush gave many evangelical clergy a brief taste of the coming struggle by temporarily upsetting the delicate balance Bushnell and others had worked so hard to maintain. The proper attitude toward prosperity, asserted religious leaders, required enough social control and sense of common purpose to keep in check the desires of individual attainment. Yet, what would happen in a situation where society was premised upon the acquisition of wealth and the exclusive pursuit of self-interest?[67] Where prosperity demanded not steady perseverance, but often simple luck and little time? What sustenance could traditional religion provide in such a situation?

Ministers from Maine to New Jersey grappled with the ethical ramifications of the gold discovery. The rush for wealth was an undeniable catalyst that brought to the surface deep-seated ethical tensions, challenging the Protestant ideal of frugality and the slow accumulation of wealth. It upset the necessary balance between merit and rewards, so crucial to the perceived justice of the work ethic. In their farewell sermons, ministers anxiously imparted words of advice to departing adventurers. Some, like Nathaniel Frothingham, concentrated on the moral dangers that wealth represented for the individual. Gold, he warned, was only a currency, "It will build houses, but not character or content." Frothingham urged that his listeners "be cleansed of covetous affections" and avoid the trap of the "Phrygian king" who discovered, after receiving his wish that all he touched should turn to gold, that grasping after money was the root of all evil. The method of financial acquisition, not its object, was his focus.[68] William Thayer emphasized that gold came at a much higher cost than most people realized. He warned his audience that in assessing the cost of a trip to California, one had to take into account the darker side, the higher price such a journey would exact. In his listing of these costs he included everything a son of New England would hold dear: home, health, religious privileges ("it is a great change to a young man from this favored soil of the Puritans, and a stupendous sacrifice if he loves the service of God"), and the security of his own soul.[69]

Most ministers emphasized temptation not as a feature of the human heart or a necessary component of original sin; instead, California itself was often depicted as the locus of evil. One clergyman warned his congregants about the "great slaughter-house of character and of souls" they would soon enter. Another likened the region to the "California Pox," a disease that infected its victims, "who on breathing that peculiar atmosphere, have imbibed the spirit, and been ruined by it." In these ominous admonitions, the spiritual landscape itself had been objectified, and the struggle between good and evil now took place on the far-off shores of the Pacific. Accordingly, some evangelicals depicted the journey westward as a pilgrimage of the soul, a test of individual spiritual mettle. Brigham comforted those bidding farewell to loved ones leaving for the mother lode, "away from the influences of order and temperance and a christian home, through the perils of a wintry sea, to the corruptions of a profligate shore."[70]

Even while recognizing the perils California represented for the soul, other clergy took more optimistic views. Communal prosperity was necessary for the spread of Christian values and institutions; no one knew this better than advocates of missions. But wealth proved to be a two-edged sword. Some ministers therefore tried to steer a middle course between their pastoral and prophetic roles, between imparting necessary words of caution to individual miners and acknowledging the obvious importance of California's wealth to the national destiny. Rather than concentrating exclusively on the temptations of greed to the individual, they attempted to place the gold rush within a larger ethical context that made sense of such an embarrassment of riches.

The Reverend Charles Farley, preaching to the First Unitarian Church of San Francisco in 1850, construed California's mineral deposits as an opportunity to prove the virtues of hard work. Implicitly chiding those who looked upon forty-niners as inherently immoral, Farley compared gold-digging to other types of industry: "Gold is dug in no meaner manner here than coal or lead at home; and our merchants in Montgomery Street have no more passion for 'filthy lucre' than those of State Street or Wall Street." Farley asserted that California was a unique society, where "a nation has literally been born in a day; a nation the strangest and most miscellaneous ever brought together." He also acknowledged that the community was "animated primarily . . . by one passion, and that a passion for money." He insisted, however, that fears of moral corruption did little justice to the strength of the American character. "It is paying but a poor compliment to our brethren at home, to suppose that the thousands and tens of thousands who have come hither . . . are such miserable specimens of humanity, without any principles of self-restraint, with dispositions wholly inclined to all sin, and wholly disinclined to all goodness. Are such, indeed, the fruits of our boasted civilization? . . . These the descendants of the Puritans? Have our families from the North, South, East and West, sent out from their very bosoms none but moral monsters?" Farley was convinced that the ethics of industry and frugality would finally triumph and that those who labored hardest would prosper. He dismissed the idea that the glittering gold would exert some kind of overpowering control over human passions. "When, in a word, the Genius of our American Institutions has fairly developed itself, we shall see . . . these black clouds disappear from our horizon."[71]

For pastors interested in the systemic benefits of gold production, the good of developing California's natural resources far outweighed the temporary insanities of gold mania. The Republic would prosper from this source of wealth, thus allowing for the strengthening of American institutions and values. A few individual souls, such commentaries implied, were a small price to pay for the greater glory of God. As in the case of the spoils of the war with Mexico, evangelicals quickly turned necessity—and even individual misfortune—into social virtue. "We are bound to believe that some great advantage to the world, ultimately to be realized, will be more than a compensation for all the temporary mischief done in the case of individuals," philosophized William Lunt.[72] Samuel Roosevelt Johnson, the Episcopal rector of St. John's Church in Brooklyn, admitted that some people saw in the exodus to California only a greed for gold. He urged a more charitable view of the situation:

"Temptations doubtless will come of it; some injurious consequences will befall; but God means the general result for good; and doubtless purposes to fill up suddenly that great Pacific region of the North with the children of our favored nation, so that our blood, our language, our institutions, our spirit, our industry, our energy, our morality and our practical religious mind may be there the resident and victorious elements."[73]

The gold rush did not simply throw a moral impediment in the path of missionary progress. Its effects were more complex, despite the propensity of ministers to compact its import into digestible, and transportable, portions. On the one hand, it brought into greater relief preexistent ambiguities in the home mission ideology. One such equivocation concerned the meaning of wealth itself and the problem of maintaining virtue where society did not restrict or impede individual gain. Protestant ministers instinctively recognized the dangers to the soul posed by a society unregulated by Christian values; one could not expect even the most virtuous of immigrants to withstand indefinitely the onslaught of temptations such an environment bred. This dilemma, whether evangelicals fully realized it or not, brought them back to the unresolved question of the nature of sin itself. Was sin located within the human being, or was it an external force or locale? Was sin resistible? What role did human volition play in regulating ethical behavior? What kind of balance between individual and social morality was possible in a place like California? These questions would take on still greater import for missionaries to the state as they confronted directly the damaging effects of social disarray.

The ability of religious leaders to objectify the dangers of wealth, to cite California as the "great hell of the continent," also illustrates how unwilling they were to recognize the amoral nature of their own capitalist economy. Blaming the spiritual miseries of miners on the "charm" and seductive atmosphere of the region allowed clergy to ignore the fact that the machinations of industry in the mining community actually demonstrated the triumph of a market economy rather than its perversion. As some observers begrudgingly admitted, argonauts, in their mad rush for wealth, ironically manifested the very virtues of individual drive, energy, and independence extolled by Protestant leaders. Paradoxically, the Protestant-inspired myth of the self-made man, a virtue preached from the pulpits of many eastern churches, intensified the allure of the gold rush.[74]

Furthermore, as much as evangelicals preached about the providence of California, the wonders of its instant civilization, and the morality of its mineral stores, they remained insensitive to the regional conflicts of interest its settlement could provoke. The migration of thousands of young men from the Northeast demonstrated the extent to which the religious needs of eastern evangelical leaders, eastern parish ministers, and western missionaries were connected but not identical. These differing investments in the westering enterprise emerged clearly in the sermons of departure. Mission leaders encouraged the notion that the preservation of community stability at home was entirely compatible with the extension of evangelical values to the mining regions. In practice, however, eastern parish ministers resisted the depopulation of their own congregations for the good of the Pacific Coast. Ministers engaged in a subtle turf war for the loyalty of the laity, particularly their young male parishioners. Even as home mission organizations tried to unite the interests of East and West, they pitted the ethics of family and community order against those of Christian missionary expansion.

This conflict resulted in a complicated chorus of advice to departing miners. Begrudgingly acknowledging that they could do nothing to stop their parishioners from venturing to El Dorado, many clergy encouraged aspiring miners to look upon their trip as a test of their souls, a trial during which they should work to preserve their religious characters. Brigham cautioned that even the journey west presented moral perils and that while on shipboard or wagon, men should discipline their spirits for the greater temptations to come. The migration was to be used as a time to cultivate the intellect, he suggested, a time to read good books, not works of amusement. The monotony of sea travel, in particular, could tempt one to games of cards and dice. A Christian, he advised, must beware, for "what is merely an innocent amusement for the occasional leisure of general society here, may become there a fatal passion." If one maintained a cheerful temper and did not complain, the privations of life on shipboard would serve as good discipline for the "half savage life of the wilderness."[75] Several ministers, in conjunction with the Young Men's Bible Society or religious tract societies, presented edifying literature to departing adventurers. Like S. L. Caldwell, they considered the company of good books a blessing. He reminded his listeners that the "New England mind and character and society is such as it is, because of the Bible. . . . The Bible, the Bible, has made New England the best place to be born in, on the whole round globe."[76]

Ministers, then, instructed immigrants to inure themselves to the evils of California by thoroughly internalizing their faith. Like their Bibles, faith could be packed up and transported to the Pacific; piety was not simply a product of eastern culture and its institutions, but was a quality of character that men could carry within themselves. Despite external temptations, true Christians, through proper spiritual and mental preparation, could adhere to evangelical standards of morality. This notion, of course, was hardly new: evangelicalism itself was a movement that fostered an individual relation to the divine through an internalized system of discipline and devotion. The prospect of California life, then, only magnified its significance. A popular song distributed during the 1850s articulated this idea of religion as buried treasure:

> And while you seek, with earnest toil,
>   The glittering prize to win,
> Remember that a treasure lies
>   Embedded deep within.
>
> Oh! Guard it that it not grow dim;
>   'Twill well repay your care,
> If often on your bended knee,
>   You burnish it with prayer.
>
> 'Twill throw a radiance round your path,
>   And in its pure, rich light,
> You'll walk amid a thousand wrongs,
>   And always keep the right.[77]

Funeral sermons for deceased miners served an important didactic purpose in driving home these points, as well as reminding mourning relatives about the fragility of life. Often such cautionary tales required extrapolation on the part of the minister, who did not necessarily know the precise fate of the late adventurer's soul; nonetheless, grieving families sustained great comfort from the thought that, in the midst of a sinful land, their sons had retained their religious principles. One eastern minister, A. Boutelle, comforted the relatives of Newell Marsh, a young man who died of disease soon after his arrival in Shasta City, by speculating that Newell had used his time at sea as a period of contemplation. Boutelle noted that in a letter Marsh wrote to a friend, "he speaks of reading the Bible through once, and some besides while on the way, which, in his circumstances, he could hardly have done without thinking seriously of the concerns of his soul."[78] Joseph C. Foster, pastor of the Baptist Church of Brattleboro, Vermont, eulogized Henry Bemis, a twenty-three-year-old who died after a strenuous trip around Cape Horn. Foster thought it likely that Bemis had turned to God in his last hours, and he noted the last-minute visit to his bedside of a missionary "who had gone to gladden those moral wastes."[79] By dwelling on the moral dangers of California (while assuring families that their late relatives were exceptions to the rule), ministers reinforced the importance of preserving and protecting evangelical values.

In keeping with their belief that spirituality was a private matter, and concerned lest their congregants stay in the land of Ophir for too long, eastern clergy rarely encouraged miners to work actively for the evangelical cause in California. Some assumed that the Christian example of their parishioners would lead necessarily to social transformation. The Reverend George Caldwell, while imploring his listeners to go forth fortified and entrenched, defending themselves with true religious principles, also asserted that such behavior would set an example for others. "We hope you will take with you New England principles and habits, and the New England character, and be good specimens on those distant shores, and among those motly groups . . . and there increase and diffuse as you can the New England element."[80] More often, however, clergy used the idioms of battle—*fortify, entrench, guard*—and employed metaphors of defense, of a bastion to be protected rather than an external change to be effected. Ministers advised that argonauts would best help themselves by getting in and out of California as fast as possible. Like Charles Brigham, J. H. Avery cautioned easterners to stick together, "for you'll find none in California, probably, who will be more true to you than the members of your own company." "Keep your own counsel," he continued, and beware of strangers, for there is always someone around "who wants to swindle you." Miners were always to bear in mind that their goal was to make money in order to return home; the cautious man, therefore, should never get too settled. "Avoid politics. What's California politics to a man that's not going to remain in California? Besides, it will consume time, and waste energy."[81]

Avery never mentioned the problems that might arise for the establishment of a "New England on the Pacific" if thousands of New England men, prospecting in California, completely avoided political or social involvement. This was not his major concern, just as it was not the primary consideration for most eastern clergy witnessing the flight of their parishioners. It would be left to the home missionaries themselves to contradict the counsel of parish ministers, and to convince immigrants that their true Christian duty lay not in avoiding involvements in California, but instead in transforming it into a home.

Chapter 3

Taming the
Physical Landscape

I hear the tread of pioneers
  Of nations yet to be;
*The first low wash of waves where soon
  Shall roll a human sea.*

The rudiments of empire here
  Are plastic yet, and warm;
The chaos of a mighty world
  Is rounding into form!
—Samuel H. Willey, *Decade Sermons*

In 1859, the Presbyterian missionary Samuel Hopkins Willey, far removed from eastern debates over the evangelization of the Pacific Coast, vividly described the "peculiarities" of California as a mission field. The minister was called to a great variety of occupations, Willey explained; he had to find a place to worship, publicize services himself, visit potential congregants, raise funds for and subsequently build a house of worship, organize and superintend its construction, and dedicate it. These duties were added to the usual rounds of funerals, Sunday services, prayer meetings, marriages, and visiting of the sick. Even more significantly, Willey continued, these activities all had to take place within a culture where the inhabitants were "extraordinarily ready" to ignore religion.[1] Missionaries and their societies, as Willey indicated, faced the challenge of bringing a Protestant-inspired order to the new state. This was a task that proved to be both multifaceted and utterly elusive. On the one hand, the minister served as fund-raiser, promoter, preacher, educator, and counselor of his flock. On the other hand, his broader goal was to instill and internalize a sense of Christian community and civic pride among the diverse inhabitants of gold rush society, and to create an ethical climate in which supporting religious work was desired rather than obligatory.

The work embraced by ministers fell into three broad categories. Although the objectives were pursued neither systematically nor with equal vigor by all clergy, they nonetheless point out the complexity of the missionary task and its utter detachment from the theoretical concerns that animated missionary rhetoric in the northeastern states. First, clergy attempted to impose a physical order on the California landscape in order to render the distinctions between sacred and profane time, space, and activity clear and discernible. Second, they worked to overcome the tendency toward internalized, spiritual disorder among the men in the mines and booming towns by encouraging church attendance and conversion among the unregenerate and by enlisting the aid of sympathetic Protestant immigrants. Finally, they strove to perpetuate the institutions and activities of the churches by bringing more ministers to the state and by founding societies and organizations that would sustain the Christian message. In this chapter I present a group portrait of California missionaries, describe their reasons for going west, and discuss their efforts to impose their own brand of sacred order on the physical landscape.

If the fate of the Christian faith temporarily relied on the settlement of an evangelical society in gold rush California, the primary responsibility for the success of the venture rested with the strength and talent of individual missionaries. As one correspondent informed the AHMS, "If the West is ever evangelized, it must be by the living PREACHER, under God, aided by such other collateral means as Christian benevolence has devised."[2] Religious leaders in the East could theorize, strategize, and even keep public interest and funding for the cause alive, but their efforts were futile without the cooperation of a talented and energetic clergy, men willing to sacrifice home, family, and public acclaim for the glory of God on the Pacific.

Who were these young men? The unsettled nature of frontier society makes it difficult to draw conclusions about the missionaries who volunteered their labors in California during the 1850s and 1860s, just as it is difficult to generalize about the thousands of settlers who headed west to seek other kinds of fortunes. All saw in the discovery of gold the providence that best suited their own needs and desires. Further complicating a collective biography is the fact of clerical transiency. Many clergy, particularly those among the Methodist and Baptist ranks, allied themselves with the church only months or years after their arrival in the state, preaching to crowds or stray pedestrians on an informal and intermittent basis. Others, their heads turned by economic opportunities, abandoned preaching for the mines, bringing down on themselves the wrath of their more institutionally oriented colleagues.

In sum, estimating the numbers of ministers who passed through California during the 1850s is guesswork: even the commissioned agents struggled to report the size of their ranks. Baptist agent J. W. Capen told the editors of the *Home Mission Record*: "There are quite a number of Baptist preachers in various parts of the country, most of them from the west and all engaged in secular employments." Adding his own commentary, Capen concluded that "many of them . . . I grieve to say, have failed to exhibit any zeal to promote the glory of our redeemer."[3] Ministers, like miners, had a way of disappearing into the swirl of El Dorado. Osgood Church Wheeler, the senior Baptist missionary in the state, reported that of the forty-six pastors he had registered in good standing between April 1849 and August 1850, "all wearing the vestments," not one had helped to further religious work in the region.[4] An educated estimate would place the total number of evangelical ministers who spent time in missionary service during the 1850s at between four and five hundred.[5]

California missionaries came from a wide variety of backgrounds, but the centrality of upstate New York in the origins of many testifies to the persistent importance of the "burned-over district" well into the 1840s as a breeding ground for missionary zeal. A handful of Congregationalists, estimated at about twenty in 1860 and limited in their geographical scope by the Plan of Union, came almost exclusively from New England, although several had been educated outside of the Puritan orbit.[6] New School Presbyterians represented a wider region, from Maine to New Jersey and west to Ohio, with the single largest contingent coming from upstate New York.[7] Educated at seminaries such as Auburn, Lane, and New York's Union, where student missionary societies were popular, New School ministers exhibited a zealous commitment to evangelical social reform. In California, leaders such as Willey, born in New Hampshire and educated at Dartmouth and Union, took the lead in organizing schools and moral reform societies. The small contingent of ABHMS agents in California, estimated at less than a dozen prior to 1860, gained numerical strength from the Boston area, owing to its proximity to Newton Seminary, and from upstate New York. Northern Methodists, the most numerous of the northern clergy, are also the most difficult to trace. Like their Baptist and Presbyterian brethren, the largest contingent received its spiritual nurture in the agricultural regions of the burned-over district. This was particularly true of the Methodist leadership: of thirteen of the most notable denominational representatives in the state, five traced their roots to New York, two to Indiana, two to Ohio, two to Vermont, and one each to New Jersey and Pennsylvania.[8]

For ministers and for other western migrants, gold rush society was a permeable membrane with few fixed traditions or institutions to regulate the flow of adventurers. Even clergy with official appointments reached the state by a wide variety of routes. Most typical of AHMS appointees were the young men, fresh from seminary, whose religious zeal had been ignited by the emphasis on foreign missionary work in vogue among students of divinity in the years following the religious awakenings of the 1810s. Campus organizations across the Northeast drew potential laborers with their appeals to the spiritual energies of young manhood. The first student organization at Union Theological Seminary, founded in 1835 by New School Presbyterians, was the Society of Inquiry Respecting Missions.[9] At Union and at other evangelical schools such as Andover, Yale, Brown, and Newton Seminary, eager scholars, invoking the urgency of the millennial struggle, impelled one another to work for the Lord in Burma, India, or China—regions where "the soldiers are few, the battle is hot, and the enemy are strong." Taking their cue from the original Haystack Revival at Williams College, groups of students pledged to pursue missionary labors after graduation.[10] Those who hesitated while in school often capitulated later at the urging of their peers. Edward B. Walsworth, a graduate of Union, served a church near his home in East Avon, New York, for several years after his graduation. In 1852, a friend urged him to think about a foreign field, if not for himself, then for the good of the congregation: "This will bind them to you & you to them & you can wield a double influence."[11]

Favorable publicity and boosterism also convinced some young men to volunteer for missionary service in California. Willey, newly graduated from Union Theological Seminary in 1848, was approached that summer by the AHMS as a possible candidate for a missionary post. He initially refused, preferring to stay in New England because of the uncertainty of religious prospects on the Pacific Coast. Subsequently, he read Edwin Bryant's recently published *What I Saw in California* and was startled by the assessment of the enormous spiritual and social potential of the state. Within months he was on a ship headed west.[12] Survey reports also provided useful information that was published in evangelical periodicals. In its first article on California in November 1848, the *Home Missionary* described the urgent need to send two ministers immediately to the promising region. The editor barraged his readers with all manner of statistics—square mileage, precise boundaries, weather patterns, the kinds of crops that would thrive in such a climate, and an ethnic delineation of the population—as if these facts, in and of themselves, rendered self-evident the spiritual promise of the state.[13] As literature multiplied, so did evangelical interest. Two months later, in January 1849, the same journal published extracts from John Fremont's memoir. Fremont provided his own detailed description of the geography, climate, and soil condition of the territory, including a valley-by-valley assessment of its agricultural potential.[14]

At the same time, fundamental changes in the economic, social, and religious structure of the Northeast in the first part of the century affected the professional prospects of ministers at home. The same factors that impelled other settlers to move westward also moved the clergy: the two migrations were, in many respects, mutually reinforcing. As intensive agriculture depleted soil fertility in the older eastern settlements and as newly built canals and turnpikes opened markets farther inland, people migrated to more profitable locations. The resulting social instability affected the employment patterns of the clergy, many of whom found themselves coping with shrinking congregations and uncertain prospects. Consequently, clerical mobility increased dramatically: in Connecticut, for example, the average term of employment for a Congregational pastor in the eighteenth century was between twenty and thirty years. By 1825, the average had dropped to six years.[15] Simultaneously, a host of new colleges nurtured by revivalist zeal offered access to education to a generation of young men for whom agricultural prospects looked increasingly dim.[16] With more educated clergy and fewer available jobs, the mission movement provided a new outlet for professional aspirations.

But why California? The interest of young men in overseas labor did not necessarily lead them directly to the Golden State. Indeed, for most of the first generation of California missionaries, the field served as either a substitute or a compromise for work in foreign countries. Many Americans considered the region, still a laborious three- or four-month journey from the East Coast, to be a foreign appointment. Charles Maclay, a Methodist from Pennsylvania, volunteered his services as a missionary in 1850, asserting that he was "ready for any missionary field, China, California, &c."[17]

The Reverend William C. Pond, son of a professor and later president of Bangor Theological Seminary, Enoch Pond, expressed considerable defensiveness about his appointment to California, indicating, perhaps, that he looked upon it as an unavoidable second choice. After graduating from Bowdoin College in 1848, recognizing that his career opportunities in Maine were limited, the younger Pond resolved to become a foreign missionary. Two months before finishing his seminary training at Bangor, he spied an appeal in the *Home Missionary* for volunteers to labor on the Pacific Coast: "Going to

California at that time was every way equivalent, so far as the feeling of the people was concerned, to going to the foreign field," he later explained.[18] The challenges to spirit and character, he maintained in a defense that bordered on defensiveness, were just as significant on this side of the Pacific as they were across it. Whether he was trying to convince himself or his audience, it is now difficult to discern. Clearly, California looked attractive because it embodied the spiritual and physical deprivations—and concomitant romantic attractions—of overseas posts. "All that had made me resolve to be a foreign missionary—the probable encountering of hardship, the distance from the old home, the encountering of physical difficulties such as not all young men could sustain—these existed in regard to California, as we then viewed it, and the preaching would be done in my mother tongue."[19]

For other young men, anxious for a taste of the exotic but well accustomed to the comforts of home, California offered an appealing middle ground—not quite foreign, but indisputably cosmopolitan. George Burrowes described how, as a student at Princeton in the 1830s, he had "determined to devote" himself "to the life of a foreign missionary." Whether through illness or accident, his plans changed, and he remained in the East for over twenty years. In the late 1850s, he began to think seriously of California as a field, seeing it as a place that would provide an opportunity for work in religious education, rather than the rigors of continual preaching. He traveled to Philadelphia to offer his services to the Presbyterian Board of Education and Board of Home Missions and was sent West in 1859 to help establish the first Presbyterian seminary in the state.[20] William C. Anderson, another Presbyterian living in New Albany, Indiana, agonized to a friend over whether to accept a post in Calcutta that had just been offered to him. Anderson explained that although he was ready to go if duty called, he disliked both the climate and the government of India and "the thought of expatriation is terrible to me—I sincerely distrust my qualifications for the post." Instead, he came to California several years later.[21]

The perceived urgency of the missionary struggle, the institutional and collegial pressures felt by many young men to take up the cause, and the dearth of job opportunities in the Northeast thus pushed more than a few young seminarians to volunteer for foreign work, despite their misgivings about their own spiritual preparation. Compounding their unease was the advice of mission leaders who, anxious to add to their ranks abroad, encouraged young clerics not to let their preference for a particular field outweigh their general dedication to the worldwide cause. Young men, therefore, did not control their own fate with respect to their choice of appointment. The California field, somewhat ironically, benefited from this administrative encouragement of flexibility: falling between the interstices of home regions and foreign posts, it looked alien enough to appeal to the adventurousness of younger men but domesticated enough to assuage fears of complete cultural dislocation.[22]

Yet this view is still retrospective. Mission proponents throughout the 1850s had difficulty convincing anyone to accept a commission to California; few ministers who ended up there as agents saw it as a first choice. Converting the heathen in foreign parts seemed a much more challenging and rewarding occupation. Nonetheless many men, once they had landed on the Pacific Coast, by choice or persuasion, found it to be the answer to their unease, and they embraced the compromise that it offered. Timothy Dwight Hunt represents a most poignant example of how California combined the exotic lure of distant lands with the comfortable familiarity—not to mention the presumed cultural superiority—of an American population.

Hunt, a New York Presbyterian reared in Genessee County, descended from the Mayflower Elder William Brewster, and named after the Yale divine, sought an overseas missionary appointment. As a student at Yale College and later at Auburn Theological Seminary, he expressed his interest to the ABCFM. The board responded by directing his attention to India "as the probable field of my missionary toils."[23] Instead, he was appointed to a post in the Sandwich Islands in 1843, where he labored to train native seminarians with little apparent success. By 1847, his letters to his family and to his supervisors in New York, tinged with bitterness toward the indolence of the heathen population, revealed a growing sense of isolation from the northern culture and values he cherished. "I am not & have not been happy in my personal labors for this people," he confided to ABCFM secretary Rufus Anderson. "I have no enthusiasm. I have no attachments. I have been transplanted here, but my roots have not found a genial soil."[24]

Hunt faced two difficulties. The first was a growing awareness that his preconceptions of missionary life had been faulty, formulated in the blind passions of youthful zeal. "I came out under impressions formed during the revivals of '38, '39, & '40. I must humble myself enough to say that I was influenced more by the romance than the reality of missionary work. . . . I felt certain of an enthusiasm that would lighten every burden, & bear me far above the trials incident to missionary life."[25] To his parents, presumably with even more candor, he admitted that he had never wanted to come there in the first place; he had realized that his preference was "decidedly for the labors of the home field." "I am like a branch transplanted that has sent down no roots, whose leaf already withering can survive only [if] its stock is returned & replanted in its parent soil."[26]

Changing his course midstream, however, presented a second dilemma. Foreign missionaries, once commissioned, were not given a hero's welcome if they chose to return to the states. Hunt's decision to come home to the East, he knew, would be likened to a dishonorable discharge, a form of embarrassment that would discredit him in the eyes of his colleagues. "How will my return affect me in the opinion of God's people?" he fretted. "You know the prejudice existing respecting the return of missionaries. It is hardly bearable in cases of affliction & bereavement: how will they look upon one who leaves the foreign because he prefered the home work. Will they at all appreciate my motives & feelings. Will they not look upon me as a deserter?"[27] Hunt saw no face-saving means of escape from the work he had chosen. His wife, Mary, less convinced than her husband that they should abandon the work, also feared the effects of a hasty return: in the fall of 1847 she confided to her parents, "I am afraid [Dwight] will go home next fall, or try to make arrangements to do so."[28]

News of the California gold rush reached the Sandwich Islands in the spring of 1848, before Hunt could act on his resolution. As islanders quickly left for the gold fields, Hunt almost immediately decided to join them. Although the official explanation for his departure in October 1848 was that he wanted to minister to his immigrating flock, both his personal correspondence and his ensuing actions indicate that he used the flight of his parishioners as a pretext to pursue a ministry among a Euro-American population. California was the perfect compromise for Hunt, in that he could labor among his own people yet remain in a "foreign" field. As early as March 1848, Hunt's justification for the significance of this new work was firmly in place: "Perhaps the Lord designed us for that station & sent us here for the discipline & experience we needed that we might thus be better prepared to undertake so great a work," he wrote to his wife's parents. "The influence we do exert will not only be fundamental, but perpetual—i.e., exerted in the formation of a people who will grow up to fill the land & more or less affect the world."[29] In California, as the interdenominational chaplain of San Francisco and later as an agent of the AHMS, Hunt found the combination of spiritual energy and cultural sophistication he desired: "I have a feeling of contentment which I was a stranger to at the Islands. . . . I am satisfied that I occupy a much wider & more promising field among a growing & an energetic people than that I occupied there among an indolent & wasting race."[30]

Although he failed to appreciate the indigenous Hawaiian culture and doubted whether evangelicalism could ever take hold among them, Hunt reacted positively to California society. He embraced the region as a fertile seedbed for the Puritan heritage and eventually told his brother-in-law that his love for the area surpassed his affections for his eastern home: "Dear to me as is my native land my Pacific home is dearer."[31] Hunt came to look upon California as the "New England of the Pacific," positing a direct line of cultural influence from east to west. After the birth of a boy in 1852, Hunt explained to his in-laws that he and Mary were thinking of naming the child William Brewster: "Did you ever think of it, that a descendent in a direct line from one of the prominent men in that band of pilgrims was the first minister of California? . . . I have but few things to be proud of, & they are my wife, my boys & my puritan blood! The blood of olden times & better men flowing in my veins is all of myself of which I boast. Shame on me, nay rather, 'woe is me' if I do not here advocate puritan principles & build up puritan institutions. I am glad on the whole, that I organized on these shores the first old fashioned orthodox Congregational Church. I can almost see the shade of the old elder rising up & blessing me."[32] California provided T. D. Hunt with a greater sense of mission than he would have found anywhere, including, most likely, his place of birth.

Like Hunt, nearly all Presbyterian and Congregationalist ministers in California during the 1850s and 1860s were commissioned by home mission societies, as were a number of northern Baptists. With their emphasis on an educated and socially polished clergy, these agencies assumed that missionaries would make sacred pursuits their sole concern. Samuel Willey, worried about the reputations of ministers who themselves mined gold, wrote to his supervisors: "We most earnestly hope no minister will come here, without making a solemn covenant with God & his own soul, to know nothing here but Christ & him crucified, & not to meddle with digging gold or speculating in lands. If a class of men should come here & do these things they would destroy their own power to do good, & cripple that of others."[33] Striving to maintain purity among their ranks, commissioned clergy frowned on the apparent lack of spiritual commitment evidenced by itinerants: "Not many clergymen who have gone to California," observed the *Home Missionary,* "make the ministerial work their exclusive business, except those who have gone out in connexion with missionary societies."[34]

In contrast, the vast majority of Baptist and Methodist clergy came to California independent of denominational appointments. Although a few Methodists, such as William Taylor and Isaac Owen, also came with official commissions, the particular situation of Methodism as a missionary movement, staffed largely by itinerants, meant that many preachers traveled through California during the gold rush for short periods and without the official acknowledgement of the church. The same was true of many Baptists, who found their way to the Golden State independently of denominational ties. For this majority of the clergy, motivations for coming were identical to those of the miners: economic opportunities beckoned them. Methodists drew large numbers of itinerants from among the ranks of adventurers like Charles V. Anthony, who found his way to the church after his arrival. Born in Portage, New York, in 1831, Anthony moved with his parents to Fort Wayne, Indiana, at the age of seven. The Anthony family had descended from a long line of Quakers in the colonies, dating back to the seventeenth century. Charles's grandfather, Elihu, served as a Quaker leader in Saratoga County, New York, for more than sixty years. Shortly before Charles's birth, his father was disowned by the Friends for his "universalist ideas." In 1851, Charles went to California to stay with his brother, and within a year he converted to Methodism. By 1855, he was a prominent preacher in the region.[35] Another young miner, Peter J. Cool, came to California from New York at the age of twenty, anxious to earn enough money so that he could finish college. Converted to Methodism just prior to his trip, Cool attended services and camp meetings during his years of prospecting. Eventually, he obtained a license to preach, and in 1854 he joined the Methodist Conference in California.[36]

Much to the chagrin of their commissioned colleagues, Methodist and Baptist preachers took up the ministry more often as a vocation than as a profession. Because they were not paid for their labors, they were forced to work at other occupations. During the gold rush, of course, the most lucrative alternative was mining. Elihu Anthony, brother of Charles, left his previous work as a blacksmith to join the rush for gold, "most of his neighbors having left, and hearing wonderful reports of rich deposits found."[37] A few ministers already preaching in the state temporarily put aside their Bibles to take advantage of the gold strikes.

Yet in spite of the proclivities of some Congregationalists and Presbyterians to label their Methodist and Baptist brethren as lower-class and immoral, missionary motivations were not easily categorized as sacred or profane. Given the high cost of living in California and the meager state of home mission salaries, all missionaries felt keenly the financial strain of living on extremely limited means. By the late 1850s, the more prestigious San Francisco churches offered generous salaries to star orators as a means of luring them westward, but these few exceptions were starkly opposed to the general rule of ministerial poverty. Even Thomas Starr King, the famous Unitarian orator and most well known California minister, struggled financially before leaving for the West; the support he paid to his mother's family almost certainly played a part in his willingness to accept a lucrative San Francisco pulpit.[38]

At the same time, not all Methodists and Baptists came for the money. A significant number apparently went West looking for opportunities of a different sort, including the desire to escape the confines of a theological tradition-alism that stifled them. Few were as outspoken as Martin Clock Briggs, born in Oneida County, New York, in 1823, and reared in Lake County, Ohio. Briggs returned to the East Coast to attend the Concord Biblical Institute in New Hampshire before continuing his studies of Greek and Hebrew in Boston in 1849–50. More than most Methodist preachers, his cast of mind was well suited to the educational and theological rigors of New England. It was this intellectual sophistication, perhaps, that caused him to express a lack of ease with northeastern life, where "the crabbed roots of old-fashioned Calvinism fill all this soil." Briggs missed the "general cordiality" of the West (by which he meant, apparently, regions like Ohio). This condemnation was not without its measure of respect: "There are some charms in the land of the Pilgrims to the patriot and Christian," he conceded. "One can not forget that young liberty was nursed on this rocky soil."[39] After a brief stint in a city mission in Boston, however, Briggs headed for California in 1850 to spread both a love of liberty and a less hindered theological message.

In sum, motivations for westward movement extended along a broad spec-trum, from institutional commitments to personal gains, with most men exhibiting a combination of the two. Once in California, the familiar cate-gories of class, educational status, and denomination became less relevant. Their unfamiliarity with the land to which they journeyed and a lack of prac-tical experience to help them cope with the social maelstrom of the gold rush served to level many distinctions. The dearth of realistic and useful informa-tion available about the new state in the early months of immigration also tended to equalize spiritual and social differences, creating an atmosphere of common cause and common confusion. Typical was the experience of Wil-ley, who tried to buy a map of the region in New York in 1848 and discovered that "the only approach to it was an appendage to a map of Mexico, covering a space not larger than my hand."[40] Even more significant was the youth of the men—almost a prerequisite for the arduous life of a western mission-ary—which often implied a lack of professional perspective that might oth-erwise have tempered their reactions to a strange and complicated world. As William Pond recollected about the 1850s, "those who wrought here were almost without exception young men, sometimes more eager than wise, and . . . for us all the circumstances in which we wrought were unprecedented. Lessons of experience were yet to be learned, and experience is a pitiless teacher whose lessons are beaten into us by hard blows."[41] In attempting cul-turally to replicate the Northeast, home mission leaders sent a delegation of men who were, despite their energy and enthusiasm, only partially equipped to do so.

The relative youth of home missionaries was also important because experientially they were the equals of the men they had been sent to evangelize. With respect to age and region of origin, the migration of eastern ministers to California closely paralleled the movement of male immigrants as a whole, and their purposes for coming were not as divergent as evangelicals would like to have believed. Most forty-niners were relatively young men who saw California as an opportunity to start a career. These similarities meant that even as ministers tried to set the terms of communal interaction in California and to serve as voices of religious tradition and moral authority, their efforts were necessarily tempered by their empathy with the plight of miners.

In important ways, of course, missionary motives were also quite different from those of the laity. While many miners merely wished to use California as a way of "making their bundle" before heading home, ministers hoped to transform the state itself into a home, to impose on it the Protestant distinctions of sacred and secular that it lacked. In this respect evangelical ministers, despite differences of education and class, shared a common bond with one another and with their sponsors that differentiated them from other argonauts, and that drew them together in a fraternity that continued to outweigh denominational distinctions. Notwithstanding occasional sectarian rumblings, gold rush missionaries generally resisted the growing ecclesiological quarrels that were splintering the eastern Evangelical United Front. Even as the organizational foundation for home missions broke apart, the social context of California united ministers in an appreciation for their common battle. As Willey wrote to his sponsors, "I assure you, we have a most excellent body of Christian men in this city, firm in every good course, & unsectarian."[42]

Once in California, ministers discovered that the moral terrain was just as murky as the undersized maps of the area. Socially and culturally, both San Francisco, a rapidly expanding urban frontier, and the teeming mining regions differed drastically from the relatively homogeneous northern towns and cities from which missionaries came. The decade of the gold rush witnessed an expansion of the region that was, as one historian put it, "neither inevitable nor tidy." By the 1860s, San Francisco would be the ninth largest city in the nation, an active banking center, and hub for the Pacific trade.[43] As early as 1850, the entire region was characterized by unparalleled human diversity and activity: Irish, Italians, Chinese, African-Americans, Hispanics, and Mormons lived alongside and amid the small population of Anglo-Protestants. "Everything & everybody is in motion," explained one preacher. "We here in these ends of the earth live in a constant whirl of excitement."[44] Willey, with uncharacteristic understatement, termed it an "era of bewilderment."[45]

Heterogeneity, however, was in reality only a matter of degree. Increased European immigration to the Northeast starting in the 1820s had begun to disrupt the relative cultural homogeneity of that region as well. This influx of new cultural groups, coupled with the growing internal migrations of workers to meet the labor demands of an emerging industrial marketplace, and the movement of farmers westward in search of more productive land, increasingly gave lie to the image of a solidly Euro-Protestant Northeast.[46] The concept of community that home mission advocates sought to replicate in the West no longer existed in its place of origin, if indeed it had ever existed at all.

What most distinguished the bustling activity on the Pacific Coast from its eastern counterparts was not its multicultural character, but the perpetual mobility of its populace. With the abrupt intrusion of the mining industry in 1848, frontier California was shaped largely by the economy of prospecting, with its cycles of booms and busts, its fluidity of class structure, and its transient populations. People migrated not to settle but to earn their money and move on. Mining towns, and to a lesser extent urban centers that supplied them, faced the dilemma of impermanence in an exaggerated form; miners were most often young, unmarried, and without property. Even if the lure of gold farther upstream did not keep men moving, the gold rush credo to "get rich and get out" sent them home, with or without their fortunes. Society began to settle by the mid-1850s, as forms of mining that required large outlays of capital and a steady labor supply displaced placer mining, but throughout the 1860s, the towns of the mother lode filled and emptied with every rumor of fortune to be found, and the cities of San Francisco and Sacramento served as stopping points for the many immigrants moving in and out of the state.[47]

The realities of California society were worse than missionaries had anticipated. Social and material conditions worked directly against the evangelical desire to promote community spirit. Indeed, the most difficult task faced by missionaries in the state in the early 1850s was finding the people they had come to save. The social maelstrom of the migration seemed beyond the ability of religious leaders to control or temper. By the summer of 1849, tens of thousands of hopeful prospectors from all over the world poured into the region. When hotel accommodations in the small town of San Francisco ran out, those men who could not find lodging in private homes pitched tents or slept aboard abandoned ships in the clogged port. "It is difficult for one in your older settled towns to conceive of the transient character of our population," explained one missionary in a complaint that swelled to a chorus. "This centre is like an eddy in the tide—where the drift of the world whirls round and round awhile, then floats off again with the passing flood."[48]

In the early 1850s the greatest threat to social stability, from the standpoint of missionaries, was the seasonal and sporadic character of mining itself. Crude technology for mineral extraction varied according to the specific location and in turn dictated the level of cooperation among workers: the individual use of the pan and rocker soon gave way to the "long tom," a large device operated by three or four men at a time. By early 1850, most miners had turned to river mining, a labor highly dependent on rainfall and chance.[49] Men followed rumors of strikes and stayed in one place only as long as their luck held out. Osgood C. Wheeler noted that the reported abundance of gold tended "to hurry them onward in almost every pursuit of life, too frequently, without proper reference to the moral character of their acts."[50] Even in the best of circumstances, mining operations sometimes came to a halt during the rainy winter season, when streams draining the mother lode swelled their banks and rising waters inundated the camps and broke through the laborers' barriers. Some men then spent the off-season in Sacramento or San Francisco, trying to increase their earnings in the gambling houses while awaiting the end of the rains.

Such social fluidity worked directly against the interests of missionaries to establish churches. Worship services often were well attended, but loyalty to community was clearly lacking. It was difficult to keep men in one place long enough to bring them into fellowship or to interest them in the long-term welfare of a local church. Presbyterian James Pierpont wrote from Placerville, "Often, we have hardly become acquainted with those whose hearts are with us, and may be just beginning to think of them, perhaps, as officers in our church, when they leave for other cities, or the call of home affections and interest takes them back again to their eastern home."[51]

Missionaries also confronted the problem of the erratic and unpredictable development of towns. Unlike the growth of upstate New York, the Ohio River valley, or even the fertile Willamette River valley in Oregon, where population growth followed predictable patterns based upon proximity to waterways and farmlands, the social consequences of the mining industry made the early development of California highly capricious. Smaller towns rose rapidly and fell just as quickly, defying the attempts of Protestant leaders to allocate resources and laborers rationally. In a letter to the New York *Evangelist,* Willey described the problem of steady development: "As immigration pours in, new centers of settlement will form, in places now unthought of. We cannot tell beforehand where they will be, because they depend on circumstances so very different from what they would be in other parts of our country. But we know that next November will bring down a population from the mines to all these important towns, now hardly anticipated."[52] This situation improved somewhat by 1853–54, as the energy of the gold rush exhausted itself and

more stable agricultural communities grew in California's Central Valley. Ironically, in direct contrast to the situation in the East, where urban centers were
coming to be seen as loci for transience and moral disorder, San Francisco
and Sacramento became relative havens of stability, where settled congregations built and maintained large, commodious churches. As late as 1857,
however, reports of strikes along the Frazier River in British Columbia deci-
mated the populations of the small mining towns in the Sierra foothills. As
long as the economy of a town was connected to the mining industry, its
sense of community was tied to the migrant, striving nature of its citizens. As
W. W. Brier put it, "It would be just as well to send missionaries among the
sailors in the port of New York, with the expectation of building up the Zion of
California, as to send them to these *mining towns* because these miners may
be sailors in two years, and the sailors miners—We know not what a year
will bring forth, no not even a month in this land."[53]

In this context of rapid change, Protestant success was difficult to measure.
Missionaries often felt as though they were taking two steps forward and
three back. One correspondent from the gold regions wrote to the *Home Missionary* that he had finally begun to build up a small congregation, only to
lose one member, "an active Christian," to emigration. Another congregant
had died the month before. "I feel like giving up the battle," the minister
wrote. "We build up churches, only to have the choicest stones swept away
by emigration. When a man acquires wealth, he goes back to the States to
enjoy it."[54] James Pierpont, having reported several months before that he
finally had convinced local storekeepers in Placerville to observe the Sabbath, noted in July 1854 that the situation quickly had reverted to its former
secular state. All places of business remained open on Sundays, "and now
there is not one in our city where the Sabbath day is kept."[55] Pierpont and others lamented the unbroken succession of days, all taken up by an unrelenting
pursuit of worldly gain.

In towns where missionaries managed to gather viable and stable congregations, the vagaries of the California economy often sabotaged the fund-raising capabilities of the church. The experience of S. S. Harmon, a Presbyterian
clergyman laboring in Sonora in the Southern Mines in 1854, illustrates the
far-reaching effects that runaway speculation could have on religious development. Because the financial well-being of churches depended on the support of people whose fortunes rose and fell, business failures could and often
did threaten the very existence of the church. Harmon had been working to
raise money for a meeting house. Among his subscribers were "some dozen
or twenty" people associated with the Tuolumne Hydraulic Association, a
company engaged in hydraulic mining in the gold regions. When the com-

pany failed "to the tune of $300,000," among the sufferers were those who had promised money to Harmon, "footing up, in the aggregate, to over $1,000."[56] In agricultural districts times were just as hard, and price fluctuations in a volatile market ruined whole towns. Samuel Bell of Oakland reported in 1853 that potatoes had been selling for thirty-seven cents a pound; all of the rancheros in town, seeing a profit to be made, invested exclusively in potatoes, paying enormous prices for seeds and labor. By the following autumn, potato prices had plummeted to a quarter cent a pound. It was no longer worthwhile for farmers even to dig the produce out of the ground. "We are in a pitiable state," Bell lamented.[57]

As gold fever ebbed in the mid-1850s, the economy began to settle and allow for the construction of large church edifices in San Francisco and Sacramento. Yet even with relative stability, the progress of Protestant culture was neither smooth nor steady. Severe financial depressions in 1854–55 and again in 1857–58 reminded missionaries of the economic vulnerability of their efforts. The Reverend William Rollinson of the Bush Street Baptist Church, San Francisco, oversaw the construction of a large new building in 1854, incurring debts in his attempt to demonstrate and embody the religious prosperity of the city. When depression hit near the end of that year and the debts mounted, Rollinson, recognizing the difficulties of his situation, quickly resigned to make a "lengthy visit" to the East with his family. Soon after, the congregation was forced to sell the $40,000 building to a French Catholic congregation for $15,000.[58] Samuel Bell, in a moment of nostalgia for the early years of the gold rush, reflected in 1856 that in spite of the anxiety and volatility of the era there had always been some people with money: "You could scarce find a man who had not a 'slug' (fifty-dollar piece) in his pocket." By the late 1850s, poverty was more uniform and progress less sure: "We have in this place no money, no commerce, no manufactures; in all things connected with monetary prosperity we have been steadily retrograding during the last two years."[59]

Agricultural districts held out greater hope for missionaries because a life of farming was more settled and presumably would attract families to the state. Mining centers remained unstable much longer than did the valley and coastal towns. Ministers came to agree with the Reverend William Bartlett's assessment that "there is nothing attractive to a minister in these mining towns, save the opportunity to preach the Gospel. They are totally unlike the valley and coast towns—the population is unstable—one engrossing interest with all its vicissitudes . . . a small proportion of families. Men cut loose from social and family ties."[60] Yet even with the potential of the agricultural districts to increase the stability of society, the problem of unsettled land claims inhibited the growth of family farming for several decades. Before 1846, the Mexican government had been liberal in issuing land grants in the region. Just as American speculators later bought up large tracts of land in the state, shutting out the growth of small farms, so too was land in the 1840s somewhat haphazardly distributed to a small group of Mexican families. By 1848, approximately two hundred families owned 14 million acres of land, but their interests were protected by imperfect titles, overlapping and conflicting claims, and lots that were only partially surveyed. In the early 1850s, as the population increased dramatically, Yankee squatters took advantage of the confusion and claimed the largely "unimproved" land for themselves. In 1851, the federal government established a board of land commissioners to rule on the validity of the Mexican land-grant titles, but cases were tied up in local courts well into the 1870s, preventing any parties from laying permanent claim to the land.[61]

Such an impediment to settlement was another obstacle to the creation of that "home feeling" so desired by the clergy. "The general topics that form the basis of conversation and argument in the Atlantic States, are all lost here in the great land question," noted one observer.[62] Samuel Willey was particularly anxious about the forced transiency of a population that could not settle down even if it wanted to. He compared the situation to the ease of obtaining land in regions like Minnesota or Oregon, a facility that encouraged the creation of community feeling. "I have always seen this difficulty, & that it was in the way of our progress," he commented, "but I never half appreciated how great an obstacle it was herein. It is well nigh *insuperable* till removed."[63] The worst fears of the clergy were realized in events like that which occurred in the farming community of Healdsburg in 1858, when an entire congregation moved to Oregon because of the unsettled land claims in the vicinity. "Had these brethren been able to purchase a home, they would gladly have made our State their permanent residence," reported the Reverend James Pierpont.[64]

The very real threat of natural disaster compounded the challenges posed by the economy and the state of land ownership. Fire was a chief hazard, given the large number of wooden structures in early California towns. In the early 1850s, wood was cheaper and more available than brick and much faster to assemble in a culture that placed a premium on immediacy. Missionaries in the early years of the gold rush characteristically chose to erect churches as quickly as possible, recognizing their importance as emblems of civilization. Yet with alarming frequency, conflagrations consumed years of steady subscription gathering in a matter of minutes. In June 1852, the Methodist Church of Sacramento laid the cornerstone for a new edifice, which was to be dedicated the following November. The night before the service, a fire destroyed $5 million worth of property in the city, including the newly completed church.[65] Similar fires destroyed church property in Marysville and San Francisco in the early 1850s.[66] After three fires had swept through Sonora within a year, Silas Harmon decided to raise the $7,000 necessary for a brick building rather than the $4,500 that a wooden one would have cost.[67] In the eyes of most ministers, the investment was a prudent one.

Religious development was thus closely linked to both economic circumstances and to natural cycles of fire, rainfall, and flooding. Not only did environmental disasters directly threaten the handiwork of missionaries by destroying buildings, they also threatened congregational support by hindering the laity, persons already inclined to flight, from devoting time and effort to religious life. Ironically, a lack of rainfall or too much rainfall could, for different reasons, spell disaster for California communities. Yet ministers never failed to glean from catastrophe a pertinent theological message, a jeremiad directed at the failures of California society. "Surely, California presents an interesting lesson for the moral philosopher," the Methodist David Diehl cautioned after storms had ravaged the coastal town of Santa Cruz. Weather may indeed be the result of luck, he conceded, but "I think it just as reasonable and consistent to believe that these terrible disasters are the voice of God saying to mamon worshipers: In your unholy devotion to gold—in your hot haste to be rich, you have trampled on my law."[68]

In their desire to overcome the perceived physical disorder of California, missionaries shared the assumptions of many easterners in associating the wilderness of the West with spiritual chaos.[69] The need to make religious distinctions in a world in fundamental disarray proved to be a morally charged assignment. For California missionaries, however, the need for such discrimination extended beyond the goal of bounding and thus taming the land.[70] It also corresponded closely with Mircea Eliade's description of the perception by religious people of time and space as differentiated, nonhomogeneous. Certain spaces and moments are, he argues, qualitatively different from others. Sacred space, for example, is "strong, significant space—for Christians and Jews, the space of Exodus 3:5: 'Do not come near; put off your shoes from your feet, for the place on which you are standing is holy ground.'" Eliade asserts that this "spatial nonhomogeneity" is expressed "in the experience of an opposition between space that is sacred—the only *real* and *really* existing space—and all other space, the formless expanse surrounding it." Sacred space in the midst of chaos allows for existential orientation; the formation of religious community, therefore, requires that the boundaries between what is called religious and what is not be made clear. "*If the world is to be lived in,* it must be *founded,"* Eliade concludes, "and no world can come to birth in the chaos of the homogeneity and relativity of profane space."[71]

Surrounded by what they had been taught to consider physical and social chaos, California missionaries set out to consecrate their new territory, to imbue it with religious significance. God had provided an unmistakable sign in the discovery of gold that California held particular importance in the providential plan.[72] Now it was left to the clergy to continue the labor, to make room for the sacred alongside the profane aspects of life. Their comments indicate that the struggle was often characterized in remarkably physical terms. "There is nothing that marks more clearly the progress of refinement, morality and religion," noted the editor of the *California Christian Advocate,* "than neat church edifices, eligibly located."[73]

Church buildings were the most visible manifestation of sacred space in El Dorado, and ministers viewed church construction as one of their primary tasks. Missionaries, upon arrival in the state, held services in rented rooms, above gambling houses, in the streets, or anywhere else they felt that they could gain an attentive audience.[74] In describing these arrangements, however, most commented anxiously upon their proximity to centers of immorality—the brothels, bars, and casinos that lined the main streets of cities and camps. The presence of a church, therefore, served as more than a convenient (and quiet) meeting place; it also disrupted the otherwise seamless garment of sinfulness. After the dedication of a Congregational church in Nevada City in 1851, the minister, J. H. Warren, reported on the significance of the consecration for the twenty-odd members of the congregation: "As we arose from the sermon, we felt that we had indeed made ourselves stronger, and had not only beautified and adorned our Mountain City, but also raised it in the scale of civilization and humanity, by having in our midst, the sanctuary of God."[75] Warren looked upon his new building as a sanctuary in the broader sense of that term, as a refuge from the disorder of society, and as a geographical delimitation of the sacred.

Many AHMS missionaries also indicated the extent to which they sought to replicate physically the New England landscape, as if a similar physiognomy would redeem California spiritually. "I think we have been favored greatly," wrote the Reverend Isaac Brayton enthusiastically from San Jose. "A neat chapel, one of the pleasantest in California, has been erected; it is small, only 25 feet broad by 40 long, surmounted by a neat cupola, in which swings a bell of 200 lbs.; its inviting tones now sounding out on the sweet air of these plains every Sabbath. . . . The pews have a history: they were taken down from the old first church in Brooklyn, and placed in Mr. Beecher's temporary Tabernacle; with the other parts of this building they were freighted around Cape Horn."[76] Altars, communion sets, pews, and sometimes whole buildings were shipped from the East to recreate a familiar setting. The symbolic importance of these reminders of a more civilized world should not be underestimated. Elements of eastern culture, hallowed by association with a Beecher or a well-known church, sanctified the labor of clergy otherwise cut off from their former communities. The Howard Street Presbyterian Church in San Francisco, where Samuel Willey served through the 1850s, pleased him immensely because it presented "the appearance of a New England church, probably because it was designed & built by a man who has built several churches, I think in Massachusetts."[77]

Sound as well as space could be sacralized. Itinerants recognized that their preaching broke into the profane activities of the community. The Methodist William Taylor was the best-known street preacher in early California. Eschewing offers to speak indoors, Taylor stood on empty, overturned crates and delivered his message wherever he could. One of his favorite locales was Portsmouth Square, in the heart of San Francisco, a place he described as "nearly surrounded by gambling and drinking houses," where the music and laughter continued night and day. It was here, he asserted, that a poor preacher could bring down the rich and powerful gamblers, like "waking up a lion in his lair."[78]

Spatial and aural demarcations were not the only boundaries used by California missionaries as bearers of the sacred. Time could also be sacralized, and Sabbath desecration was a moral issue against which evangelicals continuously battled. The Unitarian pastor Rufus Cutler commented on the importance of temporal respites from sinfulness in his call for more holidays and national days of observance: "We need these grateful breathing spaces, and periods of pastime and release, to break in upon the iron and relentless sway of Mammon."[79] Throughout the decade Sabbatarian societies fought unsuccessfully against Sunday commerce, as well as the many amusements that marked the day.[80]

Other symbols of religious order proved more efficacious. Samuel B. Bell, while serving as pastor of an AHMS congregation in Contra Costa, noted that "church bells are an essential requisite whereby to arrest the attention, and bring to the place of worship, a California population."[81] Bells, a feature of religious life mentioned by numerous ministers, had the advantage of marking both temporal and spatial limits. They simultaneously evoked memories of home, indicated the location of the worship service, and told hearers when the services began and ended. Missionaries often went without proper shelter for their families or adequate resources for writing sermons, but bells were practically indispensable as a modest way of staving off the spiritual chaos of their surroundings. James Pierpont of Placerville predicted that his newly acquired bell "shall speak to the conscience, perhaps more effectively than the voice of the preacher."[82] In Nevada City, J. H. Warren included in his description of the dedication of the church a report about the importance of the bell: "Its clear and ringing peals reverberate among the hills and deep defiles for miles around. No sound to me was ever fraught with such soul inspiring music, as was that, when for the first time in these mountain seats, were called forth those hallowed memories which naught but the sound of the church-going bell can awake."[83]

The effort to render time and space nonhomogeneous was not merely an abstract pursuit. Missionaries assumed that the religious constituents of the California landscape would spiritually orient their congregants and ultimately shape their behavior, providing an environmental preparation for conversion. Bells and buildings were, of course, important in their own right, but they were also essential forms of appeal to the consciences and "hallowed memories" of Euro-American miners. Thus environmental modifications would lead to desirable behavioral changes. Pierpont reported that these elements did indeed shape the religious activity of the laity. In a lengthy letter published in the *Home Missionary,* Pierpont described how discouraged he had been in his work, to the point where he had seriously considered leaving his post. He feared that his parishioners were becoming resentful of his continual requests for funds for the church. Upon the suggestion of another minister who advised that "a bell would do wonders for us," Mrs. Pierpont assumed the task of raising funds for its purchase. It arrived on a Saturday night: "We hung it immediately upon the steps of our church; and ere we retired that night, we rang it right heartily. It sounded out upon our hills and ravines, was heard distinctly in both portions of our mountain city, and far away by some living in the country. The next day the bell rang the people to church, as at home." Almost immediately, Pierpont related, large numbers of people began attending services, and the church grew and prospered. Soon, this time at their own instigation, the members had raised enough money to paint the building.[84]

The creation of a sacred landscape in California, as evidenced by the importance of spatial and temporal distinctions for missionaries, can be seen as an attempt to bring eastern culture and religion to the West. Paradoxically, the very act of differentiation also set California apart from earlier American communities. In keeping with Eliade's definition of the significance of sacred space, the process of sacred boundary making brought forth a new creation, a society different from its predecessors. As the clergy strove to replicate a familiar religious environment, the fact that they did so in a different setting dictated that their results would diverge from their model. California churches, albeit edifices hewn from New England pine, designed by eastern architects, and constructed by evangelical hands, were distinctive by virtue of their placement alongside western gambling parlors and dance halls and their occupation by young male miners.

Although some men remained discouraged by the disparity between the physical landscape they hoped to create and the realities of chronic social and spiritual chaos, others began to appreciate California's physical distinctiveness. It was the inspiration of the natural setting and, ironically, its resistance to the imposition of human order that gave some missionaries hope for the future of the state. Even earthquakes and fires, events that destroyed church property and gambling parlors indiscriminately, were interpreted by some observers as a judgment from God, and as a comforting sign of divine presence. After a catastrophic fire in San Francisco in 1851, Osgood Wheeler explained that God was warning California to repent: "The earth has quaked, trembled and shook; still, what regard have we paid to it but to go forward, rebuild, and glory in the elasticity of California enterprise, and challenge the world to produce a spirit of indomitable energy equal to that of San Francisco." Wheeler ventured that perhaps Californians had boasted too much about the city's manifest destiny.[85]

Ministers also expressed a growing appreciation for the distinctive beauty of the Pacific Coast region. When waxing eloquent about the scenery in the Sierra Nevada or the dramatic coastline, evangelicals sounded more like Henry Thoreau than Timothy Dwight. God could decidedly be revealed in the hushed prayers of the sanctuary, but missionaries, touring the back country or glimpsing Lake Tahoe, increasingly discerned the divine presence in the sublime wonders of nature as well. The Methodist S. D. Simonds contributed an article to the *California Christian Advocate* about a trip he made to the northern part of the state in 1851 with a small band of Methodist clergy and their wives, including Martin Clock Briggs and David Deal. All were anxious to prove that "there was something in our hills besides gold." Simonds was fascinated by the hot mineral springs, with their fountains of steam spewing from the earth. He took from his encounter the message that God's ways were beyond the powers of scientists to comprehend: "Bow down ye tyros of science!—The God of nature hath revealed himself in the Bible! Hide not yourselves in the dust of geological science. Look up—a God—THE God appears!"[86]

Profoundly moved by his brush with the chaotic forces of nature, Simonds drew inspiration from it. "We had trodden on a thin surface, over unmeasured depths of flame." He recalled that he had been "under the deepest impressions of the sublime and the terrible." Yet unlike Thomas Jefferson, who gazed into the roaring cataract and saw only the steady turning of the waterwheel, Simonds glimpsed the revelation of God in the West: "California . . . turns a leaf in science and we read nature with more satisfaction, and the Bible more clearly and with a brighter faith." The spiritual promise of El Dorado lay not merely in the social ordering of the landscape, but also in the unmediated energies of the natural realm. "California is the New World of the Nineteenth Century, and her influence will be lasting as her majestic mountains, beautiful as her flower-starred vallies, wide as her white-winged commerce, and more precious than the gold of her quartz and placers."[87] The region's natural beauty increasingly served as an external and sacred referent, as evidence of a transcendent power that kept the chaos of communal life in perspective.

Unlike home mission theorists in the East, who saw in the physical promise of the region a colonial opportunity, reading California as *object*—for civilizing, prospecting, and evangelizing—some local ministers had begun, in modest but significant ways, to approach El Dorado on more naturalistic terms.[88] Dispirited over their inability to transplant the cultural institutions that they had inherited, many nonetheless increasingly admired the physical wonders of the strange new world around them. It was not, to be sure, the world they had anticipated, and it was not a world that they had a language to explain. Still, it was one about which they were intensely confident. Discernible in the sermons and writings of many ministers, including Joseph A. Benton, is the groping for a new religious vocabulary that would correspond to a new physiognomy. Benton gave the dedication sermon at an AHMS church in Grass Valley, where he gave voice to his sense of discovery:

> My friends, we walk amid living and vast realities. They rise
> about us in giant forms. Every day they come thickening upon
> us. . . . In these beginnings of things there is also much that is
> dim and uncertain. We move, to some extent, in the midst of a
> region of shadows. Much that we gaze on is indistinct—many
> forms we see are ill-defined. But the shadows that fall around us
> are not the shadows of the past—the remnants of things gone
> by; not the shadows of evening made by the faint beams of a
> declining sun. . . . They are rather the shadows of the future, big
> with events, the long shadows forecast with things to come . . .
> shadows which in his increasing brightness, are destined to
> shorten and change, 'til they vanish in the golden light of his
> meridian splendor.[89]

Chapter 4

Mapping the

Moral Landscape

As each one steps his foot on shore, he seems to have entered a
magic circle, in which he is under the influence of new impulses.
The wills of all seem under the control of some strong and
hidden agency.
—Daniel Woods, *Sixteen Months at the Gold Diggings*

California's spiritual geography presented a more perplexing challenge to missionaries. The establishment of physical order was, at some level,
beyond their control, in that it was related intrinsically to economic and environmental factors. On the one hand, ministers assumed that the social conditions of the gold rush represented an atypical and transient circumstance,
one that would soon settle and allow for more predictable religious development. Spiritual order, on the other hand, involved the instilling and reinforcing
of piety in the individual, a task with which ministers were quite familiar. Its
apparent failure in California therefore led clergy to considerably more soul-
searching about the moral efficacy of conversion and the revivalist strategy
itself.

Clerical optimism with respect to the spiritual growth of California
stemmed from an earnest faith in the sizable Euro-American population in
the region. As California missionaries gazed out upon the immorality of the
western landscape, they were cheered by mission society promises that eastern Protestants were heading west in large numbers. Secretary Milton Badger
of the AHMS assured Samuel Willey that "the bowie-knife and Colt's-revolver
gentlemen are not the only ones on the way. A respectable portion are from
the bone and muscle of our old settlements; young men of intelligence and

good common school education, and of good morals and professed piety. . . . So many of the better class are going out, that they must eventually give tone and character to the population."[1] Suspicious of the violence and perceived irreligiosity of immigrants from the South and border states such as Missouri, where Yankee missionaries had already encountered fierce sectional prejudice, evangelicals looked to their fellow northeasterners for the spiritual and cultural leavening of California society. Just as the Northeast had been transformed and the enthusiasms of revivalism sustained by the voluntary labor of converted Christians, so too would the Pacific Coast come under the sway of true religion. Following the models established in the Old Northwest and New York state, missionary success was premised upon the support of northeastern immigrants, settlers who retained the moral precepts of evangelical religion and who would help ministers, through benevolent activity and support of the churches, to transform the rest of society.

For practical purposes as well, home missionaries greatly depended on the co-labors of the evangelical laity. This was especially true in the Methodist tradition, where class meetings and lay leadership constituted the infrastructure of associational life. Yet even for Congregationalists and Presbyterians, psychological sustenance from the laity—even on so mundane a level as hosting the minister when he came to call—was expected and necessary. For those ministers who had come to California after considering, or even entering, foreign fields, lay support was an appealing feature of the home field.

News of the gold discovery disturbed some of the earliest missionaries because they feared it would affect the religiosity of the population. Aboard the *Falcon,* a ship bound for Central America in late 1848, Willey first heard verifications of the gold strike. Rumors had been widespread for months, but the final news came as a shock to the young missionary, who had expected to embark on his ministerial career in a neglected corner of the continent. As huge numbers of young men crowded onto his ship in New Orleans, Willey recognized the reorientation that would be necessary in his work. "I had given my life to the purpose of taking some part in the settlement and upbuilding of a new state," he recalled, one that would "be the home of industry, intelligence, civilization, and religion." The presence of mining regions, he recognized immediately, presented a profoundly different kind of challenge. Not only did it worry him that only a class of people "most loose of foot" could leave home at a moment's notice, but his previous knowledge of mining countries "represented them to my mind as poor, ignorant, dissolute and degraded."[2]

The rush for gold did affect the religious fidelity of the laity, but not in the ways that Willey had feared. Ministers initially were quite pleased with the youth and energy of the immigrants. California was not a barbarous region, explained Osgood Wheeler: "Great numbers of those who have followed us, and now surround us, are well worthy of a pilgrim ancestry." Many of them even went to church, he noted. "Our chapel is crowded, and a more attentive, interesting and intelligent audience was probably never addressed by mortal man."[3] The Methodist M. E. Willing exuberantly boasted about the religious community in the state, characterized by "a large number of men of sterling moral worth. . . . In coming to California the chaff was blown off, and those who continued steadfast are generally Christians of the right stamp."[4] The Congregational *Pacific,* while unwilling to make predictions, pointed out that despite the "rude and unsocial" manner of living of many miners, they were not uncivilized; most had, in fact, moved in "polished and refined circles" at home. There was every reason to hope they would do so eventually in California.[5]

As the decade progressed, optimism turned to despair. Missionaries reported that many Californians attended church services, but they failed to demonstrate a spirit of religious commitment. "Ministers here lack those scores of faithful and competent church members, to relieve them of some of these burdens, on whom ministers in the older States are permitted to lean," reported J. S. Zelie from Mokelumne Hill. "Nothing good seems to move forward here, unless the minister puts his shoulder to the wheel."[6] The transiency of the economic order seemed to spill over into all aspects of life; religious devotion was as ephemeral as the streams of gold dust pouring out of the mother lode. Missionary hopes careened between the extremes of exultation and desolation. In their more candid moments, clergy admitted that they simply did not know how to assess their work: "I know not what to think, nor what to say of my *prospects,*" confessed Wheeler. "My chapel is *full.* . . . and I never saw better attention, not half as much emotion. Yet my congregation presents more than one hundred new countenances every Sabbath. They hear once and are gone!"[7]

Missionaries also marveled at the wide range of spiritual persuasions represented among settlers, distinctions of character that the omnipresent cultural manifestations of evangelicalism in the Northeast tended to mask. The Reverend Martin Kellogg, ministering to an AHMS church in the northern California town of Shasta, vividly mapped the "moral geography" of the people in his region. Quite numerous, he observed, were the Roman Catholics, with three churches in town (no other denomination had more than one congregation). The "recklessly irreligious" constituted the second group; these were people with little or no sympathy for Christian efforts, "confirmed in bad habits," and "hopelessly irreclaimable." The only point to their credit, Kellogg conceded, was that they were not overtly opposed to religion. Composing the bulk of society were the "simply irreligious": "They profess no piety, but own some restraint." With encouragement, this type would become hearty sup- porters of religious influences. Smaller in numbers were the "Rusty Church Members," some of whom made "large professions of friendship," but ulti- mately were less reliable than the simply irreligious. Finally, Kellogg gratefully observed, there were a very few exemplary Christians who consistently sup- ported his efforts.[8]

Kellogg's typology was obviously simplistic. Nonetheless, it accurately con- veyed the missionary perception of an unsettling, but oddly fascinating, moral diversity in the mining population. Evangelical religion was seen as an option in California—but only one among many. Joseph Benton strove for a realistic appraisal in an 1857 report: "That we are not in a way to attain distinguished eminence as a religious people, is obvious enough; though as it is we have more religiousness than godliness. . . . There are some of the best Christians in the world in California; and, I suppose, we must admit, some of the worst."[9] Among the most troubling were those who failed to think about reli- gion at all. Wheeler referred with some frustration to the propensity of Cali- fornians to ignore religious questions altogether: "I love my work, but have never seen a harder task than to get a man to look through a lump of gold into eternity. It is more like beating the air, like contending with the elements, like confining the tide or stilling the tempest, than I have hitherto supposed could possibly exist."[10] Samuel Bell observed that in his experience such persons were seldom encountered in other parts of the country: "I notice that many of your missionaries in the Atlantic and Mississippi States have a hard lot in preaching among professors of so many party-colored 'isms,'" he wrote to the *Home Missionary*. "Here, those who do not countenance and support christian worship are, in religion, simply *nothing*. They believe in nothing. They hardly take the trouble of being atheists, or infidels. They are settled into pure *callousness*, and to boast of it, at times, is the only 'religious excitement' they ever undergo."[11]

Equally problematic were the many infidels who seemed quite able to hold a variety of beliefs simultaneously, with little regard for theological or doctri- nal consistency. The Reverend David McClure journeyed to the Pacific Coast by way of Cape Horn and was shocked by his extended voyage with a group of Spiritualists. "The infidelity and opposition to the Gospel, we met with on ship-board, was a source of much grief to me," he reminisced. "The infidelity was, in its type, a mixture of pantheism, rationalism, and spiritualism, based upon the so-called 'revelations' of spiritual mediums, of whom the chief is

Andrew Jackson Davis."[12] Ministers also commented frequently on citizens who equated all faiths and all churches, like the "Dutch man," a "profane, Sabbath-breaking man," who asked the Presbyterian pastor W. L. Jones to baptize his child at the grand ball he was holding the following Saturday evening. "I had a little talk with him, and found that his highest idea of the rite was, the *naming* of the child in public. This was all he expected or wished. I was obliged to tell him that we had no such rite. I could not make him see into it. He said he had always considered that we belonged to the same church."[13] The general confusion of California society carried over from the natural world into the theological realm, much to the chagrin of its clergy.

Evangelicals had previously combated the many forms of infidelity. More confounding were the men who showed some interest in religion but who shied away from active involvement in the church. All missionaries reported enormous discrepancies between attendance at Sunday services and active church membership. Especially worried were the Congregationalists. The AHMS required agents to fill out quarterly reports marking their progress in the field, and these documents give us some indication of the frustrations faced by the clergy. The pastor of the First Congregational Church of Petaluma, A. A. Baker, claimed a larger membership than most. He reported that in 1855 he had twenty-three church members: thirteen males and ten females. His average attendance at public worship was seventy persons, and at Sunday School and Bible classes, forty. Four members had been added to the church "by profession" and another one "by letter" (having transferred from another church). Even with these promising numbers, Baker indicated that he had had only one hopeful conversion in his congregation that year.[14] Ministers fared no better in San Francisco: William C. Pond of the Greenwich Street Congregational Church could claim only five males and three females as members, despite a large and thriving Sabbath School.[15] As late as 1880, Methodist preacher David Deal complained about the disparity between nominal membership and church interest: "It seems strange that so few of the members take any interest in the Church or its Pastor and I sometimes get discouraged at the members."[16]

Deal's comments addressed what was often the heart of the matter: ministers grew resentful that their congregants seemed to lack a personal commitment to *them*. Tensions between missionaries and members ran high. Timothy Dwight Hunt described the men in small mountain towns who would not "so readily give for a preacher as for a church. The Church is something that *shows* well. It improves the appearance of a town. But the preacher eats & wears out what is given, & what is more, perhaps they do not *like* him. Especially they will not if he be plain & God fearing, & fear not man."[17] Sarah

Walsworth, the wife of missionary Edward Walsworth, wrote to her sister-in-law about their church in Marysville. She related happily that the congregation was large and intelligent and the church finances comfortable, but that the members showed an utter lack of interest in "supporting its spiritual interests." "Californians act more from impulse than principle," she concluded. "They go to church when it is *pleasant* & *convenient* to do so, & when they anticipate a good sermon—if they do not like a minister they feel no hesitation in making it known."[18]

Ministers may have been quick to interpret religious controversy as a lack of regard for spiritual interests, but their comments also indicate that miners' behavior encompassed more than mere apathy. From all accounts, California parishioners were a remarkably opinionated and demanding clientele and were fiercely independent in their tendencies. This independence could cut both ways: it could be seen as a refreshing step away from traditionalism or as a disrespect for authority and custom. Congregationalist and Presbyterian clergy were more likely to assume the latter. When the Presbyterian Reverend Laurentine Hamilton negotiated with his church trustees about his salary, he acted as though he were being held captive by a band of immoral tyrants. He told the AHMS that his parishioners had refused to let him take up a collection for any benevolent purpose (including the AHMS itself). If he tried to do so against their wishes, "The cry w[oul]d at once be raised that I was trespassing on the rights of the Trustees. . . . If I had interfered with their peculiar arrangement the Trustees w[oul]d have been down on me. All of them save one are irreligious men, & share in the general indifference toward religious matters. If I provoke their displeasure in any way the result w[oul]d be notice to quit."[19]

The positive side of this independent spirit was noted by other pastors. Osgood Wheeler focused on the challenge that his cosmopolitan San Francisco congregation presented to him. He described the intense scrutiny under which he labored when facing "the experienced traveller, conversant with men and things of every clime," or "the piercing, apprehensive glance of the well-skilled commercialist." Wheeler saw this as a summons to improved preaching: "Never were men placed in positions more imperatively demanding thorough preparations for the pulpit, than those in California."[20] Isaac Brayton, an AHMS missionary in San Jose, also interpreted the new demands of California congregations in a positive light: "Men here deal in realities. They want religion to be made a *great reality* to them, or they have nothing to do with it. Life is real here. It is not a floating along on customs, men scarce inquiring why they do this or that."[21]

For Methodists, the atmosphere of religious independence was seen as an opportunity to gain membership. Rather than attending church simply out of custom or a sense of familial continuity, Californians could feel free to choose a new faith for themselves. The preacher M. E. Willing felt that the Pacific Coast was one of the most promising fields for Methodists: "The people here are not fettered by custom and prejudice. If they feel that they ought to have religion they have not a half a score of relatives to consult where they shall get it; and as for the finger of scorn, the people in this country treat it with perfect contempt. If they feel that they ought to get religion they go right at it, without fearing or consulting any man, woman, or child."[22]

All ministers, however, were aware of the practical constraints placed upon them by an opinionated and divided population. By the mid-1850s, for example, the subject of slavery was all but taboo in California pulpits; northern missionaries were automatically suspected of being abolitionists, although most took a more moderate free-soil line on the issue. "*Prejudices do rule* to a great extent," commented Baker.[23] Hunt rationalized his silence on the slavery issue by pointing to the greater good of evangelical progress in the state. Should the minister "possibly allude too pointedly to certain immoralities, or hint in the remotest way to the subject of slavery even in private, so as to betray his antislavery sentiments, even though not an abolitionist, some over sensitive & over prejudiced men might suddenly cut him from their sympathy & aid."[24] The Baptist missionary Francis Prevaux, head of a school in Oakland, worried that southern parents would pull out of his program if he expressed his political convictions: "Coolness meets me, the cold shoulder is presented, disapprobation is manifested. . . . I respond, to all such remarks & treatment, that if God spares my life I will vote for John Charles Fremont & if I cannot get my bread in Oakland, I thank Heaven that there are other places where I can labor & enjoy the privileges of a freeman."[25]

Some clergy did notice and comment upon a distinct "California" style of piety throughout the decade.[26] In spite of considerable evangelical optimism about the spiritual potential of the state and the intermittent support of the population for the construction of churches, the goal of personal conversion through revivalism was an unabashed failure. Even the Methodists, who boasted a membership far beyond that of other denominations, confessed that the spiritual landscape looked bleak. The Reverend William Taylor commented on the stubbornness of the populace: "This city, it is true, can exhibit as many church edifices at a greater cost, than any other city of its age in the world. The people of California are justly proverbial for their liberality in giving for charitable and religious purposes. They also treat a man's religious opinions, professions, and efforts, with more respect, probably, than any other new country. . . . But, with all these admissions . . . I believe, nevertheless, that it is . . . the hardest country in this world in which to get sinners converted to God."[27] Taylor's remarks were not the hyperbole of a neophyte itinerant; in the course of his work, he had traveled throughout the United States, Europe, and Africa, where he served as a missionary bishop for the Methodist Church. William W. Brier expressed the general frustration felt by evangelical reformers: "I am despondent," he wrote to the New York office in 1860. "Care and toil has commenced to silver my head and furrow my cheeks, and yet how little has been done. Pray for us on these shores, for our faith is sorely tried. When I consider the years gone by, and all the gloom of this sinful land, I bless God that any of us have been able to stand so long."[28]

Unlike the tumult caused by setbacks in the realm of physical order, the failure of Euro-American immigrants to provide spiritual support raised fundamental questions about the missionary task itself. In foreign mission fields, in contrast, unsuccessful ministers could and often did rationalize their failures on the basis of cultural or ethnic difference: natives either were too steeped in heathen superstitions or were inherently incapable of understanding the Gospel message. Such failure did not necessarily call into question the usefulness and importance of missionary labor; on the contrary, it often caused clergy to affirm even more stridently the truthfulness of their cause in the face of persecution and hardship.[29] In California, however, the presence of a sizable Euro-American population, whose religious status was constantly in question, inevitably pressed the issue of the efficacy of revivalism itself. What was the good of conversion, if Christians so easily lapsed into immorality? What was going on in eastern churches that exerted such a transient hold on the population? Where could one locate the workings of God's grace in the individual, if not through the process of conversion? One missionary asserted that "it would be more pleasant to labor among the heathen."[30]

The prior expectations of missionaries about the piety of Euro-Protestant settlers goes far in explaining the particularly vituperative comments aimed at eastern "backsliders." Ministers reserved their most intense wrath for immigrants who had been members of churches at home but who showed little interest in the church after coming to California. The Reverend J. S. Zelie commented that he was "frank to confess, that the worst trial that it has been my lot to encounter, has been the unfaithfulness of those who *profess religion,* and who made that profession at home—in the East."[31] John Douglas of San Jose reserved even more venom for the "busybodies, gossipers, backsliders, sabbath breakers & the like," who, if reminded of their covenant vows and their spiritual responsibilities, "look at you with amazement or the coolest indifference."[32] It was the "willful neglect" of religion that distinguished the California field, wrote Hunt, "for we deal not with an ignorant people, whom we can pity for their follies, but with a people who know their duty, but *will not* do it."[33]

Assessing blame for this failure raised problems of its own. Some condemned the eastern churches. Brier questioned the efficacy of ministers in the East, who claimed to be reviving their congregants. "The majority of those who have been members of churches at home, here neglect the ordinances of God's house, and many are openly profane," he asserted. "It is a solemn truth here demonstrated, that a large proportion of our church members in the East have never been converted. Multitudes of the impenitent go on heedless of the call to life."[34] Baker expressed surprise that "a very large majority of those who come to this State from Eastern churches, are such as are most susceptible to the allurements of wealth. . . . I sigh for the churches of New England and the older States, which can send out so many from their communions, whose influence, when away, is of so doubtful a character."[35]

Other ministers saw in the lack of conversions another communal warning, an ominous portent of the wrath of God to be visited on an unrepentant land. Editor D. B. Cheney of the Baptist *Evangel* worried that Californians were not preparing the way of the Lord and living in readiness for revival "with girded loins and burning lamps," but were instead giving their "best energies entirely to worldly things." Because of their persistence in focusing on things of this world, the Spirit of God was being withheld from the state.[36]

The failure of the national revivals of 1857–58 to ignite the piety of Californians reinforced Protestant fears that the state was being singled out for its unbridled wickedness. As reports of the progress of the Holy Spirit across the continent reached the West Coast, ministers prayed that a parallel event would finally regenerate California. Evangelicals leapt upon any sign of spiritual awakening. Early in 1858, the Tabernacle Baptist Church in San Francisco began to hold weekday meetings for local businessmen at 8:00 A.M. and 12:00 P.M., and leaders enthusiastically reported an attendance of 150–200 persons.[37] Brier also sponsored a two-week protracted meeting in Alvarado that led to a number of conversions. He and other clergy saw this small beginning as a presage of the final battle against immorality in the state: "I am much encouraged, and feel that the cloud which has, so long, hung over the horizon of our California Zion is about to break away and permit the joyous light of the Holy Ghost [to] beam in upon us."[38] In some corners, it looked as though the promise of the region finally would be fulfilled.

Predictions proved premature. From all reports, revivalism passed over the region with little evidence of individual or communal transformation. The Baptist minister Francis Prevaux wrote despondently to his parents in Massachusetts: "There has been nothing in our State that would compare with the marked interest, & the great number of conversions that have taken place in the East. Perhaps this is not to be expected; & yet why cannot the Almighty work as successfully here, in wicked California, as in any other place?"[39] Concern was so great among the Methodists that a discussion was held at the annual California Conference in 1859. The presiding bishop, O. C. Baker, addressed the subject of why the general revival had not manifested itself in California. "The mournful truth is, we are yet too worldly. The desire for wealth is too strong and too pervading to allow of such profound dedication to God as he requires. . . . There is not sufficient distinctness in the life of the Church, in contrast with the life of wicked men."[40] Once again, ministers leveled blame at the peculiar Californian inability to demarcate properly the sacred from the profane aspects of life.

For a few ministers, including William Pond, the inefficacy of revivalism rather pointedly called into question the role of conversion in the Christian life. Pond's missionary labors in California proved more challenging than most. As a young graduate from Bangor Theological Seminary, Pond greeted his commission to the Pacific Coast with enthusiasm. Assigned by the AHMS to a district in the northern part of San Francisco, he arrived expecting to be greeted by a community of Euro-American immigrants, earnestly seeking the influences of a Gospel ministry, and a modest but workable building in which to conduct services. Instead he found a church, newly constructed and paid for, with no members. "I had, in my simplicity, and in accordance with all that I had known respecting the organization of new churches in New England cities, supposed that when the edifice was ready for occupancy, if not before that, I should learn of a colony, large or small, going with me as a nucleus," he later recalled. Confused, Pond appealed to the local AHMS agent who had assigned him to the post, to ask which church members would be joining him in his work. "'I don't know of any one,'" replied the agent, "'You will have to do as the rest of us have done.'"[41]

Pond nonetheless managed to build a congregation. He commenced humbly with thirteen members and an average attendance of sixty persons; by 1855, after two years of labor, the church was independent of financial support from the AHMS. Then the San Francisco banks failed. Hunt reported to his eastern superiors about the effects of the financial catastrophe on Pond's church. Apparently "Deacon Higgins," a prominent member of the congregation, "the very member whose liberality last year enabled the church so soon to become independent," had suffered severe losses. The church had relied almost exclusively on his support, and his downfall, along with the departure of several other committed members, left Pond's efforts in disarray.[42] His was a sad but common story. Pond recollected: "Men whose presence and influence led to the founding of these churches 'went home' . . . or else caught what was called a 'fever.' . . . Villages quite substantially built with expensive brick buildings were thus left quite desolate, and churches died, or ministers, discouraged by such desertions and the uncertainty of returns for hard pioneer service, left for fairer fields."[43]

Pond dissolved the church and left for another missionary station in the farming town of Downieville. By mining standards, and compared to his experience in San Francisco, his congregation there thrived and was bolstered by the support of over thirty original members. For ten years he enjoyed great professional success. It was clear from his letters east, however, that the frustrations of his work were forcing him to question the task that had sent him West. In an epistle published in the *Home Missionary* in 1860, Pond explained that he was still convinced of the truth of the Gospel message but that he increasingly doubted the ability of Californians ever to heed it. As a way of regenerating and purifying El Dorado, he concluded, "The preaching of that truth or any other, *seems* so utterly insufficient, to the eye of worldly wisdom, that the effort appears absurd."[44] Five years later, when the mineral resources in the area had been depleted and his communicants scattered once again, Pond resigned. After a brief stay in the agricultural district of Petaluma, he devoted the rest of his career to missionary work among Chinese immigrants, a labor that emphasized education and cultural assimilation rather than spiritual revival.

For many missionaries, the failure of revivalism reinforced the importance of religious institutions in sustaining individual faith. Edward S. Lacy addressed an eastern audience at the thirty-third anniversary of the AHMS, describing how his years of missionary work made him appreciate the importance of social restraints on behavior: "I never *knew* the power of society over man until I went to California—surrounded by constant temptations; how can such a community exist without the all-pervading influence of the Gospel?" In emphasizing the need for Christian schools, reform societies, and ministers, Lacy reported on the inadequacy of personal faith. "Men who have been relied on, as pillars in the church, at home, may there be found in the depths of degradation, and bold in the effrontery thereof. . . . A place like California is wonderful for the revelations it makes of character."[45] William Taylor, in most instances a staunch advocate of the primacy of individual religious experience, reflected that, based on his encounters with former professors of religion, "it is easy to see how quickly even a Christian people will relapse into heathenism, if deprived of the wholesome restraints and elevating influences of the Gospel."[46]

But one of the confounding elements of missionary labor in California was that establishing Christian institutions and influences required the assistance of a population already committed to the task. The Reverend W. L. Jones pointed out that he could not establish a church without the help of a congregation: "I do not feel as if I am building up a permanent or self-sustaining church; & until society is entirely regenerated here I do not see how it is possible to do it. . . . This makes me feel as if I am only a 'stranger & sojourner' here, as all the other people think they are."[47] Conversely, congregations lapsed into immorality without the moral fortifications of the church. Wherever evangelical work began, these observations suggested, civilizing and christianizing had to proceed together.

Interactions between ministers and miners in gold rush California threw into disarray many previous assumptions about the necessary relation between religious belief and institutional commitment. Given the transitional state of missionary ideology at midcentury and the concomitant lack of clarity about precisely what combinations of personal and social discipline were intrinsic to the proper formation of a Christian community, it is no wonder that young ministers, unseasoned by the fires of experience, found themselves at a loss to explain, much less correct, the social maladies of gambling, prostitution, and drunkenness. A sense of community spirit was not something they knew how to create out of whole cloth. As Samuel Willey looked back on the early years of his career, he wondered at the naïveté that all immigrants—missionaries and miners alike—carried with them on the ships and trails. "I wish I could stand for once before those great congregations of men in New York again, after this beginning of California experience! I would say to them, 'You don't know yourselves! You don't know how easily your strongest resolutions may be broken down! You don't know how dependent you are on the surrounding supports of a Christian public sentiment to uphold what you think to be your own religious principles!' "[48]

Growing concern about the strategy of home missions and its adequacy in California forced ministers to rely even more heavily on their eastern sponsors for guidance. Letters home contained endless pleas for counsel. "I wish you would give me your opinion in the case," wrote Willey to the AHMS. "We are all too young to judge matters of so much importance."[49] John W. Douglas added that "I feel as if I am almost alone in this country, and I feel my weakness."[50] Separated from their families, laboring in an unfamiliar field, and spiritually alienated from the eastern peers whom they had been advised to rely upon for help, missionaries looked back to their societies to give them the organizational tools that would reinvigorate the Christian cause in El Dorado.

"It is really . . . the founding and rearing of a new Christian state" that would determine California's religious character, rationalized William Pond, S. S. Harmon, and John G. Hale in a letter to the AHMS: "This did not become a Christian state when the arms of a Protestant nation conquered it, or the money of that nation bought it; it did not become such when crowds of men, claiming the name of Christian, came to dig God's gold and profane His day, His book, His name, in all these hills and valleys. It will become a Christian state when sufficient Christian teachers come here to gather Christian churches and to bring up to sacred and believing recollection the doctrines and the Cross of Christ."[51] Frustrated in their attempts to impose order on the physical landscape and perplexed by the failure of northeastern immigrants to adhere to spiritual discipline, missionaries increasingly turned to the building of an institutional infrastructure in the state, one that would survive the present turbulence and guide the state religiously once its citizens had settled down. Colleges, seminaries, and benevolent organizations would thus become the spiritual legacy of California and the measure of clerical success. For help in this aspect of their work, ministers looked to home mission societies, agencies that eloquently and enthusiastically advertised the need for a Christian stronghold on the Pacific, for encouragement and support.

As the 1850s progressed, however, California missionaries became aware of the growing disparity between eastern views of El Dorado and the social realities of the region. Such discrepancies characterize, to some extent, the leitmotif of all missionary enterprises: proximity to the object of one's labors slants—or corrects, depending on one's perspective—the angle of vision, bringing some features into bolder relief, filling in the context, and engaging the heart and mind of the messenger. In turn, the missionary frequently becomes a cultural mediator, forced into the uncomfortable situation of explaining the ways of one society to the inhabitants of the other, while questioning the translatability of his own assumptions. But in California, the cultural empathy of ministers was rendered more problematic by the eastern certainty that traditional evangelical methods were altogether appropriate, despite the pleas of agents to the contrary. California was, after all, part of the Union; its inhabitants were, by and large, products of eastern culture. Therefore, home mission societies assumed, the revivalistic and organizational techniques that had worked from western New England to Iowa eventually would work in California.

California ministers knew otherwise. Like astronauts who had catapulted into space, exceeded the speed of light, and returned home in another era, it was nearly impossible to convey their experience to their earthbound colleagues. The Reverend J. W. Capen tried: "I am satisfied that the condition of this country, its immense resources, and the rapidity of its development, are at home very imperfectly understood," he asserted. "A single year is to us what an age is to many places in the East. During only the nine months of my residence in this State the changes in this city and in Sacramento have been truly wonderful."[52] Willey was less sanguine about the differences: "The appearance of things here to eastern Christians must be singular and contradictory. Great stories & small. Large prospects & marked failures."[53] While many missionaries "on the ground," to be sure, encountered the problem of communicating the distinctiveness of their circumstances to their sponsors, Californians faced the added problem that easterners presumed to *know* what the mission field was like and how it ought to be managed. Missionaries thus struggled to make the supposedly familiar slightly more alien to their sponsors.

These disparate perceptions contributed to a growing tension between missionaries and their backers in the 1850s. A primary subject of dispute arose from the incongruity between mission society funding and the financial hardships endured by the clergy. Theoretically, eastern leaders endeavored to pay for the support of a pastor until his church became financially independent, preferably within a year. The AHMS, for example, fixed the normal annual salary for a missionary at $400; the society paid the difference between this amount and what the congregation could afford to pay, usually between $100 and $200.[54] Baptists and Methodists, while less able to afford high salaries, provided some basic support for men in the field.

This system worked efficiently for frontiers where the economy was more or less stable and the cost of living congruent with that of the eastern seaboard, but it proved disastrous in California. The financial tumult of the gold rush, as suggested previously, had at least two decisive effects on religious activity in the state: it forced the cost of living to astronomic levels, and it rendered precarious any predictions about sustained institutional support from congregations and communities. The initial outlay required to send a missionary to the West Coast, accompanied by his wife, was about one thousand dollars. When this expenditure was combined with an average salary of two hundred dollars a month for basic sustenance, the price tag for a California missionary averaged approximately 800 percent more than that paid to missionaries in other states.[55]

Eastern boards swallowed these costs, but their grudging capitulation meant that they showed less sympathy to the many missionaries who remained on the national ledgers indefinitely, or who attained temporary independence only to request more support a year or two later. Even with this help, handed out biannually with admonishment and implicit blame for the missionary's lack of sufficient vigor and preaching talents, clergy often lived on the edge of poverty. Silas Harmon sold off his library piece by piece in order to pay his bills, telling the AHMS that he was "resolved on not being in debt while I have any books."[56] Although he preferred street preaching, William Taylor brought a frame for a church with him to California, thinking that it would save him some of his missionary appropriation of $750 a year. He was stunned to discover, upon arrival, that fellow pastor Osgood Wheeler had paid five hundred dollars a month to rent a house.[57] Others, struggling to pay their bills, succumbed to the temptation to try their own luck in the gold fields. The more outspoken missionaries, including William Brier, complained repeatedly to their boards, voicing the growing resentment that many missionaries harbored. "I could write the 'Shady Side' of ministerial life in Cal.[ifornia] which would throw all Eastern Shadows into the deepest midnight. What do you think of one of your missionaries having lived, with his family, on potatoes for three days and another reduced to *squash*. If the credit system did not prevail to an alarming degree, starvation would have cut off half the Ministry of this State."[58]

Eastern boards were understandably strapped for money, particularly as the zeal for home missions faded into hard-edged political realism in the late 1850s. Yet their inability to carry through on the operation they had set in motion seems, in retrospect, particularly self-defeating. As editor of the *Pacific* in the early 1850s, Isaac Brayton was asked by the AHMS to oversee the California field. Relinquishing his position at the paper, he took the job. By early 1857, however, he grew so angry with the board's refusal to pay him more than fifty dollars a month for his services that he quit and returned to his former post. "Your appointment is now a hindrance to me rather than a help," he wrote. "It does not give me a support, but keeps me from doing what I might otherwise do, for gaining a support."[59] Throughout the decade, the society had difficulty convincing any of its local missionaries to act as supervising agents. "Worthy ministers, who are hard pressed by debts," as Brier put it, "with difficulty sustain the reputation of honesty."[60]

Francis Prevaux, commissioned and transported to the Pacific Coast by the ABHMS, found it impossible to conduct his work once he arrived. In 1851 he began preaching in the Bethel Church, San Francisco, but he quickly realized that the average of five dollars he collected at each service would hardly cover the $3,200 he paid annually to rent the hall, let alone feed himself and his wife. Despairing of his prospects as a preacher in the state, Prevaux accepted the offer of a friend to sponsor the establishment of a school. Soon thereafter the young pastor opened the San Francisco Collegiate Institute. Yet, he feared that his career change would be looked upon badly in the East. "It is so natural for people at home to impute wrong motives to a minister in California, I feared my reputation at home must suffer," he confided to his parents. "A minister *cannot* live here for less than $2000 per year, if he live ever so poorly; and no minister can get that sum from the people here."[61] Although Prevaux hoped eventually to return to the ministry, he ran the school until his departure from California, never able to pull himself out of financial debt.[62]

The aims of eastern boosters often compounded misperceptions of California's religious situation. The fault for this obfuscation rested in part with the tension that existed between the goals of promoting and rescuing the West and the onus that these divergent objectives placed on missionaries in their letters home. Men in the field were to write good letters, advised the editor of the *Home Missionary*; they needed to state the facts clearly and graphically. They also were to be careful in their expressions of pessimism: "Unless they tell their story with vividness and force, it will make no impression; and unless they tell it in modesty and cheerfulness, with Christian simplicity and earnestness, they make a bad impression."[63] Telling concerned easterners that the religious promise of California had yet to be tapped was hardly the way to raise money; signs of progress were essential to the enterprise. Yet too much optimism might also convince supporters that there was little need for further aid. The editors therefore tried to provide a steady dose of what might be termed "urgent promise," graphically detailing California's sinfulness while praising the hearty success of church enterprises. Their careful and extensive editing of incoming correspondence from missionaries reveals how much they wished to put a good face on missionary enterprises.[64]

Correspondence filled other purposes, however, for the California clergy. Writing letters home served as a source of spiritual support for missionaries anxious for connections to the wider evangelical community. They wrote to complain, they wrote for consolation, and they wrote for advice, as well as to promote the cause. Eastern leaders were not always sensitive to the difference. Willey, generally a hearty supporter of eastern boosterism, was enraged to see one of his letters—apparently a communication requiring some discretion—appear in print. "I have been much grieved to read [?] some of my private, thoughtfully written, confidential letters in the public print!" he complained. Epistles that described the activities and frankly assessed the prospects of other denominations could come back to haunt clergy, given the intimacy of evangelical circles in California. In a subsequent letter, Willey felt that he had to specify that his words not be published: "In the case of the letter I have just written to you, in which I have spoken so freely of other denominations if by any combinations of circumstances it

should get into print & come back here, it would be most unfortunate."[65] Easterners apparently did not learn their lesson easily. In 1856, Timothy Hunt
related that a fellow worker had experienced problems because of another
published letter: "Bro. Frear is now in some trouble with the Methodists in his
place in consequence of his article in the *Home Missionary*. . . . Everything
comes *back* to us & the utmost prudence is necessary in publications."[66]

These rather mundane quarrels between missionaries and their boards
illustrate an important point. Even when California clergy and their sponsors
agreed on the need for financial support, they were beginning to conceive of
the enterprise in fundamentally different terms. The interests of the clergy
encompassed a range of considerations beyond the purview of eastern
boards, including the need to maintain close relations with co-workers outside their own denominations. One gets the distinct impression on reading
this body of correspondence that mission boards simply could not fathom
the predicament of their laborers in the field, and thus they could not respond
to missionary needs in a fully sympathetic way.

Reports of California's extensive wealth further exacerbated misunder-
standings between missionaries and their sponsors over the question of monetary support. Eastern characterizations of the Golden State had paved the
roads with precious metals and imagined a lucky strike in every swing of the
miner's pick. To society agents, the constant pleas of ministers bore little
resemblance to these depictions. In reality, the erratic and unpredictable profits of the gold rush flowed increasingly into the accounts of eastern bankers
and speculators; individual miners fortunate enough to strike it rich paid out
their earnings to the merchants and businessmen, not to mention the gambling house owners, of San Francisco. By mid-decade, furthermore, as mining
technology advanced and large-scale capitalist mining operations became
the most efficient means of gathering wealth from the mother lode, proceeds
traveled even more quickly out of the state.

This steady stream of profits eastward incensed local missionaries. With
increasing levels of impatience and occasional intimations of abandonment,
missionaries chastised their superiors for their implicit encouragement of California's dependent status, which the clergy thought contributed directly to
the spiritual malaise of the state. "It may be difficult for you to understand the
condition of our churches," explained Brayton to the AHMS. "The amount of
gold which has always flowed from this State . . . is no index to the condition
of our religious societies. . . . Little of that money belonged to the church. . . .
Then, too, that stream of gold did not even belong to the people of this State.
It was due to creditors; or it has been forwarded by men who are only work-
men, not residents, to their families."[67] James Warren, a Congregational min-

ister serving a Nevada City church that had recently burned to the ground, complained even more bitterly about the lack of help from the East. Writing in the midst of the financial panic of 1857, Warren pointedly remarked: "It is said by some writers on commercial and financial matters, that California gold has saved the East from bankruptcy. If all the gold of California is needed for this purpose, then the East is welcome to it; but certainly is it not a pity that California can not keep enough of it to prevent her own bankruptcy."[68]

Ministers were quick to underscore the extent to which easterners depended on profits from the gold fields. Their heightened awareness of California's colonial economic status placed them in the ironic situation of defending the very citizens whose lack of spiritual vigor they so often denounced in the churches. Despite constant complaints about the hard-heartedness of the Euro-American population, ministers empathized with the practical exigencies and difficulties of life in the state. Some suggested that easterners should give something to the West in return for gold. As Brayton pointed out, the thousands of men digging gold in the mountains prized the Gospel but were not privileged enough to enjoy a settled, self-supporting church. Those brethren in the East who were blind enough to criticize them, therefore, should have recognized that they were thoroughly indebted for their own prosperity to the hard labors of Californians, who were "denying themselves home, and almost everything, to start rivulets of gold from the mountains whose stream enriches all the East."[69]

On several occasions Willey took exception to comments made about Californians in eastern publications. In 1850, he returned a copy of the *Home Missionary* to the New York offices with portions marked and corrected. Of particular concern to him was the negative depiction of Euro-American immigrants by an author who had criticized the way mining companies—groups of men who banded together to make the journey westward—often disbanded upon arrival in the state. Emphasizing the importance of personal commitment, the author condemned the moral blindness of miners who could see nothing but gold once they reached El Dorado. "The writer has missed the truth," Willey insisted. The dissolution of companies "was *expected* to be done if remaining together were not profitable. Nobody regards selfishness that of necessity leads to such steps." Willey added that the writer had exaggerated the moral condition of the mines: "With all that is evil in such a life—there is not a little of good in it—and I think some will leave the mines better men than they entered."[70]

Willey felt some sympathy for the forty-niners. He also knew, apparently better than did his eastern colleagues, that miners would neither read a publication that condemned their actions outright nor worship with a pastor who wrote scathing remarks about them. Easterners should not write about Californians, Willey implied, as if they were objects to be manipulated at will. The complexity of the missionary situation with respect to their superiors and their congregants is even more vividly illustrated by a second exchange between Willey and the AHMS. Horace Bushnell spent some time in California in the years 1856–57. During his stay he served the cause of Protestantism in the state ably: he preached about California's promise, he encouraged the establishment of the College of California (later the University of California at Berkeley), and he helped scout out a site for the institution. Like other eastern supporters, however, he did not have to live with the consequences of his pronouncements. In 1857, after his return to the East, he published a speech in which he described the "California character." In it he criticized southern immigrants as "unworthy & unprofitable to the state." Further, he condemned as immoral the common practice of "squatting" on disputed land, a touchy subject at best, and labeled people who did so "unworthy usurpers." Finally, he referred to Missourians, of which there were a substantial number in the region, as "border-ruffians."[71]

Willey and other ministers were incensed. The last thing they needed to fan the flames of sectional controversy was a blanket condemnation of southerners and Missourians, people who already harbored doubts about the loyalties of missionaries. The subject of land titles, also a cause of great chagrin to local evangelicals, was no less controversial: some ministers, after all, actively encouraged Euro-American immigrants to squat on Mexican lands to ensure a settled congregation. To make matters still worse, the Methodists had obtained a copy of the speech and published it throughout the state, an action that cast popular suspicion on all of Bushnell's local colleagues. In a letter that countered the theologian's contentions point by point, Willey asserted that he had "not yet seen *the first individual* who endorsed it, or regarded its impression as truthful."[72]

Caught between loyalties to their eastern sponsors and their growing awareness of the particular demands of California life, home missionaries adopted an increasingly critical and vocal stance toward the financial priorities of the national boards. It was evident to missionaries that "civilizing" California, for mission advocates in the East, served primarily as a means of defending and redeeming their own culture by extending it to other regions. The dozens of dedication sermons delivered to miners and missionaries heading west emphasized the importance of preserving evangelical values, of not being swayed by the spiritual chaos of California for fear it eventually would taint the morality of the Northeast. On a less elevated note, home mission agents also saw the economic advantages to be gained by promoting commerce and culture in the Far West through eastern speculation, and they viewed this industry as a fair trade for the gift of Christian civilization.[73]

Another cause of friction between missionaries and their boards concerned the paucity of ministers in the state. From a sparsely settled region of several thousand inhabitants in 1847, California swiftly grew to a population of several hundred thousand, outstripping the capacity of home mission boards to respond.[74] The first missionaries in the field, sent off with a cordial farewell and the promise of immediate reinforcements, were understandably alarmed. In late 1848, just as the first reports of the discovery of gold were filtering into the Northeast, the ABHMS asked the young seminarian Osgood Wheeler of Wayne County, New York, to travel to the Pacific Coast as their pioneer missionary. Wheeler accepted the appointment with the stipulation that an assistant would be sent out to him by the next steamer. By August 1849, no helper had arrived, and Wheeler raised a plaintive cry to his board in New York: "Why will not some good, self-sacrificing ministers of Christ come to my relief? . . . Here I am in the midst of a population of upwards of 70,000 Americans, increasing at the rate of 1,000 per week . . . and not a single Baptist minister besides myself, given wholly to the work of the ministry. . . . I beg you to induce some good men to come out to our assistance as soon as possible." The next Baptist missionary arrived nearly eighteen months later.[75]

Mission boards were just as frustrated as their envoys. Although leaders published countless articles in their journals emphasizing the urgency of the situation, few ministers volunteered for duty. The predicament of the Baptists demonstrates the difficulty of finding willing candidates for the field. The first assistant named to help Wheeler stumbled upon another mission field during his westward journey, and he decided to stop there.[76] The ABHMS then designated several suitable men for posts, but both declined. Two more prospects were finally located: Levi Grenell, the son of a Baptist preacher in New Jersey (who also happened to be a member of the ABHMS Board), and Francis Prevaux, newly graduated from Newton Seminary. Both made the trip West, but Grenell stayed in California for only a short period, and Prevaux almost immediately left the ministry for a teaching career. Two more aspiring pastors received appointments shortly after their arrivals in California: Amariah Kalloch of Maine preached in Sacramento for six months before he was stricken with a fatal illness. He was replaced in his pastorate by James W. Capen, a classmate of Prevaux's at Newton who had journeyed to California independently of the mission board. Capen preached for a year before joining the Episcopal Church.[77] Throughout the decade Baptist leaders argued over whether to suspend the mission entirely because of the lack of funding and acceptable candidates.[78] No one raised the question of what more ministers would do when so few conversions were taking place. Facing this question would have meant directly confronting the failure of missionary efforts.

The trial of finding missionaries was exceeded only by the difficulties of keeping them in place upon arrival. Eastern mission leaders countered pleas from California missionaries for aid by insisting that they *were* sending young men westward to fill the region, in numbers that sometimes surpassed those sent to other areas. What had become of all these laborers? "It is true that there are ministers enough for this country, *regularly ordained*, to supply for some time to come the increasing demand for ministerial labor," conceded one observer, "*if they would only come forth* and enter upon the duties of their calling. . . . But their services are not to be had—nay, they are not to be found; hidden away in the canons of the mountains, in search of gold, toiling with the pick-axe and rocker six days in the week, to preach occasionally on the seventh to their fellows upon the vanity and insecurity of earthly riches!"[79] Judging from the "clergyman's box" in the San Francisco post office, quite a number of ministers resided in California. "But ah, there are many 'Reverends' but few preachers. They come, but nobody knows where they are. The gold-diggers probably know them—know them as diggers."[80]

Although missionaries understood the obstacles inherent in convincing able young ministers to assume the rigors of western life, their pleas also contained explicit criticisms of the home mission societies for their neglect of the region. In January 1854, at a joint meeting of the Presbytery of San Francisco and the Congregational Association of California, the assembly named three leading ministers to write to the AHMS and relate, once again, the impediments to religious progress in the state. Pointing out that only fifteen clergy from both denominations were then working in California and that the mining regions in particular were in desperate need of spiritual leadership, the authors hastened to add that "in no part of the Atlantic States with which we are acquainted would such openings be allowed to remain unentered."[81]

Evangel editor D. B. Cheney also interpreted as regional bias the failure of boards to provide more personnel. He took umbrage at the annual report of the ABHMS in 1863, which referred to California as a missionary field. "We have not been aware that the Board has expended a dollar for California the past year," he asserted in the pages of his paper. Noting that eloquent appeals had been made in the report for the Northwest and for the freedmen of the South, Cheney indignantly observed that not one word had been mentioned about the Pacific Coast. Furthermore, he insisted, the dereliction in supplying California was not for lack of volunteers, as leaders had claimed; Cheney himself knew of "good men ready to come to this field," if the way were

opened to them. "We plead for six men at once, we plead urgently, importu-
nately, but in vain." Cheney concluded that "our brethren charged with this
administration have made grave mistakes in respect to a proper occupancy of
this coast and that a very grave responsibility is connected with those mistakes is clear to us beyond a peradventure."[82]

The organizational expectations of the national boards, interpreted as east-
ern-biased and out of step with the needs of the state, came under increasing
fire from California missionaries. Not only were men in short supply, but the
difficulties of reaching miners in remote camps stretched missionaries to the
limits of their endurance and ability. Clerical responses to the realization that
their methods were of little use ranged widely, from the offering of subtle suggestions for tactical change to the outright rejection of eastern strategies.
Nearly all agreed, however, that, as Willey said, "This country offers a field of
great usefulness which does not seem likely to be supplied in any of the *ordinary ways*."[83] To those who had spent any time in California, this suggestion
of distinctiveness seemed like common sense. Samuel Blakeslee added that
ministers "cannot, they *cannot*, do this work in the old settled methods of the
eastern people and churches. They must modify their system of ministerial
work as really and essentially as the farmer or other laboring man must here,
in a new country, modify his. There must be more action, more stir, more
earnestness, more direct effort, more off hand energy & a great deal more
go-a-headitiveness . . . than at the east."[84]

Congregationalists and Presbyterians felt the disjunction between theory
and practice especially keenly because of the less flexible nature of their poli-
ties; AHMS missionaries often remarked on the Baptist and Methodist field
agents who rendered their churches more adaptable to California life.[85] Taking matters into their own hands, AHMS missionaries at the first Synod of Alta
California in 1857 officially requested traveling evangelists for California, a
new type of ministry particularly suited to western needs. Arguing that a settled ministry was still their top priority, the clergy reasoned that "the peculiar
nature of the field" required the adoption of a more flexible system than that
employed in other states.[86] After being turned down by the New York board,
several missionaries extended a personal invitation to Milton Badger, an
AHMS secretary, to come out and see for himself the spiritual predicament of
the clergy. This request was also denied.[87]

Although organizational inflexibility was a more acute problem throughout
western states for Congregationalists and Presbyterians, it should also be
noted that the Methodists expressed similar fears that traditional techniques
needed revision in California. In a letter published in the *California Christian
Advocate* in 1875, a correspondent suggested appointing a "conference evan-

gelist" as a means of reaching people in remote places; these men were to serve as assistants for local pastors and distribute tracts in the mining regions. The author argued that Methodists needed to adapt themselves to the "providential demands of circumstances," as well as offer support and direction for the men in the field.[88]

Some pastors, discouraged by the feeble support from eastern agents, devised more ingenious methods of making their appeal. Martin Kellogg, serving in the mining town of Grass Valley, asked the AHMS to send him an apprentice to serve for a limited amount of time, hoping that this pitch would appeal to seminary students. "You can assure celibate graduates that this is an admirable place to *break in,*" he wrote earnestly, clearly oblivious to the *double entendre.* Evidently increasingly desperate, he added, "Can you find a few *semi-invalids* not broken but breaking down, who would like to be made strong again by a few years' trial of our admirable climate?"[89]

The missionary desperation over the shortage of ministers also contributed to early calls for the rearing of a native ministry in the state. By the late 1850s, Congregationalists and Presbyterians had grown so worried about the shortage of pastors that they began searching for ways to open schools themselves. The AHMS, however, already crippled financially by a growing denominational consciousness in the East, would not commission teachers as missionaries in the West. Once again, California evangelicals were left to their own devices. Joseph Benton, at the meeting of the General Association and Synod in 1859, offered board and instruction to any young man who would study for the ministry; and the Association, in its recognition that the East would not provide more assistance, committed itself to founding a seminary. Warren commented that this decision "awakened a feeling of hope and inspired a zeal as nothing else has done, for a long time."[90]

This turning inward for self-help was one of the first organizational indications of a distinct religious consciousness in California. Embedded in the frustrations that missionaries articulated about the miners with whom they labored and the sponsors with whom they sparred is the feeling of distinctiveness, the sense that California religious leaders, initially out of necessity and desperation, could rely only on themselves. In 1861, Cheney informed California Baptists that they could no longer count on the eastern boards for help. The ABHMS had, over the past twelve years, Cheney observed, expended significant effort in California, "some of it wisely and some of it unwisely." The coming of the war, he predicted, would most likely mean they would stop sending "the pittance they have been bestowing." "We are left, therefore, almost entirely to ourselves . . . however unwilling we may be to have it so, however unwise we may regard it on the part of our Eastern Board to practically abandon such a field as this." Baptists must resign themselves to this desertion, he concluded.[91]

What was extraordinary, in the midst of the constant disappointments of religious work during the gold rush, was the optimism that so many clergy retained about the promise of the state. Like the ability of California's physical beauty to demonstrate the power of God, the very contradictions and chaos of society seemed, paradoxically, to manifest its potential for good. Thrown back on their own devices, ministers discovered hope not in eastern religious patterns but in the promise of the Pacific region. "It has been, probably, impossible for the different distant boards to comprehend the demands of the work," explained the editor of the *Advocate*. "California is so full of contradictions in herself, so new, so gigantic, that none at a distance can comprehend the field. Like a rain-bow spanning the whole heavens, perfect at birth, California sprang at once into greatness."[92] As California missionaries planted Protestantism in the region, they did so with a sense of distinctiveness—and defiance—born of frustration and rejection and fed by the inherent promise of their new home.

In spite of material and human impediments, evangelical ministers found ways to impose their own kind of religious order on the physical and moral landscapes of the new El Dorado. Indeed, the chaos and untamed energies in both the natural and the spiritual realms were often admired as evidence of western distinctiveness. At the same time, however, lay Euro-American immigrants brought with them and adapted other notions of moral order, notions linked only tangentially to those of the missionaries. The beliefs and behaviors that clergy repeatedly described as sinful or chaotic had their own logic and were inspired by a worldview quite distinct from anything the missionary ideology could encompass.

Chapter 5

The Moral World of
the California Miner

"Take the *Arabian Nights, add* to them *Gullivers Travels* & then
multiply them by *Baron Munchausen* & the product will be
California!"
—Charles Glass Gray, *Off at Sunrise*

If I should make another raise,
In New York sure I'll spend my days;
I'll be a merchant, buy a saw,
So good-bye, mines and Panama.
—*Old Put's Original California Songster*

Protestant missionaries were not the only California immigrants
concerned about questions of morality. "Dame Shirley," a young woman who
had traveled with her husband to the California mines in 1849, wrote home
frequently to her sister in Massachusetts about life in the town of Rich Bar.
Her letters reveal an awareness of the disjunction between eastern moral
standards and western ways as well as her own ambivalence about the gap
between the two. Amused and intrigued by a procession of drunken Chilenos
passing through the streets immediately after a funeral cortege had followed
the same path, Dame Shirley remarked on the strange circumstances that
brought together extreme misery and happiness in a single moment. Then, as
if suddenly aware of how her comments might be interpreted, she self-consciously attempted an explanation. "Of course," she apologized, "I ought to
have been shocked and horrified—to have shed salt tears, and have uttered
melancholy Jeremiads over their miserable degradation." Justifying her dis-

crepant attitude toward what ought to have been condemned as sinful and pacifying her sister's sensibilities with a breezy term of endearment, she concluded that "the world is so full of platitudes, my dear, that I think you will easily forgive me for not boring you with a temperance lecture, and will good-naturedly let me have my laugh and not think me *very* wicked after all."[1]

Dame Shirley's attitude—particularly her professed consciousness of the sinfulness of the actions she witnessed—reflected precisely the kind of moral laxity that eastern Protestants feared would develop in California society. Worse, from the perspective of home missionaries, such statements came from the pens and lips of previously pious churchgoers who, having full knowledge of right and wrong, still did not respect the difference between the two. It is no wonder that observers puzzled over this apparently sudden shift from piety to tolerance, a metamorphosis that seemed to characterize the behavior of many arrivals to the region. Hubert Howe Bancroft, one of the early historians of California, captured the essence of this mystery when he likened the discovery of gold itself to a conversion experience: "The strongest human appetite was aroused—the sum of appetites—this yellow dirt embodying the means for gratifying love, hate, lust, and domination. . . . The conversion of San Francisco was complete. Those who had hitherto denied a lurking faith now unblushingly proclaimed it."[2]

Like Bancroft, other observers and historians of the gold rush have also criticized the morality of mining society. Josiah Royce, the Harvard philosopher of the late nineteenth and early twentieth centuries, was one of the first historians of the state to pass sentence on the communal ethics of the gold rush era. Born and reared in the mining town of Grass Valley and educated at the newly established University of California at Berkeley, Royce had experienced firsthand the rigors and opportunities of pioneer life in the Golden State. Looking back on these early years from the perspective of Harvard Yard, Royce framed the development of California culture in an idealistic philosophical context. "Whoever knows that the struggle for the best things of man is a struggle against the basest passions of man," he wrote, "and that every significant historical process is full of such struggles, is ready to understand the true interest of scenes amid which civilization sometimes seemed to have lapsed into semi-barbarism."[3] For Royce, the period of the gold rush was characterized primarily by a struggle between the forces of disorder and the civilizing tendencies of eastern culture, and by a halting but steady movement from immorality to morality.

Both missionaries and historians have brought certain presuppositions to their search for the emergence of moral patterns in California society. Royce understood moral progress to mean the advance of Anglo-Saxon civilization;

as unsettled as he was by the racial and ethnic intolerance evidenced toward foreigners in the state, he nonetheless believed that Euro-Americans ought to have done more to encourage the "better sort" of immigration to California. Morality, for Royce, meant something quite specific: a system of values shaped by evangelical Protestant piety. Similarly, as we have seen, early Protestant missionaries looked for religious progress in terms that were familiar to them: they sought to recreate the communities from which they had come. Subsequent historians of California religion and scholars of the West in general have done little to challenge this paradigm. American culture and moral behavior, we are told, moved with Euro-American settlers from east to west, from the Puritans to the pioneers. Americans in the West, according to this understanding, engaged in a continuous process of cultural creation, the rendering of order from chaos.

A wealth of recent scholarship in popular religion, however, encourages us to take a closer look at what Royce and others have called chaos, barbarism, or immorality, and to question the judgments of those observers who have so characterized it. Particularly difficult to assess are those noninstitutional expressions of religion in California, the patterns of behavior that fall outside traditional clerical and organizational boundaries. Jon Butler, in his suggestive studies of the persistence of heterodox religious activity in the colonial era, points out that although historians have always treated American colonists as a singularly religious people, the rate of church membership in the colonies on the eve of the American Revolution was probably no higher than 15 percent. He suggests, therefore, that in order to understand what colonists meant by religion, "historians need to move beyond the study of ecclesiology, theology, and the ministry to recover noninstitutional religious practices."[4] In the case of California, this insight invites us to view the low rates of church attendance not as a judgment upon the religiosity of the population, but instead as an indication that we need to look outside the churches for our understanding of popular religious behavior and beliefs.

Popular religious practices are difficult to trace, of course, because they are not normally articulated systematically. Sources for their study, therefore, must be approached obliquely. In trying to explore the religious behavior and meaning of morality in the California mining community, the words of Dame Shirley suggest a starting point in the apparent disjunction between eastern evangelical morality and the moral world of the mines. If this disparity is not seen as a discrepancy between a normative morality and utter depravity—that is, if one does not accept the traditional Protestant categorization of saint and sinner as an objective rendering of reality—can one discern the articulation of alternative moral systems? Are there patterns of morality evident here that missionaries and historians have overlooked? In trying to identify patterns of religiosity at the popular level, we must also keep in mind the constant interaction between the clergy and the laity; for, as Carlo Ginzburg and others have pointed out, it is questionable whether "popular culture exists outside the act that suppresses it."[5] Yet we can no longer rely on the clerical assumption that morals are to be equated with evangelical values. What, then, did these moral worlds look like?

The letters and diaries of Anglo-Protestant immigrants to gold rush California provide an important perspective on religion in both the mining camps and the swiftly growing cities that served them.[6] By the end of 1849, nearly one hundred thousand immigrants had arrived on the Pacific Coast to try their luck; by late 1852, the number of argonauts topped 250,000. Not all dug for gold. Even at the peak of the mineral frenzy in the 1850s, less than 50 percent of the population actually engaged in mining. Many others found their "main chance" in the service industries that fed, housed, clothed, and equipped miners, as well as the ubiquitous brothels, saloons, gambling houses, and law offices that ministered to other needs. Finally, the rapid migration fueled by chimerical tales of easy money produced a large number of persons without jobs, without homes, and with uncertain prospects, persons who simply wandered around.[7] Yet because of the necessity of extending credit on all levels of exchange, merchants and prospectors alike were ultimately dependent on the mining economy and its inherent instabilities for their livelihoods. From Placerville, W. S. Newman wrote that "the Miners are in debt to the Country Merchants, Country Merchants are in debt to the City [San Francisco] Merchants, Our City Merchants are in debt to the Eastern Cities—and as *usual, all* are expecting the money from the *Honest* Miners."[8]

The most salient moral aspects of these interlocking social and economic worlds were the features that differentiated them from the East: extreme ethnic and racial diversity, a relative lack of religious institutions, a dearth of women (see chapter 6), and a new and often unfamiliar working environment with its own standards and principles of operation. Here, we begin to explore the moral landscape of California from the perspective of the nonclerical settlers in an attempt to more fully understand the religious world(s) inhabited by Californians.

Observers reported that one of the most obvious differences between eastern culture and life in California was the ethnic and racial diversity of western society. Statistics for the early years of the gold rush are particularly problematic, given the constant movement of the population.[9] Leonard Pitt estimates that of the approximately 100,000 immigrants to the state in 1849, the year after gold was discovered, 80,000 were Euro-American (predominantly from the northeastern and border states); 8,000 were Mexican; 5,000 were South American (mostly Chilean and Peruvian); 4,000 were Chinese, and the remaining 3,000 were Europeans from a variety of countries. By 1852, these groups were joined by 2,000 African-Americans (both free blacks and those brought as slaves by southern whites). These miners joined the preexisting Californio population—those native-born Californians of Mexican descent— of approximately 15,000, and as many as 150,000 American Indians.[10]

Heterogeneity varied from place to place. Some areas of the Central Mines, a region whose streams eventually flow into the Sacramento River, contained communities comprised almost exclusively of Euro-American miners. The Southern Mines, encompassing areas along tributaries of the San Joaquin River, included more cultural diversity in its social composition. More than a matter of immigration patterns, these differences can be attributed, at least in part, to cultural conflict. Foreign miners and minority groups, displaced from the richer ore deposits to the north by Euro-Americans asserting a "first right" to the diggings, were often forced to labor in the less profitable placers to the south. Widespread transiency also meant rapid shifts in settlement patterns, even in relatively homogeneous regions. Illustrative of this incessant movement is the census calculations of Nevada City: of the men listed in the 1850 census, only 7 percent reappeared in the city directory of 1856.[11]

The moral implications of such cultural diversity are difficult to evaluate. It was the confusion and lack of structure in society, however, more than its mere heterogeneity, that seems to have affected relations between miners. This is most evident in the miners' judicial systems—or rather, their lack of them. The vigilance committees of the gold rush are well known as manifestations of frontier justice. Where formal legal systems broke down or were yet to be established, inhabitants formed their own judicial structures, tried accused criminals, and often dispensed a "fitting" punishment.[12] Historians have been intrigued by such incidents since they first occurred, some interpreting these events as the instinctual American thirst for democratic process, others as the unleashed passions of nativist mobs.[13] Clearly, many Euro-American immigrants perceived California as a society on the brink of social chaos and viewed vigilante justice as a simultaneously comforting and terrifying necessity. Alfred Doten, witnessing a vigilante action in a mining camp in December 1851, expressed in his diary the profound disquiet that such events provoked: "The taking of the murderers, the trial and execution was carried on in the most quiet and orderly manner throughout—The night was dark and fearful and together with the howling and roaring of the wind through the tall pines and the warring of the elements rendered the scene awful and terrific in the extreme and one that will never be effaced from the memory of those who witnessed it."[14]

Significantly, Anglos often characterized the boundary between order and disorder as a cultural divide. Mrs. Lee Whipple-Haslam, a woman reared in the mining camps of Tuolumne County in the 1850s, wrote vividly of the frontier justice she witnessed as a child. "It is true the miners had to put the fear of the Lord, or His teachings, into the hearts of the Mexicans and Indians. . . . The punishment was not ladled out with a silver spoon, but with a solid stick, and laid on whole-heartedly, without reservation and with enthusiasm."[15] For Whipple-Haslam and others, foreignness was equated with social and moral disorder. Significantly, the murderers that Doten spoke of were a group of Mexicans. Just as Dame Shirley identified drunkenness with Chilenos and miners generally referred to prostitutes as senoritas, Doten understood criminality to be an inherent characteristic of nonwhites, particularly Mexicans and American Indians.[16] For Euro-Americans, the equation of cultural difference with social disorder provided a ready target for abuse.

Defining nonwhites as a social problem also allowed Euro-Americans to avoid the more threatening fact of their own incivility. Elisha Douglass Perkins, one of several miners from Marietta, Ohio, reported on Christmas day, 1849, that "some have passed the time in drinking & gambling, which latter vice is very prevalent everywhere in the country, a relic of old Spanish rules & customs."[17] This racial dichotomy—white and civilized, nonwhite and uncivilized—helps to explain why many Anglos expressed amazement at the honesty of men in the early days of the rush. With nonwhites to blame for crimes and corruption, these settlers felt free to look upon one another with trust. Bayard Taylor remarked with some relief that debts in California were paid punctually and that "men were obliged to place" a general confidence "in each other's honesty."[18] Peter Decker, an immigrant from Ohio, in his description of Sacramento in 1849 commented on the pervasive honesty of its inhabitants, who felt "the necessity for this state of things in the absence of houses for protection."[19] Anglos, these observers implied, were able to control themselves when circumstances demanded it; if and when they did commit crimes, as in the case of Doten's friend Charles Everbeck, who stole from the diggings of another man's claim, reason would ultimately prevail. Doten noted that afterward Everbeck felt "extremely sorry and ashamed of what he had done and swears he will never steal any more dirt."[20] With the problem of social chaos defined as a peculiar affliction of the communal outsider, Euro-Americans tended to preserve a sense of equality and honor among their own ranks. This moral stance helps to explain the double standard Anglos often applied in their social contacts. Charles D. Ferguson, a miner from

Aurora, Ohio, juxtaposed his boasting of shooting three Indians in unprovoked incidents with his description of the camaraderie that prevailed in California: "It only needed to be known that one was in want, and there were always willing hearts and hands, yes, and money too, to relieve."[21]

Religiously, the intimacy born out of common experience, at least for those migrants of northern European descent, transcended traditional confessional boundaries. California was not a paradise of religious toleration, but harsh circumstances taught men to look for companionship and solace where they could find it. Less than a decade after nativist riots had exploded in Philadelphia, and even as the anti-Catholic Know-Nothing party was gaining ground in political elections, Protestants worked peaceably alongside Irish, Belgian, French, and German Catholics in the gold diggings. John Steele, a teenager from Wisconsin who later became a Methodist minister, traveled through the northern mining country with "Donnelly," a devout Irish Catholic. Steele described their one encounter with Indians, who had surrounded them at a point along their route. Faced with possible death, the two men prayed for deliverance; Steele overheard Donnelly praying "fervently" to a variety of saints to save them. In spite of his own evangelical inclinations, Steele later insisted that it was Donnelly's pious entreaties that had proved efficacious.[22] Similarly, Jean-Nicholas Perlot, a Belgian argonaut, described his encounter with an Irish Catholic who sang the praises of the local Methodist minister. In a statement that would have appeared oxymoronic if not sacrilege in another setting, the Irishman explained to Perlot why he had asked the Protestant minister to bury his companion: "I am a Catholic, an Irishman who is not Catholic is not an Irishman; but that does not prevent me from recognizing that that Protestant is worth more than the priests of Stockton."[23] In both contexts, religious boundaries were redrawn to meet the needs of a new environment.

If the cultural diversity of California changed the map of the religious landscape by allowing men to redefine moral worth in ethnic and racial rather than confessional terms, the lack of a firmly entrenched institutional framework for religious expression left open the door for both heterodoxy and religious apathy. Some settlers, however, simply could not find churches. Miners by necessity spread out along the narrow canyons and ravines of the mother lode to protect their claims, often rendering themselves inaccessible to the hardiest of itinerant ministers. James Mason Hutchings, a devout Episcopalian, wrote to a pastor in New Orleans that he had tried to observe the Sabbath and had "tried to hear of a good preacher, but, as yet, in vain."[24] With others, it was difficult to differentiate lack of ability from lack of interest. With some dismay, L. M. Wolcott reported that "we are thousands of miles from home, and comfort ourselves by thinking that a knowledge of our indulgence in vice will never reach them. Here, there is no parents eye to guide, no wife to warn, no sister to entreat, no church, no sabbath. . . . All the animal and vicious passions are let loose, and free to indulgence without any legal or social restraint."[25]

While some lamented the dearth of Protestant churches and ministers, others noted the religious diversity afforded by the lack of an established religious influence and the concomitant willingness of Californians to give all beliefs a hearing. Indeed, what was special about religion in California was not simply the *fact* of pluralism, but the placement of a wide variety of beliefs on a relatively equal organizational footing. Unlike the situation in southern California, where a slower immigration and a stronger Catholic church impeded the Protestantization of the region well into the 1870s, the rapid influx of settlers to the north quickly overwhelmed an already weakened Catholic structure, producing a free market of religious beliefs.[26] Samuel Willey aptly observed that settlers had already relaxed their bonds to home and tradition through the process of migration; for many, the consequent psychological liberation carried over into their religious outlooks: "The minds of the mass are much *loosened* by emigration, & absence from the associations of home leaves men a kind of freedom of choice in religion & in politics, which they would not feel there. Consequently, if loose doctrines are preached under superior advantages they will feel more liberty at least to go & see & hear for themselves."[27]

Mormonism, spiritualism, phrenology, and Universalism all found sympathetic audiences among the migrants. Missionaries interpreted this diversity as indicative of the moral laxity of the culture, but some miners saw a healthy and intriguing marketplace of beliefs where religion was a matter of choice instead of custom. Rather than leading necessarily to religious apathy, observers often commented upon the earnestness with which California migrants debated theological propositions. An extreme example can be seen in a man named "Carroll," who according to one account "allowed his mind to wander and stray overmuch in the maze of theological mysteries and its (to him) apparent contradictions." As a result, he had "instituted a private and personal quarrel between himself and his Creator" and eventually came to believe in the total annihilation of the soul after death.[28] More characteristic, perhaps, was the discussion at a party in Fort Grizzly in 1855 where "the liquor flowed in abundance." As the party broke up and Doten looked for his companions, he "found one stowed away in a corner, another lying across a candle box with a pile of smoked salmon for a pillow," and two more, "arguing and discussing on the merits of Mormonism, spiritual rappings, and the Maine liquor law, across a keg of Scotch whiskey."[29] Many forty-niners were—or learned to be—religious "seekers," men who looked for religious certainty and valued its consolations, even in the highly pluralistic and religiously disordered world of the mines.

Although Anglos frequently defined themselves in moral opposition to Indians, Hispanics, and others they deemed outcasts, exposure to cultural differences greatly fascinated them and even influenced their behavior. The journey to the Pacific Coast afforded some men their first glimpses of Latin American Catholicism. Alonzo Hill admired the church he visited in Valparaiso, Chile: "The Catholic church & cementary are truly magnificent & beautiful. A representation of the crucification of Christ in solid silver, and the general display of Bullion is tremendous."[30] Minister Daniel B. Woods left Philadelphia with the Camargo Company in February 1849, determined to cross Mexico on horseback. His description of Mexican culture reflected an intense curiosity about Catholicism: in Guadalajara, he witnessed the procession of the Host, in which a priest led a large crowd of Mexicans and a band down the street. In Magdalena for Easter, Woods observed the stations of the cross. On both occasions, he was entranced by the unusual sights and sounds, and commented favorably on the extent of popular participation in the rituals.[31]

Many forty-niners were also intrigued by the customs and traditions of American Indians. A variety of Indian nations, including the Yana, the Konkow, the Nisenan, and the Miwok, inhabited the foothills of the Sierra Nevada, living both within and around the edges of mining society. Their religious festivals provided entertainment for prospectors. As much as Anglo-Americans criticized Indian ways and scorned the begging by natives around the camps, the tribal festivals engendered a certain awe and admiration among white immigrants.[32] Doten, who was not above blaming Indians for all manner of crimes, sent a lengthy description of a "Digger" medical festival to the *Plymouth Rock*, his hometown newspaper in Massachusetts. With a perceptive eye for detail, Doten carefully described the three-day event. Outlining one healing ritual, he suggested without irony that "perhaps some of our medical friends in Plymouth may understand the philosophy of it, and avail themselves of it in their future practice."[33] A female correspondent for the *California Christian Advocate* described a pow-wow or healing ritual for an ill leader that she had witnessed near Shasta City; initially shocked by the "screams of these maniacs," she was gradually drawn into the flow of the ceremony. By the time it had ended the next day, the writer could not help but contrast the life of the Indians, "their united interest—harmony among their own tribe— the sincerity of their love or hatred," to Anglos in the state, who "in their grab after gold, cannot give one hour to the sick in all their suffering—nor time to attend the dead to the grave, the last claim we all have on each other."[34]

Although it would be naive to interpret this abrupt inversion of savagery and rationalism as a wholehearted embrace of cultural difference or to deny the extent of Euro-American participation in the gradual extinction of Indian communities, it does indicate a curiosity fostered by the heterogeneity of California life. In some cases, this interest led to a new view of society; for most men, it encouraged changes that were much less sweeping and largely unconscious—small transformations that nonetheless signified a measure of cultural syncretism. Some Euro-Americans, for example, imitated Indian techniques of washing and cooking.[35] Migrants also spent their leisure time immersed in activities of Hispanic and even Chinese origin, including fandangos, certain forms of gambling, and rodeos. Most Euro-Americans, unskilled in mining, employed labor techniques imported by the more experienced Mexican prospectors. Even Doten, despite his frequently articulated hatred of Mexicans, began to use Spanish phrases in his journals; on 4 July 1854, he and some friends celebrated Independence Day: "Had a good supper at which we were unable to talk anything but Spanish, having forgotten our mother tongue entirely."[36] Doten and his companions were in no danger of abandoning their Anglo-Protestant heritage. Exposure to differences on a variety of levels did, however, complicate the missionary plan to construct traditional cultural and religious boundaries.[37] At the very least, it undermined the clerical belief that Anglo-Protestant culture was obviously superior to—or even separable from—any other.

In different ways the mining economy itself also worked to alienate Euro-American migrants from the precepts of evangelical Protestantism. The majority of Anglos coming to California were men from the middling ranks of society: farmers and skilled artisans (metalworkers, harness makers, masons, tailors, and carpenters) accounted for 70 percent of the membership of some mining companies.[38] According to Paul Johnson and others, these were the members of society most likely to be attracted to evangelicalism, a belief system that encouraged self-discipline and hard work, as well as a range of values and predispositions that were well-suited to success in an industrializing nation.[39] Indeed, most miners went to California for the purpose of getting ahead—either pulling themselves out of debt or building a nest egg to establish themselves financially. As Peter Decker pointed out, California promised an equal starting point for all takers: "Here every man is on the same equal footing. Here each stands or falls by his own merits."[40]

In fact, Decker's statement proved to be only half true. The westward migration, as John Findlay has suggested, with its dependence upon high expectations, risk taking, opportunism, and constant movement, was antithetical to the ethic of evangelical Protestantism that posited a direct correlation between wealth and hard work.[41] Ministers continually stressed the importance of perseverance and ascetic self-discipline as the keys to a faithful and rewarding life. In dozens of dedication services for departing miners, eastern clergy tried to draw the all-important but often elusive distinction between the sinful desire for quick wealth and the healthy ambitions of the entrepreneurial spirit. Examples abounded of good Christians who had fallen into utter ruin in California. Elisha Lord Cleaveland, pastor of the Third Church of New Haven, stressed to his departing congregants that the possession of wealth was not sinful; the real problem, as he saw it, lay in an "excessive, impatient, covetous desire" for riches. In a listing that would have pleased his Puritan forebears, Cleaveland asserted that true happiness required trials and hardships as a means of strengthening the faculties of invention, energy, industry, steady perseverance, self-reliance, patience, submission, self-denial, and faith. He urged emigrants to search their souls for any signs of unhealthy motivations. Were they impatient? Had they considered the needs of their families and friends? Finally, he concluded that the trip was morally permissible as a way of acquiring property or as a necessary economic step. Yet he cautioned his audience that their return to the East, even in the best of circumstances, might be a difficult one: "Will you not bring back with you a restless, morbid desire for change, excitement, and wild adventure? Are you sure you can bear the sudden acquisition of wealth? Many of the strongest minds have been unhinged by such an event, and wholly unfitted for a life of usefulness."[42]

No amount of religious self-discipline could alter the fact that traveling to California to mine for gold was a speculative risk. If disease and death did not overtake miners along the way, utter poverty could—and often did—destroy them in the mother lode. Dame Shirley, one of four women in the mining town of Indian Bar in 1851, put it most succinctly in a letter to her sister: "Gold mining is Nature's great lottery scheme. A man may work in a claim for many months, and be poorer at the end of the time than when he commenced; or he may 'take out' thousands in a few hours. It is a mere matter of chance."[43] The gold rush was, indeed, "consummately democratic," in that its dependence on luck more than merit freed men from responsibility for their own failures.[44] Miners found a variety of ways to express their astonishment at the discovery that hard work mattered little in this world. Levi Kenaga wrote to his parents that "it is not like people thinks it is to make money thay only get fifty dollars and that is not much for this cuntry a man must go and try his luck Som men has luck and som has nun."[45] Ephraim Delano confided to his wife: "Some goes to the mines and does well and others goes and does very poor I am one of the latter class about one out of ten does well it is all a lottery."[46]

Mining, to be sure, took different forms, and it is certainly true that the trend by the late 1850s was to use more cooperative techniques that required a greater initial outlay of capital and relied more heavily on wage labor. River mining, deep gravel mining, and quartz or lode mining each necessitated forms of economic organization that quickly gave the lie to the image of the lone prospector panning or digging for gold.[47] Nonetheless, the success of the enterprise—whether one worked for a company or alone, in the rivers or in the deep tunnels, and whether the payoff arrived in two days or two months—was always a speculative risk. As noted, local merchants and store-keepers, farmers, and even companies on the East Coast and in London, relied on the success of the mines to assure their own prosperity. With greater wealth came greater protection from failure. Still, no participants were entirely insulated from the speculations of the miners' world.

Even though migrants recognized that failure could not be blamed on a lack of skill or hard work, at times the contrast between eastern expectations and western realities was simply too great: "The bright and glowing pictures pre-sented to the public—the 'news from California'—'$2,000,000 in gold dust'—'rich discoveries'—'new diggings,' etc., must all be filled up with a back-ground of cloudy days, of rainy weeks, broken hopes, privations, sickness, many a gloomy death-scene, and many a lonely grave."[48] The problem of fail-ure was one that few men could explain to those at home: in eastern culture, in the world from which miners had come, failure implied personal fault. Charles Davis, cognizant of the high hopes his friends back East had for him, cautioned his wife not to tell anyone how he was faring and to "make every-thing appear as it is easy and agreable, but dont say anything further."[49] Others turned to drinking or to gambling as an escape from the pressures of their economic situations.

For some, the cognitive dissonance between these moral worlds proved to be too weighty: miners witnessed many instances of suicide among their peers. Daniel Woods wrote in October 1849 that he had recently heard of twelve cases of suicide because of money problems.[50] Among the most poignant was that of Alonzo A. Hill, a young man from Massachusetts who had met with little success in the gold mines. Hill journeyed to California with the apparent intention of making enough money to assist his family's failing dry goods business. In a series of letters to his father, he felt obligated to explain his inability to turn a profit. Although his father's letters have not sur-vived, Hill's own indicate that the burden of family obligations weighed heav-ily upon him. Even after his father began shipping him boots and liquor in bulk in order to sell them at higher California prices, Hill was not able to clear enough of a profit to aid his family. He remained in the West, but by the spring of 1857 his sense of personal futility had taken its toll. Unable to live up to the expectations of his family, Hill wrote a final letter home before taking his life: "Insanity for 9 or 10 years has preyed upon my brain, some all the time, in excess sometimes, This last year I am conscious of its increase and the weight on my brain seems crushing me, I hope when the heart which dictates this note has ceased to throb you will forgive me, & God will, too."[51]

The capriciousness of fate was the central fact of existence in the mines. Despite the arguments of ministers, immigrants found that they could make no easy equations between hard work and success. Those who found ways of coping with the moral contradictions between this world and the East were often led to the rationalization of actions that in other circumstances would have been unthinkable. John Steele explained that "the most carefully arranged plans and confidently expected success brings only disappointment, while apparent failures and expected disappointments result in unexpected success. "Sometimes," he concluded, "it seems enough to induce people to suspend judgment, abandon their plans, and trust to luck."[52]

Trusting to luck, for many unsuspecting adventurers, led down roads that previously would have seemed morally reprehensible. Gambling became a particular point of contention between clergy—who scolded miners for looking to chance as a way of settling their affairs and idling away their hours—and miners, who came to see gambling as a logical extension of their daily routine in the diggings. As Ann Fabian aptly observes, the prospect of striking it rich was often closely tied to the miners' reasons for coming to California in the first place, and it was difficult for them to discern a moral difference between the two gambles.[53] The gaming houses of San Francisco, run by legitimate and savvy businessmen, presented an enticing alternative to the cold streams of the Sierra Nevada. "Plush, glaring, and lively," situated on the main Plaza where a church might have stood in an eastern town, often the only available source of community and female companionship, gambling parlors represented one of the few signs of life and pleasure in an uncomfortable physical setting.[54] Benjamin Vicuña MacKenna, a young Chilean who arrived in California in 1855, marveled at the prominent place that these establishments occupied. He noted that "gambling houses, open day and night, were the actual churches of San Francisco, and gold was the only God worshipped." In contrast to these scenes of gaudy pleasure, MacKenna wrote that the only church he ever saw in town was a Protestant one, out in a suburb "as though they were ashamed of it."[55] Decker, an occasional churchgoer, sadly observed: "How dingy and uncomfortable the churches here and how well fited up the Gambling Houses."[56]

Like Decker, many miners were just as alarmed by the vices of California as were the ministers. But even for the pious, gambling and the world that encompassed it held a certain fascination. MacKenna, who was a practicing Catholic, described the gaming houses as places "meant to drug the senses while the soul was being gnawed by feverish greed."[57] John Steele character-ized the simultaneous curiosity and revulsion that his first sight of a gambling saloon engendered: "Boys and men, from respectable homes, from quiet vil-lages and country places in the states, here spent their evenings, and formed associations and habits which wrought their ruin." Yet, he continued, "It must be confessed that there was such a witchery in the music, instrumental and vocal, that the masses were attracted and entranced, and in passing I found it difficult to resist the temptation to go in and listen."[58] Other observers were allured by the romantic figure of the professional gambler, the man of cun-ning who consistently worked the gaming tables to his benefit. One miner insisted that among gamblers in the early days of the gold rush there were "as many good, honest and square-dealing men as could generally be found among those engaged in any other business." Great acts of charity were sometimes attributed to them: such was the case of "lucky Bill," who upon hearing of a widow and two daughters without funds to return home took up a collection in the gambling houses of San Francisco, "and ensured their pas-sage home."[59]

In religious terms, some miners found new gods to worship that better reflected their understanding of cosmic order in the mines. Gambling appealed to some men because of the advantages of comfort and pleasure it held in comparison to prospecting. Both, however, appeared to be random forms of behavior, suggestive of a cosmic order distinct from the rational pre-dictability of the evangelical worldview. One indication of how much this alternative order held sway was the appearance of divination and other mag-ical practices in mining areas. Since many prospectors attributed success in the mines to the caprices of fortune, it seemed only reasonable that one should try all means of enlisting divine aids in one's work. As Keith Thomas has suggested, divination, a practice introduced from Germany to England in the mid-sixteenth century and used widely among miners there over the next hundred years, "legitimized random behavior by enabling men to make a choice between different courses of action when on rational grounds there was nothing to choose between them."[60] Divination and other magical prac-tices thus provided a sense of cosmic order for miners that better reflected their experience of the world.

An adventurer from New Bedford, Massachusetts, C. W. Haskins provides the reader of his journal with lengthy explanations of the magical practices used by his comrades. Forty-niners, he admitted, like many other people, exhibited a "peculiar mania of belief in the efficacy of signs." Divining rods were used to help locate gold deposits. Some believers felt that it was particularly effective to fasten a small vial of quicksilver to the rod and to attach a piece of paper "upon which was written in some foreign language certain mythical words and signs, evidently from the Bible, meaning, I suppose, 'excavate and ye shall find.'" Others speculated about the significance of dreams, soliciting the advice of others in order to come up with the most reasonable interpretation. Horseshoes were a favorite means of attracting luck. Haskins describes an acquaintance who had been earning twenty dollars a day at his claim; one evening he picked up a horseshoe on his way home and hung it on a nail in his cabin "with the remark that his claim in future was 'just agoin' to pungle.'" Sure enough, he earned fifty dollars daily for the next two weeks.[61]

It is difficult to know whether California miners were actually any more attracted to divination and magical practices than other nineteenth-century Americans, or whether they were simply more open in their use of them. Recent scholarship on the origins of Mormonism suggests that the practice of non-Christian rituals was more widespread at the popular level than ministers were willing to admit.[62] California provided an atmosphere with few institutional restraints to the expression of such beliefs. It is also likely that European immigrants provided a renewed impetus for these practices in the mining community, even as evangelical Protestantism effectively confronted them in more settled regions of the country.[63] Such a theory is strengthened by Haskins's comment that among miners, Germans were the firmest believers in divination and signs. He observes that, although many Americans were nearly the equal of the Germans in their ritual practices, "the main difference between them" was that the latter "had no hesitation in acknowledging such a belief." American prospectors, unlike their German counterparts, expressed a discomfort in discussing their ritual activities; apparently they felt some level of social pressure to deny their existence. "It was not expected, of course, that the most intelligent miners would acknowledge a belief in such signs, and they were always ready to ridicule any one who did. One of the old miners in particular, who ridiculed the superstitious notion, would always close his eyes when leaving his cabin, so his partner said, and not open them till he got into the road, and faced in the right direction in order to catch the moon in the proper position over his right shoulder."[64]

If some forty-niners worshiped new gods, others wittingly or unwittingly

conflated Protestant moral categories. The sacred and profane worlds, separated so clearly by ministers, became much less distinct for their fellow Euro-
Americans in California. William Swain, a prospector from Youngstown, New
York, commented that "many religious types," including a Methodist minister
of his acquaintance, saw no inherent conflict between Bible reading and
gambling.[65] Returning from dinner for his second sermon in an outdoor area
in Coloma, the Methodist itinerant William Taylor found the same worshipers
he had left hours before playing cards in the makeshift pews.[66] Even Dame
Shirley, although more anxious to justify her concessions to vice, had trouble
upholding her evangelical principles during her first week in Rich Bar. She
met a young man who had not spoken to a woman for two years and who, in
celebration of her arrival, rushed out and bought some champagne, "which I,
on Willie's principle of 'doing in Turkey as the Turkies do,' helped to drink." By
way of explanation, she asserted that "nothing can be done in California without the sanctifying influence of the *spirit;* and it generally appears in much
more 'questionable shape' than that of sparkling wine."[67] Her comments indicate that not only was she intensely aware of the appearance her actions
would have from an eastern vantage point, but also that she was not oblivious to the humor provided by the shifting moral ground on which she found
herself.

Yet the majority of immigrants still sought comfort in the familiar rituals of
home, concrete acts that symbolically connected them to the moral order
they had left behind.[68] As reported by miners and missionaries, many men
did go to church, when and where they could. The young C. M. Welles, from
Hartford, Connecticut, reported that itinerants came through his camp regularly, preaching to "closely-attentive and keenly appreciative audiences."
Miners, in ritual preparation for services, cleaned their clothes and washed
up: "Thus cleansed and clad, the miner feels at once good-natured and independent, and prepared to give a preacher a cordial and respectful welcome,
beside paying him bountifully for his labor."[69] Yet even when men sought
solace in such activities, their observances revealed the dissonance between
ministerial expectations and social reality. Miners lived within a system of
meaning in rapid transition, informed by both evangelical values and actions
and by the alternative moral order of the mining world. Often when they did
observe traditional Protestant rituals, their compliance revealed a failure to
understand the prescribed meaning behind the ritual itself, as in the case of
the man who wanted his child to be baptized at a Saturday evening dance.
Even for those men who did understand and appreciate Protestant rituals, circumstances frequently made it difficult to perform them.

Two religious rituals that were popular in California illustrate these points.

The first involved burial rites. The high death rate from disease and accidents constantly reminded men of the vagaries of life in the mother lode. Illnesses were pervasive in the cold, damp winters of the Sierra Nevada foothills, and outbreaks of cholera, dysentery, and typhoid swept through the thin cabin walls and makeshift tents. "Philo" informed his sister that on some days in Nevada City there were more than one hundred deaths from cholera.[70] The dangers of mining life added to the mortality rates: accidents, snowslides, fires, storms, and flash floods took high tolls.[71] In letters home, men frequently commented on the uncertainties of existence in the mines. "I tell you truly," wrote miner Charles Moxley to his sisters, "people die here very fast and I think out of so great an emigration many will not return home to their friends but I think a far greater number will find a grave in Calafornia."[72]

Early and unexpected death, perhaps because it was a tragedy familiar to Euro-American immigrants, turned men consistently back to the conventional rituals of home. Death and despair were the social realities of California life that evangelical piety handled best; it is not surprising that miners felt solace in recreating the death rituals of their former lives. Funerals were one of the few indispensable religious rites observed—when possible—in El Dorado. The thought of dying alone, far from friends and relatives, with no one to stand at one's graveside, was a source of nearly universal concern. As Nathan Chase told his wife with great dismay, "If a man dies here he is very likley [sic] to die with the name of god in vane upon his lips that is the way with most men in California."[73] Elisha Perkins observed, "If I must die, let me but get home & die in the arms of my friends, & I'll not complain, but here with no one to care for me, or shed a tear of affection as my Spirit takes its flight, tis horrible." He concluded by noting that "the grim monster appears now doubly grim & the grave has more terrors than I ever before felt."[74] Friends and companions usually did everything possible to provide suitable religious tributes for their deceased comrades.

Because of inconsistent church attendance and the small number of ministers in the region, men were often hard pressed to ensure a proper burial. Ministers were scarce, and religious affiliation, in these instances, seemed to have little bearing on migrants' choices; the content of the rite mattered less than its performance. Ministers reported being stopped on the streets by men seeking their services for impromptu funerals. The Reverend Jean Leonard Ver Mehr reported that one day in 1849, while out walking with his wife near a burial ground, several men stopped him because they thought he had a "clerical appearance." They asked him to read prayers over the man they were burying.[75] In most instances, men were compelled to perform their own brief rites, like the one Levi Kenaga described to his brother: "I have ben on a miners funerell that day i recive your letter one of my nabores he dide verry suden it is hard to see a poor miner die without a friend around him We buried him as good as we new how."[76] Thus, while forty-niners longed for the comforting rituals of home at key points in their lives, they could not always find the solace they sought. In these instances, miners' views of what constituted acceptable substitutions reveal the nature of their spiritual priorities.

Happier occasions also merited observance. The second and perhaps the most important ritual occasion in California, as for evangelicals elsewhere, was the Sabbath. For miners, Sunday was the one day of rest from their normal labors; men gathered in the nearest town or camp to visit, to sell their gold dust, and to buy supplies and equipment for the coming week. It was also the only opportunity for relaxation and entertainment: gambling saloons, bowling alleys, pool rooms, and racetracks stayed open to cater to their clientele. Men and women who spent their weeks in cramped cabins or tents looked forward to the opportunity to meet friends.[77] One minister described the favorite Sunday pastimes of gold seekers as bearbaiting and balloon ascensions.[78] For most, the day was spent in less exotic pursuits. On a typical Sabbath in 1851, Alfred Doten noted in his journal: "Clear and pleasant—As usual in about all other diggin's this day was spent by some in drinking and gambling—by others in reading the Bible and singing psalms, or washing their dirty clothes or going out hunting."[79]

Although miners generally did not express the level of anger and sorrow voiced by missionaries about Sabbath-breaking and their practices did not strictly conform to evangelical standards, many registered a decided unease about working on Sundays. The voluntary cessation of prospecting was a positive religious option, reflecting at least a partial internalization of Protestant values: it was an otherwise arbitrary choice made by men who felt that the day should be separated qualitatively from the rest of the week. Some mining groups voted to keep the Sabbath instead of laboring.[80] Even the generally irreligious Doten expressed compunction about mining on Sunday; 27 February 1853, he duly noted, was the "first Sunday I have yet worked in California at mining—but I was obliged to."[81] Although many men agreed that work should cease for the day, fewer commented negatively about the widespread practices of gambling, drinking, and dancing that constituted the "Sabbath rest."

Sabbath observance was also determined by the demands of the economy. Merchants were in an especially difficult situation. Because much of their business was transacted on Sundays, they could ill afford to close their doors. Peter Decker felt keenly the lack of observance of the Sabbath. On his way across the plains from Ohio with the Columbus and California Industrial Association the twenty-six-year-old merchant spent as many Sundays as possible reading his Bible. During a stop in Independence, Missouri, Decker joined up with several other young men, "They being both professors & Methodists," and spent the afternoon with them: "We talked on religious subjects, each had his Bible & we read a while in Testament & asked & answered questions in regard to what we read." In May 1849, when the company decided to travel on Sundays in the interests of time, Decker registered his objections with the captain. Expediency, however, soon conquered his hesitation. By July, he commented that he was "so used to traveling on Sunday that one hardly thinks of it unless reminded of it," adding that "I hope to get to a land of Sundays again before long."[82]

Decker was not a strict evangelical, judging from his interest in buying liquor from a Mormon family he encountered on the trail.[83] Nonetheless, the Sabbath held a particularly important place in his life. Once in California, he looked forward to the psychological transformation brought about by the washing and donning of clean clothes once a week. "A change makes me feel as though it really was Sunday," he remarked.[84] He filled his Sunday diary entries with talk of home and family. Glimpses of women and children, dressed for church, would often touch a nerve of nostalgia. For Decker and others, Sabbath observance was more than a religious injunction; it marked a day on which they allowed themselves to remember the world they had left behind and to forget the hardships of the society they had entered.

Decker found work in a store and was thus forced to work on Sundays to make ends meet. The Sabbath soon became a source of frustration for him. "This is an unpleasant day to me," he remarked on one Sabbath, "stores all open & is contrary to my feelings to do business on Sunday, but could not close here as this is *the* business day of all others. So I spent the day in the store." Yet he continued to be troubled by his predicament. A week later he recorded that "this is the day on which many miners camped out of town come in to do their trading & all stores are open & could not do business otherwise."[85] Decker never reconciled himself to his situation.

Miners also celebrated other holidays as best they could; but again, such occasions looked very different in this new environment and did not necessarily fulfill traditional Protestant expectations. Doten loved these excuses for revelry. On Thanksgiving in 1854, he and his friends celebrated when they thought the time was near: "We know of no *'proclamation'* to that effect as yet, but as it is about the right time, we kept today as a day of *feasting* and *praying.*" Christmas was a time of more frivolity. In 1850, Doten stayed home for the day, baked some "Grizzly" mince pies, and fired a twelve-gun salute in honor of the day. "Christmas in the mines is generally a pretty jovial day, whether from any regard for religion or not I cannot say, but this day is always a festive day in the diggin's—And then at night if there is a fiddler about his services are called into requisition and all have an extremely tall time. On that occasion each one feels himself privileged to get 'tight' and go in deep for fun and of course 'the ardent' has a quick and ready sale—but Dame Nature next morning gently chides them with headaches &c and reminds them of the glories of last night."[86] Migrants celebrated New Years' Day in much the same style, with the "burning of powder, explosions of huge logs, gambling, drinking, &c." Perkins commented that "the amount of gambling done is astonishing. . . . Hundreds from the sober portion of the states who hardly ever saw a card before leaving, now work hard for nothing else but to try their hand at some game of chance."[87] Such holidays provided a chance to intensify the pleasures of the Sabbath.

If participants attributed the moral world of the mines to the magical properties of California itself and evangelical missionaries categorized it as sin, how are we to understand the behavior of Euro-Americans? Had some migrants always combined evangelical precepts creatively with what Ann Fabian calls an "alternative culture of irrational economics," and had the social chaos of the gold rush merely given these preexisting tendencies a chance to flourish?[88] Was the migration to California a self-selecting process, in which those who were already somewhat disaffected with evangelical Protestant culture were most likely to move? Or, can we see on the Pacific Coast the development of a new religious culture, one distinct from eastern precursors?

All these explanations are to some extent persuasive, and perhaps all are necessary to account for the diverse nature of gold rush society. The first explanation echoes the findings of David D. Hall, Jon Butler, and D. Michael Quinn, who have demonstrated that at both the popular and even the clerical levels Protestant beliefs and practices have existed, often quite comfortably, alongside magical worldviews from the seventeenth century up to at least the 1840s.[89] The second corresponds to the observation of John D. Unruh, Jr., and other historians of the American West, that westward migration was indeed a selective process and that certain types of people—particularly young, single men, who were already less loyal to the churches—were more willing to assume the risks of going to California.[90] The latter theory, however, corroborates the accounts of contemporary writers that the moral world of mining society was, at least for a limited period, a singular entity, one that drew upon elements of popular religious culture and Anglo-Protestantism but that for some participants necessitated a spiritual reorientation. In spite of other factors that may have contributed to California's distinctive religiosity, we must consider this final explanation, the reason given by many participants, in more detail.

Clifford Geertz has suggested that questions of ultimate meaning, "religious" questions, tend to confront human beings in at least three types of situations: those events that challenge us at the limits of our analytical capacities; those that push us to the borders of our moral insights; and those that test the boundaries of our physical endurance. In all of these contexts, human beings grapple with moral questions—questions of cosmic order, divine justice, and the meaning of human suffering. Rather than living with absurdity (an option that a few sturdy souls do embrace), most of us fashion worldviews that make sense of our existential situations; we adopt perspectives of reality that complete and transcend the "partial truths" of the sensory world.[91] Most people do not cling to a belief in a transcendent order that consistently contradicts the mundane facts of daily existence. Instead, we alter our views, slightly or momentously, to bring religious beliefs into alignment with the known world. In Geertz's terms, worldview and ethos thus become congruent.

The evangelical worldview, so well-suited to the ethos of agrarian regions and small towns in the Northeast, came into conflict with the moral world inhabited by California gold miners. Our brief glance at some of the features of this society—its cultural diversity, its lack of institutional religious structures, and the moral implications of its economy—suggests some of the difficulties of transporting evangelical beliefs to this new environment. The fault lay not merely with young and eager missionaries, frustrated by the logistical handicaps of the physical environment, nor with bold and openly rebellious adventurers, anxious to flaunt their sinfulness in the faces of their more pious compatriots. At least part of the problem was intellectual: Protestant evangelicalism could not fully explain or make sense of life in the mines. Ethnic and racial heterogeneity did not necessarily challenge the beliefs of miners, but it did shift the boundaries of what people considered morally acceptable forms of difference. The luck and chance of mining proved a more aggressive blow to evangelical faith, however, given the centrality of ascetic self-discipline and rational cosmic order to evangelical ideology. Some clearly struggled to make sense of the disparity, while others adopted alternative visions of ultimate reality (held, in some instances, simultaneously with Protestant theology).

Because gold rush society was not in itself a stable alternative to eastern culture but was instead a community founded on the values of mobility and rapid change, it was never possible to construct a static worldview to meet the needs of its varied constituents. Rather than making sense of this world on its own terms, most Anglo-Americans located their time in California within larger frameworks of meaning, frameworks whose horizons stretched well beyond the chaotic boundaries of El Dorado. By doing so, by viewing the moral dimensions of their lives as grounded elsewhere, they could justify doing in Turkey as the Turkies do.

In an 1854 edition of the *Home Missionary*, the editor fretted about the perils of California: "When shall serious and truly rational thoughts be born in those breasts? When shall those perturbed spirits pause, that they may see God? The truth—they have lost sight of it. When shall they find it again? In the retirement of *home*? But they have no home. They live hither and yon, just as it happens—now with these, then with those; ever pursuing the same objects, gain and pleasure, pleasure and gain; and the division of the weeks is only a division made in the almanac, and not in their hearts; their life is wild, unrooted, groveling, degrading. What hope is there?"[92] Along with most home mission advocates, the author assumed that California immigrants lacked self-discipline and that the perceived disorder of mining society reflected a more pervasive and frightening chaos within the souls of individual argonauts. To be sure, men in the mines did not order their lives in the ways that missionaries desired; they attended church sporadically, they broke the Sabbath regularly, and they drank and gambled and fraternized with the unregenerate. Yet most faced the question of discipline on a regular basis and struggled to find an internalized structure for their lives amid the disarray they saw around them. Contrary to the suspicions of the clergy, communal turmoil often highlighted rather than reduced the necessity for personal control in the lives of immigrants.

To understand fully the moral dimensions of life in frontier California, it is important to locate the often confusing and contradictory elements of the mining economy within the context of entire life stories. Mechal Sobel has wisely pointed to the distinction between "culture as lived and culture as analyzed," between the frequently noncoherent practices and beliefs that constitute a human life and the "overall functional coherence" of which these values and acts can be a part.[93] As we have seen, some Anglo immigrants felt no incongruities between their commitments to Protestant churches and their mining, gambling, or failure to observe the Sabbath. Many others did, and to appreciate the worldviews of these settlers, we must first look at their reasons for coming to California and assess the moral dimensions of this journey in their lives. Put simply, motivations for going West affected the way migrants thought about and acted in their new home. Finally, we will view the world of the mines through the story of one miner, John Doten, a man who struggled with questions of self-control for much of his life.

No two people came to California in the 1840s and 1850s for exactly the same reasons. Census figures, however, and the repetition of certain themes in the writings of Anglo immigrants reveal several distinct patterns of movement and subsequent moral discernment. For nearly all argonauts, the adventure of life in the West was seen initially as temporary, a fact that allowed men to enter a world qualitatively distinct from both their pasts and their futures. Such men lived in the West assuming that they would return eastward, that El Dorado was a temporary escape from—or a solution to problems in—the "real world" of home and loved ones.[94] Outcomes did not always match expectations. Most, but not all, migrants did return. For example, Charles Ferguson disobeyed his parents and headed westward at age seventeen for what he considered a brief adventure and stayed in the West for over thirty years. Yet most important in the behavior of migrants was the self-perception of persistent mobility, the notion that their lives were not defined primarily by their experiences in California. Given this casting of the gold rush into a temporary moral arena, the ramifications of people's actions held a peculiarly tangential relation to their sense of identity.

This means of conceptualizing the California experience was most common among younger, single miners. As we have seen, the emerging community on the Pacific, compared to its eastern counterparts and even, to a lesser extent, to other frontiers, was exceptionally young. Like California missionaries, many prospectors came West before they had been seasoned by life experience. According to the 1850 census, fully 76 percent of the Anglo community was twenty to thirty-nine years old. A modest sampling of the members of three northern mining companies corroborates the youthfulness of the immigration: nearly two-thirds were between the ages of seventeen and twenty-eight, and the final third between twenty-nine and forty-five. Only four in one hundred men were over the age of forty-five.[95] "Gold fever" proved particularly communicable for young men, as Ferguson demonstrated: "Visions of gold excited my brain. It was not the gold alone, but an awakening of a strong desire of adventure which had pervaded my spirit from a small schoolboy taking my first lesson in geography."[96]

Adventurers in this age bracket often portrayed the trip to California as a great escape, a temporary respite from familial and communal responsibilities before they returned to settle down. Welles was haunted as a boy by his desire to see the world. In the early 1850s he departed with seven associates, "poor but virtuous men" who had been "ill-used by fortune," on an around-the-world adventure. Traveling by way of Panama and Australia, Welles arrived in San Francisco in June 1854 and was immediately captivated by the differences between California and his "comparatively conventional and humdrum life" in the East.[97] For him and for many other young men, the trip to California served as a brief foray into a world of excitement and adventure before the obligations of family and society took control of one's destiny. In keeping with the romantic mood of the era, the perceived innocence and wildness of California provided these self-proclaimed adventurers with a test of identity and a chance at fortune, in an Iliad-like return to an epic world of shipwrecks and buried treasure.

From a demographic perspective, this group of adventurers was not the type most likely to join churches. Religious observance tended to be closely associated with the ties of home and tradition they eschewed. Yet most of them did not consider themselves to be immoral. In an Emersonian manner, the quest for identity carried moral connotations and entailed an explicit criticism of traditional religious doctrines and polity. Welles, interestingly enough, attended several religious services during his stay in California. His experiences apparently only reinforced his negative attitudes toward eastern religion. In a log schoolhouse in Petaluma Flat, he encountered a young home missionary, "a spruce, dignified young graduate from an eastern theological seminary,—clad in garments of spotless black." Welles commented on the differences between the "religious exercises of the eastern seminary" and the plain but rough nature of the western heart. He concluded, after the service, that the minister would have done well in the East, where everything is "done by a kind of rule," but here, "the poor man was as helpless with his theology and his ways, as if he had come to swim in the ocean with fetters on."[98]

Welles's comments are telling. Highly critical of the missionary's style, his statements reflect an attitude of moral skepticism, not the moral indifference that missionaries often assumed and lamented. Miners were particularly suspicious of clergy asking for money to build churches since swindlers and thieves were legion. Even worse in the eyes of many were the ministers who both preached and mined for gold themselves. The Reverend J. H. Warren described the immense time and effort he spent simply gaining the trust of his supporters. "I have to go to the miners at their work," he wrote to his superior in New York, "in their tunnels, sluices, cayole holes. . . . I meet with all kinds of success and defeat. As I am becoming better known, and people learn that I am here to preach, and for nothing else, they are more and more inclined to give me their confidence and their aid."[99] Popular criticisms of ministers often implied that a higher moral standard was expected of the clergy, one that missionaries frequently failed to meet. One pious prospector reported to his wife that he knew of men "who have been Preachers and Home Missionaries in Massachusetts that have given all up" after coming to California. They "have made ship rack of Faith and have return'd to the beggerly elements of the world, and is to be fear'd are two fold more the children of the devil than ever[?]."[100]

Other young men actively reveled in the moral freedoms of California life. Doten was from an established Plymouth, Massachusetts family and seemed to take immense pleasure in defying the strict Calvinist morality of his New England upbringing. He went on benders four or five nights a week and made frequent visits to the local "senoritas."[101] He also recorded his feats meticulously in dozens of leatherbound volumes, and in an ironic attempt to wrestle with the ghosts of his past, he eventually became a correspondent for the *Plymouth Rock,* reporting back to his hometown about the customs and conventions of life in the gold regions.[102] These dispatches convey a mixture of pride and defiance, reinforcing the sense that Doten's travels served as a way for him to differentiate himself from the evangelical moral climate of his childhood. After the Maine Liquor Law was passed in 1851, Doten wrote snidely that such a law "has not yet extended its protecting arm over the benighted denizens of this barbarous region, where men are allowed to carry a bottle or a jug in their hand if they choose, and no official superintendent of the public welfare to make a descent upon him."[103]

As much as Doten enjoyed defying the authorities of his past, he struggled to reconcile himself to them. His desire to write home can be seen as an attempt to bridge the gaps—generational, moral, and spatial—between the old world of the East and the new West. In moments of nostalgia, Doten noted that hearing the church bells ring and seeing the women and children going to Sunday meeting, "reminded me forcibly of home."[104] After describing a stag dance that he had attended, a common form of socializing in a society with few women, Doten somewhat defensively cautioned his eastern readers about judging California mores too harshly: "Let no 'old fogy,' when he reads this, turn up his immaculate nose with a grim smile, at what he may term 'follies.' Just let him be situated precisely as we are situated here, and then see how he would act. If he has any warm blood at all about his heart, he might easily do worse than we did."[105] In many respects, Doten never emerged from under the shadow cast by his upbringing; he may well have been saved by it. For a time, his journey to California provided him with the distance to explore his own moral and religious sensibilities.

The youthfulness of many prospectors also suggests that the trip to California closely resembled another kind of ritual. The stance of openness, the vitality with which both Welles and Doten seemed open to "pure possibility," bears a functional resemblance to Victor Turner's description of the ritual coming of age, the experience in many cultures through which young boys are initiated into manhood. This rite of passage often includes what Turner calls a *liminal* period, a time during which neophytes are neither boys nor men. They inhabit a realm outside the bounds of normal society, in which, technically speaking, they have no status whatsoever and thus are temporarily beyond the authority of custom or law. "Liminality may perhaps be regarded . . . as a realm of pure possibility whence novel configurations of ideas and relations may arise." In a liminal period, the usual distinctions and gradations of rank or status are eliminated and the liminal group sees itself as "a community or comity of comrades and not a structure of hierarchically arrayed positions."[106]

In the societies from which most miners came, such rituals were not articulated in explicitly religious terms, for example, among the upper classes a passage to manhood might have taken the form of a grand tour of Europe. Nonetheless, the attitudes that many men exhibited during their time in California indicate that their western sojourn expressed these qualities of liminality. This was the main chance for aspiring artisans and farmers—or even for educated gentlemen seeking more adventure than Europe could offer— not only to strike it rich but also to gain a new status in life, to attain adulthood.[107] Prentice Mulford described the common attitude in his Long Island village: "An unspoken sentiment prevailed there . . . that a young man must move away to seek his fortune."[108]

The temporary lack of moral and social differentiation that defines liminality came into direct conflict with the desire of ministers in California, who wanted to make sharp contrasts, sort out the sacred from the profane, and define and classify certain types of behavior as good and others as sinful. It also varied sharply from the conversion experience itself, the evangelical rite of passage that separated the sinner from the new saint. For many immigrants, the chaos of California religious life was experienced as a realm of pure possibility. "They live hither and yon, just as it happens—now with these, then with those," fretted ministers. Looking at the same phenomenon, describing it in precisely the same way, young men instead saw temporary liberation and the acquisition of life experience.

Yet if many men sought freedom and adventure in California, a second group conceived of their journey as the fulfillment of familial responsibility. Mining company reports indicate that as many as one-third of the prospectors that left the Northeast for the gold mines were married men. For this group, as well as for many other miners who had financial and familial obligations or who wanted to set themselves on a firm financial footing to begin their married lives, the moral world of the mines presented a different sort of challenge. Charles Elisha Boyle explained that he was leaving Ohio for California in order to rid himself of "the detested sin of being poor."[109] In traveling to

California, these men were trying to earn enough money to repay old debts or to gain an independent living; the promise of wealth in a relatively short time lured them away from their jobs as artisans and farmers, often to the dismay of their families. For different reasons, they, too, saw California as a temporary stopping point, a place conceptually distinct from their lives at home. To be sure, some married men also desired liberation and adventure and an escape from an oppressive or tedious life. But journals and correspondence suggest that many men were pushed westward in order to support beloved parents, wives, and children, giving rise to a more poignant but equally strong sense of impermanence.

Nathan Chase, with a wife and two small sons in the East, thought only of working so that he could return home quickly. In a series of emotional letters to his wife, Chase described his life in the mines and the rigors of his work. He continually assured his wife that the only reason he left was to gain some property so "that i mite not be a dog for other people any longer." For Chase and others like him, the memories of loved ones often helped to preserve the values of self-discipline that were easily lost sight of or voluntarily cast off by other miners. Throughout their months of correspondence, Chase remained optimistic about his prospects for saving money in California, but only "if a man will be stidy and tend to his business and keep out of licker shops and gambling houses." He lived and worked in the mines, always keeping in front of him his goal of returning home: "I am very ancious to do what i can in California and then i shell fly to the arms of those who i love the best on earth."[110]

Not all men who sought gold shared Chase's single-minded determination. Some, like Alonzo Hill, were discouraged and eventually defeated by their ill fortune. Others, who were lured by the possibility of making their fortunes more quickly than they could in the mother lode, lost their earnings at the gambling tables and thereby lengthened their stays by months or even years. Some men, even as they worked for money to take home, felt that the transitory nature of their situation sanctioned behavior that in normal circumstances they would not have considered appropriate. In each of these cases, it was difficult to keep one's eye on the future in view of the enticements of the present. In the final analysis, however, the world of the mines was not home, and present actions related only peripherally to the moral core of one's life. Charles Davis, perhaps reminding himself even while he wrote to his wife, asserted that "every consolation that a person can have here is in the future, for however well he may be doing on the way, he has arrived to no point that will be comfortable to him untill he is ready to leave the mines for his native home."[111]

Few of these miners saw themselves as irreligious or immoral. Especially for the select few who chose to write about their experiences, questions of faith and morality proved salient and pressing and even motivated some of them to make the trip in the first place. Yet their patterns of religious expression diverged from and even conflicted with the patterns embraced by local religious leaders. Missionaries and miners thus often worked at cross-purposes: missionaries worked to build communities and create churches and religious institutions that would foster a "home feeling"; some miners, on the other hand, did everything they could to remind themselves that home was somewhere else. As one immigrant put it, "How priceless, when thus deprived of them, become our homes—better than fine gold!"[112]

Not all men experienced California as a temporary stopping place, however. Some stayed on, intent on earning money and building a life for themselves. For these miners, the world of El Dorado required another kind of self-discipline—the discipline to fashion a moral identity in a society with few external restraints. The journal and letters of John Doble, a prospector from the Midwest, illustrate one man's responses to, and continuing participation in, the moral world of the mines.

Like that of most Euro-American immigrants, Doble's life was neither particularly adventurous nor heroic. He was born in 1828 in Sugar Creek Township, Shelby County, Indiana, the fifth of eight children of William and Catherine Huffman Doble. Never quite convinced of his proper path in life, the young John trained first as a blacksmith and subsequently embarked on a career in bookkeeping. Yet his inner restlessness apparently did not subside. When war broke out against Mexico in 1846, the eighteen-year-old volunteered for military service and fought in the Battle of Buena Vista with the Third Regiment of Indiana volunteers. It was not long after his return that the news of the discovery of gold in California reached Shelby County. Abner, John's younger brother, left in November 1849 to seek his fortune on the Pacific Coast. As reports of Abner's growing success as a businessman in San Francisco filtered eastward, John must have begun to contemplate making the trip himself. He departed for California by way of Cape Horn in November 1851, little realizing that he would never return to his family home. John spent the next fifteen years mining and later served as Justice of the Peace in the mining camp of Volcano and surrounding communities. He died in San Francisco in October 1866. In his obituary, the San Francisco *Daily Morning Call* listed his occupation as blacksmith.[113]

In an important sense, Doble's experiences of migration, mining, and settlement fit the pattern of the young adventurer. Exhilarated by his travels through Mexico (to which he would return in the early 1860s), brimming with curiosity about the world beyond Sugar Creek, Doble looked upon his expedition to California as an impromptu exploration of his own capabilities and dreams, a chance for adventure and financial gain before settling into life in the rural Midwest. The announcement of his journey could hardly have been more casual in tone. His diary begins on 27 October 1851, the day that J. W. Reid, a friend from nearby Indianapolis, wrote to him and suggested that they travel together to California. In his characteristically declarative style, revealing little inner turmoil over the magnitude of this decision, Doble noted that "I answered him immediately that I would try and make ready to go and forthwith commenced preparations." Although details of his family background are sketchy, the fact that Doble's father was living and that he had several siblings in neighboring villages must have made the prospect of his departure less traumatic. He knew that his family was not dependent upon his labor or his income. Indeed, his father apparently loaned him money for the trip. Cutting his ties, therefore, entailed settling a few old debts and packing his trunk. Within three weeks, Doble was in New York City with his companions where they compared the comforts of various sailing vessels and equipped themselves with Colt revolvers for the journey. At the same time, Doble and his friends reveled in the boyish world of adventure that they were already creating for themselves, visiting the Anatomical Museum and dissecting rooms of the New York University Medical College, dining on oysters and ale, and settling "on the names that we should each be known and called by."[114]

In spite of the enthusiasm with which Doble entered into these festivities, he was by nature a careful man, not a creature of spontaneity, and he set his sights in California on the accumulation of money. With caution and careful planning befitting an accountant, Doble kept track of his small sums. As revealed in his diary, his main reason for keeping such a record was not to document the romantic wanderings of youth but to tally his profits: "I intended to have made this a journal of all I made & lost or spent & all I received & payed out until I returned home again." When his book was lost temporarily, the resigned youth conceded that "I must let that go" and determined instead to write "whatever happens to my mind while writing." Nonetheless, he continued to enter meticulous tallies of each dollar earned and every ale consumed. Doble was not a provider; he had no family to whom he sent the sums he earned. His fastidious temperament, however, obligated him to work until he had repaid his parents, who had made his trip possible, and the local loans that had established him in the mining regions. So single-minded was he that when word reached him of his father's death in the fall of 1852 and Abner urged him to return home to attend to family business, Doble painfully insisted that he could not leave until all his debts were paid. As was the case for many miners, the specter of failure and its implication of personal fault hung low over Doble's small tent. Ironically, it was his ingrained sense of duty to those at home and to himself, more than any other factor, that kept him in California for the rest of his life.[115]

Soon after his arrival, Doble articulated the principles that governed his career in El Dorado. He initially planned to open a cigar and tobacco store in Stockton, one of the large central valley towns that served as supply centers for the mining camps. When prospects looked inauspicious there, Doble headed for the Southern Mines. He first came in contact with the world of the miners along the Mokelumne River. "I have Noticed the population of the Mines are very unsettled," he wrote in February 1852. "I have got acquainted with men here who have been here in this neighborhood for 2 & 3 years and known every thing that man can know of the Mines yet these men are nearly worthless." But rather than attributing these failures to the caprices of fate, as did many observers, Doble gleaned from them the virtue of self-discipline. "As soon as they get a little ahead," he noted, "they go to drinking and keep it up until the money is out and go back to digging again until they get another start when again the same course is pursued."[116]

For Doble, self-restraint and perseverance distinguished the successful from the unfortunate in the mines. If ever a prospector worked at his trade with steady habits, it was John Doble. Digging six days a week, sometimes returning to his claim after his evening meal when other miners retired or headed for the saloons, Doble saved all the money he could. He was not a big drinker: he took his first tastes of whiskey and champagne in California and noted that he did not like either very much. When invited by his companions to join them for an evening of revelry, Doble remarked simply, "I did not think it would suit me."[117]

Much of Doble's asceticism, to be sure, was idiosyncratic. Nonetheless, it is a striking feature in light of the many enticements and amusements that California offered to a young man, and his tenacity motivates the reader of his diary to seek a further accounting of his actions. What kind of moral self-understanding underlay Doble's behavior? Do evangelical patterns of self-discipline, part of a religious culture imported from the East, explain his worldview? Or is there a coherent pattern to his life that can give us further insight into the extraordinary ethical world of the gold mines?

On the surface, the vocabulary that Doble used to talk about his own efforts at self-control appears to have less to do with morality than with purely pecuniary matters. In one of his rare bouts with alcohol, during a period of depression, Doble set out to get tight. "I felt very bad all day so got a bottle of Brandy to drive away dull care," he wrote. Later, he checked his actions, explaining that he "did not drink to drunkeness as I did not think it would pay." Similarly, after an all night poker game on a Sunday evening in April 1852, Doble expressed remorse for his behavior: "I ought to quit this gambling alltogather. . . . I have a love for that game but have no desire to gain money by it as I know Money thus gained is of no value to the winner or at least I have never known it to do any good."[118] Like the young Benjamin Franklin, Doble measured moral value in terms of social exchange; rather than relying on an internal ethic of self-control, he perceived restraint to be important insofar as it contributed to his good name.

One could reasonably argue, of course, that the use of the terms *pay* and *value* are highly ambiguous in these contexts and could, in fact, be charged with religious significance. The negative value of winning money at the card table could have referred to the detrimental effects it would have upon the soul of the winner, for example. Doble, in keeping with evangelical Protestantism's moral calculus of the relation between worldly activities and the lasting welfare of the soul, might have seen gambling and drinking as spiritually dangerous. Yet his attitudes in other areas reflect little of the antipathy toward these worldly behaviors that antebellum evangelical culture sought to instill. When Doble looked at men who were drinking and gambling away their earnings, he saw not sinners in need of redemption, separated from Christians by a lack of providential grace, but men who simply lacked the proper measure of control: "Some of them are good men or appear to have once been," he commented. "When one is found to be a reckless dissipated man he is most sure to be a man of some information & talent."[119]

Doble, like many immigrants to California, was neither a thoroughgoing materialist nor a strict evangelical. Rather, he made creative use of both the religious teachings of his upbringing and the hard lessons of mining life to fashion an ethic for survival in the mother lode. He articulated his understandings most fully in a series of letters to a woman whom, oddly enough, he never met. Lizzie Lucas, of Pleasant Ridge, Pennsylvania, was the cousin of Margaret Doble, the wife of Abner Doble. Thinking that the shy John was in need of female friendship and perhaps hoping that she could also arrange a suitable match for Lizzie (who was fast approaching the onset of "spinsterhood"), Margaret facilitated a correspondence between the two that lasted over five years, well after the end of Doble's mining career. In his letters to the pious Presbyterian woman, Doble poignantly and somewhat obliquely expressed a longing for the stability of home and family life that female companionship represented. Cowed by the male attentions bestowed upon the few available women in California, Doble complained to Lizzie about the "airs" of local females.[120] He never worked up the courage to ask for Lizzie's hand in marriage, although throughout the leap year of 1864 he filled his lengthy epistles with broad hints about his yearning for a proposal, such as "I wish some Lady would take compassion on my desolate condition and make herself happy by offering to convey my uncertain & wandering barque down the stream of time."[121] When Lizzie did not take advantage of his indirect advances and instead accepted the proposal of a local suitor, Doble continued to look upon their correspondence as a form of moral improvement, "so that I might have some profit from your extended experience and perhaps by your example I might be bettered in this world if not in the world to come."[122]

Yet ironically, it was precisely in his attempts morally and spiritually to connect with Lizzie's Christian devotion that Doble revealed the chasm that had developed between eastern evangelical values and his own moral worldview. In Indiana, he explained, he used to attend "the various churches and enjoyed it much. . . . Were I there now no doubt but that I should resume old habits and attend church regularly as formerly."[123] Life in California had led him down a different path: "Here we are all in a measure eagerly chasing the fickle Goddess Fortune," he reflected, "and in our zeal forget partially that we are human and surrounded by beings of our kind and are only awakened to a full sense of this situation when we are down in the world or when fortune deceives us. I have chased the Taunting Goddess for 10 years now and several times had my hands upon her but always by some Magic that I could not understand she has managed to elude my eager grasp and I have thus found plenty of time to moralize over it."[124]

In his moralizing, Doble came to the conclusion that self-discipline was the basis for a life of value in California. "Self-control which but few possess in any considerable degree is in my estimation one of the finest attributes of the human character," he confided to Lizzie. It was an ethic based on a familiarity with the teachings of the Bible, in that Doble believed that the nearer we come to self-discipline, "the nearer we come to the standard of perfection" taught by "him who was sent to save the world."[125] Yet in spite of the theological phrases in which he couched some of his ideas, Doble separated these moral precepts from the rest of the Biblical narrative; his interpretation of Christian beliefs hinged upon the ethic of the golden rule, which for him formed the core of the religious message. "I am not a church member," he wrote, "but never interfere with those who wish to be. . . . I take for my religion the words of Christ, 'As ye would that others should do unto you, etc.' And I do try to live up to it but I sometimes fail in it which is nothing but human."[126] Religion, for Doble, was an ethical imperative, a highly internalized code of behavior that, having been distilled from its theological context, became an end in itself because "the value of life is measured by the good we do in the world."[127]

We should keep in mind, given this individualistic moral outlook, that ministers sending off miners to the gold fields had worked to promote exactly this end. One could argue that western religious leaders were reaping the values that their eastern counterparts had sown. In accentuating the perilous moral climate prospectors would soon be encountering, clergy emphasized inner moral strength as the only sure source of value: "You will need more force to be saved from *yourselves*—more inward power to sustain you when outward restraints are taken off."[128] Advising miners to read books, keep diaries, avoid drinking and gambling, and to stay away from social and political involvements in the "half savage life of the wilderness," ministers implicitly warned their congregants not to trust the external manifestations of religion they might encounter.[129] The religious message, for purposes of easy transport, had become a code of ethics.

For eastern Protestant leaders, these teachings were a temporary measure, a means of guarding the souls of their flocks during a brief sojourn through a world of dangers. For men like Doble, this message took on added relevance in light of the social realities of California. As they saw it, mining society was akin to a moral barter economy. In a sphere in which people of different beliefs lived and cooperated together without benefit of long-standing rules and traditions, exchange was crucial to the viability of the entire community. Where religious beliefs ranged widely, one could either impose one's own values upon others or reduce all moral exchange to its lowest common denominator. Ministers often advised migrants to stay together with those of "their own kind," knowing that only within a group with similar values could miners avoid confrontation with cultural and moral difference. Within the mining communities, however, social isolation was impossible; men were forced to depend upon the kindness of strangers.

Many miners, like Doble, found ways of understanding their own moral values within this diverse setting. Getting along well in society was important to Doble. He was, by nature, a generous and amiable man. Echoing Dame Shirley, he told Lizzie that "it is an old adage that 'when you are in Rome you must do as Rome does,' and to get along smothly this adage must be in part followed." Thus the value of certain actions meant not simply monetary value or even their value to the individual's soul; it also referred to value within the moral barter system of the mines: "A person need not loose any of their self respect but may yield to the Notions of others without giving up their own that is let others acts as they may still *appear* to consider it alright not by words but by saying *nothing*."[130]

In keeping with his desire to oil the cogs of social intercourse, Doble often showed acts of great kindness to complete strangers. These gestures at times interfered with the primary goal of making money, but Doble thought them worth the effort. He spent several nights in October 1852 sitting at the bedside of a very ill man. "Charly" was not a close friend, Doble elaborated in his journal, but "watchers are hard to get here & I may be sick & want attention too. . . . so I do all I can for him." Doble's sense of the fragility and solitude of California life thus reinforced his adherence to the golden rule: one never knew when one would be needing help from others.[131]

When Doble did talk about a social ethic, there were pragmatic reasons for his interest. Tolerance and self-control made community life in the shifting world of the mines possible. Working a claim, for example, was most often the joint venture of two or more men, and one's livelihood depended on the diligence of one's mates. For Doble, the one characteristic he could not abide in his partners was a lack of self-control, inasmuch as it interfered with the success of the entire mining operation. He denounced his tentmate, Tom, who during his week of cooking made bread late one night after an evening of drinking. After putting the loaf in the oven, Tom promptly passed out and the bread burned, "so he gave us a lecture on intemperance & said he would quit drink." Doble also noted that "subsequent circumstance have proven he did not keep his word."[132] Soon after, Doble sought out new partners, ones who would not "drink up all they make." Clearly, drinking, gambling, and visiting prostitutes were blameworthy in that they demonstrated a lack of self-control that was detrimental to the ability of the community to go about its business. Doble did not find these activities sinful in any absolute sense, but within the moral barter of the mines, they made social and economic survival nearly impossible.

Doble's priorities in this respect also help to explain the rather odd emphasis he placed on the keeping of one's word. In his view, the breaking of verbal commitments was the worst of evils. After a night of gambling, for example, he meditated in his journal about his actions: "I played a game of Rounce this evening for Liquors & Cigars & lost $1.50 & I now think I shall never play again for Money or property of any kind & unless I forget this I now swear never to play again for any thing of any intrinsic value." Such a promise was not made lightly; as much as Doble disliked gambling and chastised himself the few times that he went on a binge, he had hitherto avoided making any absolute declarations about stopping. Just a year earlier he had considered renouncing the sport but decided instead to "risk no more money at it but will make no promises least I might break them." On this occasion he apparently contemplated anew the notion of making a vow: "I have frequently thought of renouncing all togather," he continued, "but have always been afraid to say positively or swear to it for fear circumstances would make me break my word (which I have late tried to keep in all cases)."[133] In Doble's mind, the keeping of one's promises was far more crucial to the functioning of society than was a total abstinence from gaming: the latter might temporarily set back one's financial gains, but the former made the moral world of mining tenable.

The central tenets of this ethical system—self-control and tolerance of difference—go far in providing a rationale for the relation miners like Doble had to organized religion in the state. According to the logic of evangelical reform, the experience of conversion served to educate Christians about the absolute sinfulness of habits such as drinking and gambling. Protestant ministers denounced these vices as *inherently* sinful, aside from the detrimental social and physical repercussions they might have. Converted Christians, therefore, would embark on moral reform as a consequence of the experience of God's grace. Revivalism and church growth would lead to temperance, antislavery, and antigambling societies. For Doble, however, the ethic of self-control was essentially a pragmatic imperative. It gave life meaning and value insofar as it made society possible. Thus, it was fitting that he attended temperance meetings long before he set foot inside a California church.[134] When he occasionally did attend services (not coincidentally, more often after he began his correspondence with Lizzie), he did so haphazardly, expressing displeasure with the "weak" ministers who all too frequently talked politics instead of religion: "Those [who] do come usually do the cause of Religion more harm than good by their poor preaching and curious conduct." Doble viewed his attendance at church not as an occasion to worship his God in the company of Christians, but as part of his "duty to encourage all moral institutions whether I am a member or not." He therefore attended all four churches in town, including both the Methodist Episcopal church and its southern counterpart, the Baptist church, and the Catholic church.[135]

These habits of attendance also suggest how Doble's moral worldview made distinctions that had little to do with theology or ecclesiology. All churches were moral institutions insofar as they promoted the virtue of self-discipline. In this context, denominational differences and questions of belief had little social meaning. Faith was a matter of private concern. In a description of his recently deceased friend Jim, a man he felt closer to than anyone else he had met, Doble articulated his version of the truly good man:

> He was entirely clear of all the Vices for which *Cal* is so noted he used strong drink in no form not even Tea & coffee he made use of no profane Language at all nor did he ever grumble in any

> Manner to my knowledge he was raised a strict Methodist
> (Episcopalian) & his actions remained the same until his death
> although he has for the last six months been a firm believer in
> Deism which belief he adopted as soon as he knew what it was
> & he futher has told me he always doubted some of the
> Doctrines taught by his Church though he never permitted his
> mind to run on the subject until he had seen what Deism was &
> then the more he thought the more he believed the Doctrine
> This love of the truth was very great I never knew him not in the
> least things to vary from it & falsehood he always denounced
> whenever he saw or knew of it.[136]

Doble saw in Jim all the qualities that he strove for in his own life: thorough-going self-discipline, constancy toward one's principles, and honesty in all encounters. The intense theological controversies between evangelical ministers and Deist infidels had no bearing upon the value of Jim's character.

In like manner, Doble himself sought virtue wherever he could find it. A listing of his expenses for the month of July 1853 indicates the wide-ranging nature of his interests. Alongside the laundry expenses, the beer, and the food purchased, Doble listed one "phrenological examination," one "chart of head," and a guide for bachelors entitled *Fowler on Matrimony*. His evening activities included going to hear a Mormon speaker (his only observation was that he "spoke well"), attending an "exhibition of Spiritual Manifestations," (he "did not learn any thing nor see anything but what I thought was verry natural"), and witnessing a traveling necromancer's performance (in which he "showed some slight of hand & some magic lanthorn tricks").[137] None of this seemed to conflict with his occasional church attendance; he regarded all of these activities as potentially conducive to moral and physical well-being.

We can only guess at the reasons John Doble arrived at this particular style of moral discernment. On one level, his was not a surprising or unusual set of ethics. Ascetic self-discipline, as has been suggested, was one of the principal features of evangelical Protestantism, a guide for conduct in which miners leaving for California had been instructed by their ministers. Habits of self-control also had practical uses in the mining camps, as Doble's experiences illustrate. Western reality thus reinforced certain kinds of behavior for many individuals. Still, somewhere along the way, the theological reasoning behind evangelical behavioral proscriptions had been lost or put aside in order to facilitate social order in a heterogeneous society. Tolerance was a more valuable and helpful asset than its opposite. Robbed of the moral absolutism that accompanied evangelical modes of behavior, self-discipline was reduced to a set of guidelines to which men could attach belief systems as they saw fit.

Beyond the socioeconomic advantages of a life of discipline, however, Doble's reflections also indicate a more profound, if muted, awareness of the importance of self-control. Reminiscing about his participation in the Battle of Buena Vista on the fifth anniversary of the encounter, Doble compared the world of the mines with his memories of war. "I could not help but look at the changing scenes & places a man will pass through in a few years," he mused. "This day 5 years ago I was at the Battle of Buena Vista loading and firing dodging & laughing at & to the Mexican balls with a determination to kill as often as possible & to day in a tent again some thousands of miles from there but instead of the Musket a pick & shovl & instead of men to kill rocks & Earth to move with the determination to get as much Gold as possible."[138] Like war, the gold rush was a period of upheaval, of concentrated effort divorced from the fullness of ordinary life. It was also, like war, a time in which one's fate was beyond one's control: like many miners, Doble expressed a dazed consciousness that life was careening out of his grasp, that larger forces governed his future. For Doble, the only choice allowed in this setting, the only voluntary means by which to hold off the chaos that threatened to engulf the individual, was that of self-control. Control allowed one to exercise a small measure of will over the anarchy of the mines. Many men, Doble included, instinctively knew that the only glue that could possibly hold together the unstable compound of California society was the will to say no.

In June 1854, Alfred Doten reported to the *Plymouth Rock* that the mines were on the decline. He concluded that "the cream, certainly, has been skimmed off, and a 'green one,' just into the mines, stands rather of a poor chance even of making a living, unless he hires out."[139] From a peak gold production of over $80 million in 1852, the output of the mines had dropped off gradually until by 1860 it stood at just under $45 million. Concomitantly, daily wages decreased sharply, from an average of twenty dollars in 1848 to three dollars in 1860. When strikes were made on the Fraser River in British Columbia in 1858, as much as 25 percent of the population of some mining towns joined the exodus.[140] The days when an ambitious and energetic California miner could earn an independent living were over. Many men died during their adventure; those remaining who could afford to returned home, and a number, including Charles Ferguson, Alfred Doten, and John Doble, stayed in the West, as witnesses to the slow settling of society after 1860. After 1869, the opening of the transcontinental railroad and the resolution of Mexican land claims heralded a new era of growth in the state, one marked conspicuously by more women and families, along with more ministers and churches, the latter supported by the growing incomes of capitalist financiers. The moral bewilderment of the boom days faded as more familiar patterns of religiosity gained a foothold.

Yet western states, including California, never replicated the precise religious configurations of the East, despite the best attempts of home missionaries. The rush for gold gave rise to a generation of men, invigorated by the excitement of the era, who could not resume the slower pace of life in the towns and on the farms of the northeastern states. Rodman Paul has observed that well into the 1860s mineral rushes in British Columbia, Nevada, Colorado, Idaho, and Montana drew crowds of itinerant prospectors, led by "old Californians," to move abruptly and rapidly around the West. Miners invariably were followed by merchants, mechanics, and boardinghouse keepers, all ready to supply their needs. "They are a fast people," observed John Hittell in 1861, "They will attempt to outrun old Time himself, and if they succeed once, it pays them for a dozen failures."[141] For some, then, the ephemeral quality of California living became a way of life, and the moral world of the mines was recreated in other regions.

Chapter 6

The "Wondrous Efficacy"
of Womanhood

Thou'rt going forth alone, father,
   To a far distant shore,
Thou'lt mingle in life's busy scenes,
   We *may* ne'er see thee more;

But a daughter's heart, with filial love,
   Beats anxiously for thee,
Before His throne of grace above,
   She'll daily pray for thee.
—Mary J. Tallant, "On the Departure of a Father for California"

An observer of California society during the early years of the gold rush furnished a description of one of the masquerade balls frequently held in San Francisco in the early 1850s. Unlike some of the more exclusive gatherings of the day, these balls were open to all, and the writer aptly captured the human variety that they attracted: "By the private entrance came the maskers, male and female. The Spanish bandit, with his high tapering hat, ornamented with ribbons; the gipsy, with her basket and cards; the Bloomer, bountiful in short skirts and satin-covered extremities; the ardent young militaire . . . the flaunting Cyprian, not veiled by domino or mask; and the curious, but *respectable* lady, hidden by cloak and false visage. There is the French-man in a fantastical dress; and Gallic count imitating the Yankee; the Yankee affecting 'Aunty Vermont'; and men already feeling the force of their libations affecting sobriety."[1] Miners and merchants in the young city flocked to these affairs, and reveled in the confusion of social roles that the masquerade represented. The swirling and intoxicated chaos of gypsies and soldiers, ladies and prostitutes, reflected in microcosm the diversity of life on the far western mining frontier, a place where the swift pace of settlement, the heterogeneity of community, and the transiency of population made social order an elusive goal. The masquerade balls, in this context, provided a controlled outlet for the anxieties and passions of a community with few cultural demarcations.

In a contrasting scene, Sarah Royce, a young wife and mother from New York State who had traveled across the plains in 1849, attended another party in San Francisco in 1850, a festival sponsored by the female members of the four Protestant churches in town. A pious woman, Royce had been troubled by the "reckless speculation" and wild habits of new arrivals to the city. She breathed a sigh of relief at the church party, an event that she claimed made many people feel that "even in California there was society worth having." Sometime during the evening, she noted the arrival of a very prominent, wealthy businessman with his "disreputable companion," and she approved when almost immediately, a "committee of gentlemen" asked them both to leave. Royce later reflected righteously on this incident: "The events of that evening proved to him, as well as to others, that while Christian women would forego ease and endure much labor . . . they would not welcome into friendly association any who trampled upon institutions which lie at the foundation of morality and civilization."[2] In Royce's mind, the businessman's arrival with a woman presumed to be a prostitute represented a direct assault on her most cherished beliefs and values and, indeed, on her sense of self. Yet the other woman was not held up for direct criticism. She was, in Royce's recreation of the evening, a nearly invisible pawn in a larger moral battle between men and women.

These two scenes are revealing for their differences as well as their similarities. Both depict important truths about the relation between religion and gender in gold rush California. As discussed previously, divergent moral worlds coexisted on the western frontier, worlds that valued relations between men and women in different ways. Although the male authors of the first account took pleasure in the mixing of class and gender at the masquerade, Royce seemed determined to sort and classify, to make absolutely clear, the distinctions between various types of people. Yet these narratives are not as easily distinguished as Sarah Royce's moral implies, for these battles were not merely binary fights between men and women over gendered understandings of human relations. With many players in turn opposing and allying with one another, these disputes more closely approximated the hands of poker dealt at the local gambling halls, where various participants pressed for their own advantages and staked their own moral claims.

Yet gender distinctions and the moral and spiritual virtues ascribed to each sex were crucial aspects of the evangelical piety that Euro-Americans brought with them to frontier California. In theory, if not always in practice, antebellum Protestants prized women as "naturally" religious. Both male and female religious leaders agreed that it was the woman's duty to guide and protect the Christian virtue of her husband and family. Correspondingly, as women assumed the role of spiritual nurturer, the private sphere of the home became the locus for piety. The "proper Christian home," as Colleen McDannell has suggested, "worked toward the salvation of the family." Indeed, it could be argued that Protestant evangelicalism was principally a "domestic" religion, centered not around the church or the altar but around the hearth and home. The father, as head of this idealized household, supported his wife and children by striking out into the amoral world of the marketplace and braving the competitive and increasingly impersonal arena of commerce for the sake of his brood. The ideal wife and mother remained in the home as a moral beacon to her husband, exemplifying religious virtue and gently guiding him in his own spiritual growth. In sum, the separate spheres of private and public worlds occupied by antebellum men and women meshed with the evangelical understanding of the proper functioning of a Christian society.[3]

In direct contrast to the familial environments from which missionaries and many Euro-American immigrants had come—communities in which the rhetoric of "separate spheres" of influence was at least approachable in theory—California in the 1850s was virtually an all-male culture. To be sure, other regions of the American West also contained predominantly male populations. Yet statistics bear out California's early singularity. In 1850 the ratio of men to women in the United States was 106 to 100. In rural Oregon at the same time, the proportion hovered at 137 to 100. New settlements in Nebraska, Kansas, and Iowa in the 1850s, promising fields for home mission organizations, boasted populations of approximately three men for every two women. In contrast, of the 68,813 Euro-American inhabitants in 1850 California between the ages of twenty and thirty-nine (which constituted 76 percent of the total Euro-American population), 2,583, or slightly under 4 percent, were female. By 1860 the discrepancy had moderated, but an imbalance still prevailed: females made up only 30 percent of the Euro-American population. Middle-aged women, furthermore, were still greatly outnumbered: only 20 percent of the population thirty to forty-nine years of age was female. In the towns of the mother lode, these percentages were still lower. Some estimates place sex ratios in the mining regions in 1860 at roughly twenty-three men for every woman.[4]

Compounding the demographic distinctiveness of gold rush society was the transiency encouraged by the economic vagaries of placer mining itself. Migration to agricultural regions most often involved the entire family; with women and children came the religious institutions and patterns of belief that had ordered their lives back home. Similarly, on the Plains and in the early settlements of the Pacific Northwest, women and religion arrived alongside men. In contrast, men generally came to California by themselves or in single-sex groups, well aware of the advantages that mobility represented in the search for gold.[5] With a population that was, at best, 8 percent female, the Pacific Coast came closer than any other settled American community to being, quite literally, a man's world.[6]

For all of the difficulties that missionaries encountered in trying to transplant eastern evangelicalism to the California frontier, the obstacle of gender proved most troubling. One early missionary estimated that approximately one out of every eighty to one hundred arrivals on the coast was female, and concluded that "in the present state of society and of the country, this is an undesirable place for a lady; and especially for a family of children. Take out your most highly favored towns, nine-tenths of your respectable families, divide the other tenth, between the high and the low, the virtuous and the lewd; and then devote your excessive male population exclusively to speculations and to trade; shut up your large churches, and assemble on the Sabbath, what few of the worshippers of Mammon you can, into small schoolhouses and dwellings; surround your public squares with gambling saloons and dram shops, and you will have a picture of any of our rising towns, particularly the emporium of the Pacific."[7]

Yet even as the relative absence of women created problems for missionaries, it affords a singular opportunity to test the limits of what has typically been characterized as a nationally influential ideology of gender difference. How influential was it, both for ministers and for other immigrants? If indeed antebellum Americans looked upon women as the nurturers of virtue and evangelical piety, how did Californians characterize religious adherence in a community with few women? Were understandings of ideal gender roles transformed to compensate for the lack of female presence? Could women still influence men spiritually from a distance of several thousand miles? Or was the evangelical message so dependent upon "virtuous womanhood" that in her absence it languished? Finally, how did the small number of Euro-Protestant women living in California understand their religious and domestic roles in the western environment? These questions prompt no simple answers. During the gold rush, miners and ministers and men and women all dealt differently with the religious consequences of the gender imbalance. It is fair to say, however, that the linkage of domesticity and spirituality remained a compelling ideal for many Euro-Americans, and it continued to shape the way people acted even when their behavior did not seem obviously religious. Ironically, the lack of women seems to have heightened the religious significance of womanhood in the eyes of ministers and ordinary adventurers alike.

Home missionaries themselves occupy a curious but crucial role in this analysis. They, too, were men, subject to the aggressions and passions that all males, according to domestic ideology, presumably experienced. But they were also the principal transmitters and sustainers of a feminized religious faith, a belief system that questioned the inherent piety of their own sex. By the late nineteenth century, home mission societies were seen as the province of evangelical women, who took it as their specific mission to carry the qualities of home—with all of its connotations of feminine piety, virtue, and honor—into the world.[8] Yet in the transitional period of the 1850s, before the incipient movement for woman's rights had affected the leadership structure of religious organizations, the male leadership continued the increasingly paradoxical practice of promoting hearth and home over "masculine" virtues. It was inevitable that this nascent feminization eventually would call into question male control over the vocation of the ministry itself, as well as over the leadership of the benevolent arms of evangelical social reform. In the antebellum era, however, most Protestant men and women failed to trace the contradiction between natural female religiosity and male ministry to this logical conclusion. Instead, they were content to let a feminized piety serve the functions of social control and communal stability for which it was obviously intended.

Female religious influence had multiple meanings for the home mission movement. At the most basic level, the national home mission societies often appealed specifically to woman's innate piety for financial support. The *Home Missionary* published numerous articles with titles such as "A Voice to Ladies, In Behalf of the Destitute Portions of our Land." The editors asked not that women engage in special kinds of work, but that they heed the call of their superior religious sense in aiding the work of men: "The considerateness, the sympathy of woman's heart, her self-denial in promoting any object which her judgment and conscience select for her efforts, will not allow her to hear, unmoved, the cry of the destitute."[9] Female promotion, as missionary leaders recognized, was not limited to moral support. Rallying women's sympathies drew on the organizational skills of what Mary Ryan refers to as the "voluntary, affectionate, and private networks of women" mobilized during the Second Great Awakening. Although the directors and boards of home mission societies were male, lay women funded and assembled the thousands of local chapters that provided the ongoing financial sustenance for the organizations.[10] Men may have taken up the reins, but it was women who kept the carriage moving.

In California, small but dedicated cadres of migrant eastern women proved integral to the task of organizing churches. Missionaries could not have accomplished their tasks of visiting and fund-raising—and even constructing the meeting houses—without the day-to-day labors of the few female church members. In December 1850, the ladies of the First Presbyterian Church, San Francisco, "ever helpful in furthering its interests," held a fair to raise money for the new church building, netting a total of nearly $4,000. Female members of the Congregational Church in Grass Valley earned $1,200 for construction costs in a fourth of July fair in 1853, contributing significantly to the $4,500 price of the edifice. And their efforts did not stop with fund-raising: once the money was obtained, the women constructed the building. The pastor, J. G. Hale, proudly reported on the end product: "It is finished with a singing gallery and lobby underneath. It is ceiled overhead and on the sides, up to the windows, with matched boards. The walls are covered with 'California plastering'—plain white cloth, sewed together by the ladies of the Sewing Circle, and tacked to the frame."[11] Similar scenes were repeated throughout the towns of the mother lode.

As important as these contributions to missionary work were, the significance of evangelical women extended far beyond their daily labors. By the 1850s, the pervasive Protestant identification of piety with female influence suggested that western regions could not be fully christianized until they were populated by families, and more specifically, until women arrived who could guide the spiritual growth and nurture of men and children alike. Much of the reasoning behind this belief was purely pragmatic; as the clergy well knew, men would settle down in the presence of family. The Presbyterian Timothy Dwight Hunt, in a sermon outlining the dangers of life in the mines, noted that "not till loved ones are here and the charms of 'sweet, sweet home' adorn the shores of our bay and beautify and enrich our valleys and the banks of our streams, will men plant and cherish institutions for coming time, and live for the benefit of immediate and remote generations."[12]

If the mere presence of women did not induce men to live for the benefit of future generations, the California clergy assumed that women would practice more forceful techniques. Hunt concluded his sermon by likening familial influence to law enforcement: "Our wives and our children would be a better safeguard than a police or a day patrol," he asserted.[13] Ministers assured their audiences that the presence of women would help to correct the numerous social ills that threatened California—problems that the ministers could not seem to combat on their own. Religious newspapers like the *California Christian Advocate* juxtaposed complaints about "the times"—wherein everything seemed defective and gambling, dueling, and prostitution desecrated the community—to the promise of woman's influence. The passage of laws, the growth of literary and scientific societies, and the founding of the YMCA were all hopeful signs, asserted one editor, but something essential was still lacking: "We want society. We want virtuous females, children and homes."[14]

These repeated invocations of evangelical womanhood suggest that the clergy viewed women as more than moral enforcers. Embedded in these calls for female influence lay the belief that women could redeem and order the chaos of California life—a chaos felt just as keenly by ministers as by miners. "In whatever land you find a family circle," explained the *California Christian Advocate* in its first issue, "that land has been visited with the Gospel of Christ."[15] The Reverend Joseph Benton, a Congregationalist, asserted that woman's presence would add a needed spiritual element to the future greatness of the Pacific Coast, completing the work started by men: "The softening influence of female character—the warmth and earnestness of female piety; the strength and devotion of woman's love, are needed to restore, restrain and renew our population—to sweeten and refine all our pleasures—to deepen and inspire all our grateful and sacred emotions."[16] Ministers hailed women as the civilizers of California society, as angelic creatures who could evoke an otherwise latent piety from the depths of male character, and who could reinvigorate a spiritual landscape that seemed to be quickly eroding.

In no small measure, the efficacy of woman's influence, for ministers, lay in the rhetorical use of gender as a technique of persuasion. Clergy frequently evoked images of virtuous womanhood, in its various manifestations, as a homiletic device to appeal to a restless male population. Women may have been scarce in California, but every argonaut had a family back home. Recognizing the power of domestic images, missionaries used them generously as a way to keep their male congregants in line. A mention of a mother, a description of a sister grieving for the soul of her wandering brother—these evocations prompted memories of home and emotional ties with beloved women that stirred male consciences, filling the place of woman's immediate presence. The publication of poems and stories in local papers also reminded men of their religious obligations not just to God or to the church, but to family back home. One such song, reprinted in several San Francisco religious periodicals, stressed the notion that the eyes of kith and kin were watching:

> We miss thee at home. Yes! We miss thee
>   Since the hour we bade thee adieu,
> And prayers have encircled thy pathway
>   From anxious hearts, loving and true,
>
> That the savior would guide and protect thee
>   As far from the loved ones you roam,
> And whisper, when e'er thou wert saddened,
>   They miss thee—ALL miss thee at home![17]

This emphasis on family at home proved particularly useful for clergy because it provided a message both specific and universal, an emotional appeal that transcended the increasingly brittle boundary between North and South. As sectional tensions mounted in the 1850s, ministers fretted over how to preach to diverse audiences of men; not surprisingly, some of the most powerful and emotional—and thus religiously persuasive—images also had political and social implications that provoked intense regional sentiments. Antislavery, for example, was a brand that few northern missionaries cared to display to their congregations, whatever their own feelings; many of the clergy felt that the hostility it evoked among southern evangelicals was too damaging to make it worth the effort.

Motherhood, conversely, was a symbol lacking regional bias. The Reverend Charles Wadsworth made great use of its universalism in a sermon delivered to the YMCA of San Francisco. He preached on Prov. 10:1, "A foolish son is the heaviness of his mother," and the Old School Presbyterian's plea to his listeners self-consciously rose above distinctions of culture and region. "Every one of you has a mother somewhere. . . . You are all sons! You have all mothers! And I know—for in all these faces there looks up to me no soul that has been brutalized into shame or scorn of a mother's gentle love." He implored California men to be worthy of a mother's love, and to use the "holy memory" of mother as a guiding star in their travels. He colorfully envisaged a woman, "bowed down before the Mercy-seat praying" for the soul of her boy. For the young man who had lost his spiritual way, or who was engaging in sinful practices, Wadsworth held out a mother's love as the final lifeline: "I fling myself in that young man's path . . . and I say to him now: REMEMBER YOUR MOTHER! . . . You are not yet a fiend; and the last angel that deserts your soul will be your mother's memory!"[18]

Another means of promoting the proper kind of female influence was actively to encourage the institution of marriage. Lamenting the inability of men in California to settle down, ministers diagnosed the problem as a lack of family: by encouraging marriage and family life, missionaries knew that they would encourage communal stability, and they hoped that male conversion would follow in its wake. As early as mid-1849, J. W. Douglas wrote to the AHMS about the need for families. "I wish that colonies of true hearted Christians would come out here & settle, on some of these waste lands, & make this now waste wilderness of California (a double waste at present) to rejoice & blossom as the rose."[19] Methodist minister S. D. Simonds promoted the addition of a tearoom as a regular feature of the church, hoping that this re-creation of feminine presence would enable men to "cultivate the social life more."[20]

Evangelical leaders hoped that the edifying influence of pious Christian families would also extend outward into the community. As the leading San Francisco Presbyterian pastor, Samuel Willey rejoiced when the wife of Maj. Amos B. Eaton of the United States Army joined her husband in the state. Eaton himself had been a "model Christian": he abstained from intoxicating drinks, he faithfully attended church and weekly prayer meetings, and for several years he superintended the Sunday School at the Howard Street Presbyterian Church in San Francisco. When joined by his wife, however, the luster of his example shone even brighter in her presence, according to Willey, for "then there was another precious Christian home, throwing its influence around a large circle of homeless young men here." In short order, sure enough, the Eatons had organized the San Francisco Ladies Protection and Relief Society, proving to Willey that the powers of the home were indeed potent.[21]

The frequent use that ministers made of images of evangelical womanhood raises the important question of precisely how clergy understood feminine influence to function in society. Traditional evangelical theology—Reformed and Arminian alike—emphasized the crucial distinction between the female ability to civilize men in preparation for their conversion to Christ and the capacity to christianize them, that is, to participate integrally in the actual process of their conversion. Horace Bushnell's notions of spiritual nurture notwithstanding, most evangelicals would have shrunk from the idea that women played an instrumental role in male conversion; they still believed that only through the workings of God's grace could sinners receive salvation. Women, like revivalists, could facilitate a man's spiritual preparation by evoking a desire to receive God's forgiveness, but they could not take the final step for him. Hearth and home were no substitute, in the eyes of the clergy, for the sweet outpourings of the Holy Spirit.

Debates over strategy within the home mission movement complicated the traditional understanding of conversion as the prerequisite for salvation. For practical purposes, revivalists in the West relied on the promotion of Christian institutions—primarily schools, churches, and families—as the principal means of advancing the cause of Christ. Evangelicals understood converting and civilizing, the twin aspects of the missionary push that had always existed in a certain tension with one another, to be mutually reinforcing aspects of the religious community.[22] In gold rush California, ministers who agonized over the apparent failure of revivalism to ignite the piety of the laity naturally turned to the promotion of religious institutions. If gold seekers would not convert, they at least would be restrained by the familiar features of the eastern moral landscape.

In this context the promise of woman's influence, a primary purveyor of all that Christianity and morality symbolized, attained a heightened religious significance. Theological nicety was often lost in the clerical effort to emphasize the power of evangelical womanhood. One Methodist writer, for example, comforted his listeners when he expressed confidence that women would solve the town of Stockton's drinking problems through their mere presence. "The great moving power, the lever which we trust will eventually cleanse our city of the 'whiskey shops' that still infest it, is the steady but constant acquisition of mothers and daughters to our society. . . . To the ladies (God bless them!) we look for protection from the spread of intemperance."[23] Missionaries may not have said that women would show men the road to divine glory, but they implied as much in the stress they placed on domestic values and the institution of the family.

Ironically, the fairer sex also attained the status of the spiritual protector and defender of men, inverting traditional notions of the power of males and the authority of the clergy. As home mission organizers and fund-raisers, active reformers in the California community, evokers of feeling and piety, objects of veneration, and caretakers of men's weaker spiritual natures, women shaped the way evangelical clergy presented religious faith to the mining population. Yet rather than acting merely as male aiders and abettors in a gendered morality play, in a curious way, missionaries voluntarily undermined their own moral authority by singing the praises of female virtue. "Ladies of California!" proclaimed a correspondent for the *Pacific*, "It is for you to say how soon our State shall be distinguished for purity and virtue." Ministers agreed that the piety of *all* males had suffered from the lack of woman's influence. "We Californians have been so long away from the restraining and humanizing influence of our families, and of ladies' society," the writer continued, "that we are prepared to welcome it now and yield to it, far more than we were wont to do in former days."[24] The clergy seemed ready to acknowledge their own need for the kind of moral authority that could be exerted only by hearth and home.

Other Euro-American immigrants responded to these invocations of the religious importance of women in varying ways, but their reactions generally did not lead them into the churches. The intense appeal to evangelical womanhood had at least three ironic and certainly unintended consequences for the men in the pews. First, if the line between woman's religious role as civilizer and savior became blurred for California missionaries, miners unabashedly deified women and looked to them for spiritual protection. Reversing popular fictions of endangered females being rescued by dashing heroes, miners spoke about themselves as the helpless victims of a corrupt society, waiting for female protection and salvation. In what was clearly a metaphor for the perceived disjunction between the moral world of the home and the dissolute arena of gold mining, apocryphal stories abounded of faithful women who journeyed West to rescue their men from the clutches of evil. The miner John Steele described one "Dr. Y," a surgeon in the United States Army during the Mexican war who was discharged for drunkenness on duty somewhere near Mexico City. Dispirited and ashamed, he drifted north into California. Back in Kentucky, his wife, "knowing his proud spirit" and suspecting his fate, resolved to save him with a "woman's love, constancy and devotion." She tracked him to Sacramento where they set up a home, had a son, and where, for a time, she "appealed to his better nature" and "sustained his nobler manhood in the desperate struggle to assert itself." Eventually, however, he succumbed to gambling and drinking, despite his wife's unfailing attempts to save him. One night, in a drunken state, he accidentally shot her to death. He was immediately lynched by a mob, and their son was raised by a good Christian family.[25]

Fortunately, not all such stories ended so unhappily. Generally, the virtuous woman triumphed over the weaknesses of her man. In *Philip Thaxter,* a long and often tedious novel published in 1861 by Charles Washburn, a former miner, the fears of forty-niners about the vicissitudes of fate and the religious importance of a good woman attained fuller and happier expression. Thaxter, a young New England school teacher and farmer with a loving wife and family, struggles under constant debt. When gold is discovered, Thaxter catches the fever and sees a trip to California as a way out from under his financial obligations. He joins a company of miners without consulting his wife, and when he finally tells her of his plan to leave for two years, she emphasizes the lack of home life he will be forced to endure: "It is a dreadful country to go to," she tells him. "When you have been to work hard all day, you will not have such a nice home as this to come to. No good, warm supper—no nice, warm, dry clothes to put on, and no big fire to warm yourself by. And you will have no wife there, no Benny, no George. And when you lie down at night, to sleep on the cold ground, you will think you would give all the world if you were back to your old home again."[26]

Against his better judgment and the prophetic advice of his wife, Thaxter decides to try his luck in the mines. Here his slide down the slippery slope of moral degeneracy begins. Although his intentions are honorable, the lure of quick wealth mesmerizes the poor man, and he is helpless to combat it once he leaves the sanctifying influences of his family life. Within a year, Thaxter is drinking whiskey, carrying weapons, living openly with a married woman in San Francisco, and running a gambling house. Washburn describes him in a characteristically Victorian turn of phrase: "His self-respect was literally and absolutely gone. He was embarked on the sea of dissipation and sin, and he rushed headlong into anything that promised gold and excitement."[27] Finally his wife, hearing nothing from him for months, comes to California to look for him. When they are at last reunited and happily living on a ranch south of San Francisco, Thaxter once again regains his moral bearings and is able to lead a virtuous life.

As steeped in Victorian sentiment as they are, these stories reveal a great deal about religion and gender roles in El Dorado. Miners often saw their religious destinies as being controlled by the women in their lives; without women to guide them, they were merely the passive victims of a moral chaos, helpless to alter their own spiritual fate. Women were thus the conduits and the gatekeepers of male religiosity. Even wives assumed the role of maternal nurturers, from whom, as one miner put it, "Many a poor suffering soul received assistance, comfort and consolation from their motherly and sisterly hands and gentle spirits."[28] Paradoxically, the stress that California ministers placed on women's influence only blurred the already hazy moral boundaries experienced by forty-niners, in that it reinforced the conflation of female moral suasion with female salvation. In turn, it displaced moral responsibility from the shoulders of men who interpreted their own spiritual rootlessness as understandable—and even natural—in a community without women.

By the admission of both missionaries and laypeople, female moral persuasion was considerably more efficacious in furthering the cause of evangelical Protestantism than was clerical preaching. Charles Ferguson attended a bazaar sponsored by the women of Nevada City during which kisses, smiles, and other feminine charms were sold off to benefit the local church: "The miners were captivated with the smiles of the ladies and were willing to pay liberal for one; nor were the ladies sparing of their blandishments, so long as the miners' money held out."[29] From the town of Columbia, the Presbyterian Reverend Laurentine Hamilton wrote about his own failed efforts to convince shopkeepers to close their doors on Sundays, in contrast to the town's women, who passed around a petition and easily collected the signatures of a majority of merchants who promised to observe the Sabbath. Hamilton could only admire the efficacy of this concerted female action.[30] Forty-niners, in the estimation of the clergy, desired the esteem and companionship of women much more than the respect of the minister.

The equation of domesticity with religious devotion also unintentionally encouraged a conceptual separation between the community of the mines and a life of faith. Many adventurers considered both religion and home to be life experiences that existed somewhere else. As the Reverend Daniel Woods expressed it, in the mines "there is a respect for religion, as there is a respect for everything which reminds one of home." *Respect,* however, did not compel attendance at church; indeed, it only encouraged a wistful longing for a return to normal life, domesticity, and consequently, piety. Like John Doble, men in California may well have gone to church more often if women like Lizzie had agreed to marry them. In so thoroughly associating evangelicalism with an eastern pattern of household and familial arrangements and by not stressing the sanctity of California society as it was lived and experienced by most men, ministers may actually have discouraged argonauts from establishing ties to worshiping communities in California.

What emerged instead was a considerably more privatized and individualized understanding of religious faith. Eschewing the struggling churches, many otherwise pious men relied on their letters to wives and families as their only form of devotional exercise. Charles Westover spent Sunday afternoons writing home to his wife and five children in Ripley, Indiana, using his letters to recreate the home life he yearned for: "Now Betsey if I could here some one nock at the cabbin door & could open it & see you with your little brood around I do think I would give all the gold in California if I had it but that cant be."[31] Others wrote to their ministers at home, describing the loyalty to family and friends that motivated their work: "I am now thrown for religious enjoyment upon my bible, secret communion with the Saviour and meditation upon his word," wrote one man, "together with correspondence with christian friends & what my memory retains of religious instruction received in bygone days."[32] Religion in the mines often consisted of private rituals in which men gave vent to their longing for the homes and religious ties they had left behind.

The necessary domestic activities performed by men in the absence of women also attained moral status because of the inescapable identification with home and family life. Daniel Woods noted that on rainy days his companions would all go visiting together, and "like the ladies at home, we often take our sewing with us." Woods looked back on these afternoons fondly: "While we plied our needles, our tongues were equally busy speaking of mutual friends and hopes."[33] Another miner, writing to his sister, acknowledged a certain pleasure with his domestic arrangements: "I am beginning to think as all the girls do, that there is nothing so bad about housekeeping after all."[34] Within these alternative familial arrangements, some miners were also able to express the piety that had become so individualized. Woods and his companions, for example, held family vespers at a certain hour every day, attempting to have them coincide with worship services back home. As he put it, "These were meetings of the heart—the reunions of faith."[35]

The missionary message also inadvertently encouraged an "indiscriminate" desire for female companionship. Try as ministers might, the linkage of womanhood with morality was not easily qualified by Christian admonitions. Consequently, local prostitutes and gambling house operators learned to play the gender game more successfully than evangelicals, manipulating the yearning for domesticity and emotional intimacy to their own ends. Prostitution was a common fact of life in gold rush society, as demonstrated by the casual mixing of "Cyprians" and "respectable ladies" at the masquerade balls (significantly, the ladies were the ones who wore masks).[36] The more observant ministers recognized the psychological and emotional appeal of prostitutes. William Taylor, a Methodist itinerant with more than his share of sympathy for the plight of the lone forty-niner, described how prostitutes "became the leading conservators of social life" in California because of the shortage of women. Houses of ill repute, he continued (with little explanation as to where he had collected his evidence), seduced otherwise virtuous men precisely because they contained many of the features of home, with "curtains of the purest white lace, embroidered, and crimson damask." Given their obvious appeal, Taylor concluded that "you would not suspect that you were in one of those dreadful places so vividly described by Solomon."[37] Gambling halls and saloons also offered domesticated environments that featured plush fabrics, comfortable furnishings, and female companionship.[38]

To avoid misinterpretation, missionaries continually refined their emphasis on innate female religiosity. They reminded their congregations that woman's presence was not adequate without the hallowing influence of the church. One woman was not as good as any other—a message that contained racial and cultural, as well as moral, admonitions. Christianity, ultimately, was the social force that put male-female relations aright. The clergy made it clear to men that women and churches belonged together, that the more "unmentionable" forms of social intercourse between the sexes hardly constituted appropriate female influence. In a sermon given at the dedication of an AHMS church in the mining town of Grass Valley, Joseph Benton explained that "the Christian House of Worship has been the foundation of our happier social condition, and has . . . raised woman from her thraldom and degradation to her position of equality; as before God a responsible being—and as beside her man, a companion."[39] Still, many immigrants continued to seek out intimacy and domesticity even if they had to pay for it. Doing so, ironically, linked them emotionally to a familiar and deeply spiritual world.

Finally, both ministers and other male immigrants not infrequently expressed resentment at women for their failure to live up to the ideal, even as they extolled woman's *potential* social and religious influence. Some men, perhaps those adventurers for whom the trip to California represented a youthful lark or those anxious to justify their departure to female family members, insisted that El Dorado was a man's world and ought to remain so. By the mid-1850s, however, some ministers also voiced disappointment that women were not living up to male expectations by improving western society. Because of the male vulnerability to female influence, warned several clergy, an erring woman was much more dangerous to society than a sinful man. "Women in this country have acted shamefully," wrote one minister. They had not helped the spiritual condition of the land as much as he had expected; therefore, he concluded, Christians must look for a general revival of religion, "like what was seen in the early history of the Church in the Western States." Another expressed less a sense of indignation than of chagrin: "As a general thing, I am sorry to say, the influence of woman in California, so far, *has not been what was expected of her*. Women of religious professions step into the deep stream of worldliness, along with their husbands, and instead of leading them out, drag them down. . . . I have seen more liquor drunk in the last two months, by those who are styled *ladies,* than in all my life before."[40]

This overt hostility and anger undoubtedly reflected more than a disappointment with individuals. Implicit in the criticisms against women is a somewhat oblique acknowledgment of the male dependence on female presence in order to make community whole. Yet this dependence was not without its resentment, and the hostility directed toward "wayward" women may have been an expression of male ambivalence about the power of evangelical womanhood to complete the task of social conversion they felt unable to accomplish. Some men could not live *with* women, but they most certainly could not live without them.

The comments of men tempt one to conclude that the few Euro-American women in frontier California served merely as the objects of male projection of their own hopes and fears, or as the pawns of ministers in an elaborate scheme to organize and control mining society. Such readings, however, fail to take into account the women's own perceptions of life on the mining frontier. They also downplay both the extent to which some females served as active partners in the venture of bringing evangelical religion to the state and the many ways in which other females, like males, vigorously thwarted missionary plans for the building of a Christian society. On the whole, the received wisdom of missionaries was true: women in western communities often did labor to control and civilize men. Taking this argument further, Robert Griswold contends that the West frequently became a battleground between the sexes over differing understandings of moral order. Men without a critical mass of women to guide them, he argues, displayed little interest in founding schools and churches and in donating to charities; they often demonstrated an open disdain for "female" patterns of domestic morality. According to this line of reasoning, ministers and women would indeed have banded together to promote and impose their own, feminized communal ethic upon an unwilling male population.[41]

There are still several problems with this type of argument, as well as it may account for the overtly antimale campaigns used by some Protestant women to advance a variety of reform causes. First, it fails to acknowledge the deep-seated ambivalence evident in men's protests against women in western communities. Men may have often complained about female attempts, literally and figuratively, to clean up their communities; some, certainly, thought that women ought to stay in the East and not venture into what they considered to be a masculine domain. Yet even the men who made these comments also yearned for reminders of home and for feminine influence; reports abounded of men lining up on the doorsteps of recent widows to seek their hands in marriage and of single young women receiving dozens of marriage proposals from lonely adventurers. Many men vacillated between desperate homesickness and the active enjoyment of newfound freedoms.[42] To categorize the former as an inherently male attitude, therefore, is to oversimplify the obvious complexities of relations between men and women.

Griswold's analysis also does a disservice to many women by overestimating their desire to reform a male world. He seems to have accepted the truism of the day that women were inherently more religious, more domestic, and more intent on social order. Although many women did fit this pattern, there was a wide variety of female responses to life on the frontier. Women, like men, came West for many different reasons: some sought to recreate the world of eastern culture and civilization from which they had come, while others, with equally moral intentions, looked for escape from the restrictions that their former communities had imposed upon them.[43]

Other factors may help to explain why many women worked for social and religious reform. Most important, the small number of Euro-American women in frontier California did not represent the same cross-section of the population constituted by males. The vast majority of women traveling overland to the West in the antebellum period were married or were under eighteen; perhaps 2 percent traveled alone.[44] Although this sampling includes westward immigrants as a whole, and significant numbers of single women did come by ship from other countries,[45] it is highly unlikely that their numbers approached that of young single men.[46] Moreover, as many as one-quarter of married female immigrants were pregnant or had recently delivered children.[47] These physical and biological differences meant that women were much less likely than men to interpret their migration as a liminal or transitory period in their lives. Unlike most men, they came intending to settle down, or were forced to remain relatively settled because of the physical realities of birth and child rearing. Women, therefore, may have been a civilizing influence in California in part because those who chose to migrate desired social stability and not necessarily because women, as a group, were inherently more civilized than men.

Stability, however, came in many different shapes, and particularly in the 1850s, many Euro-American women did not conform to the idealized image of the domestic, nurturing, and pious wife, mother, or sister. Like men, women came West to make money and interpreted the undertaking in moral terms. Mary Jane Megquier, the wife of a physician from Maine, traveled to California with her husband in 1849 to seek new economic opportunities. Megquier's practice in Maine had floundered; the couple hoped to save enough money in California to support their family more comfortably. Leaving their children with relatives, they settled in San Francisco, where Mary Jane ran a boarding house while her husband practiced medicine. Just before their departure, she wrote to a friend that "when I found how much the ladies were appreciated in the far west, be assured I was ready to start."[48] Her intention, however, was not to bring morality and right living to the gold seekers, nor did she desire simply to feel useful in a fulfillment of religious obligations. What she meant, as she explained, was that the scarcity of females would place her domestic skills in much higher demand and would yield the kind of financial profit she desired. Like many other forty-niners, Mary Jane Megquier wanted to earn her living.

Once in California, Megquier did little to further the cause of religious or moral organization, despite her churchgoing background. In fact, she was precisely the kind of woman that missionaries excoriated for their failure to impart proper feminine influence. Megquier appreciated the freedoms that California life offered, noting that there were "churches in abundance but you can do as you please about attending, it is all the same whether you go to church or play monte, that is why I like, you very well know that I am a worshipper at the shrine of liberty." To her mother, she admitted, "I suppose you will think it very strange when I tell you I have not attended church for one year not even heard a prayer but I cannot see but every thing goes on as well as when I was home." In a letter to her young daughter, she intimated jokingly that, far from seeking to restrain the natural impulses of the men around her, Mary Jane herself was being kept in check by her husband: "I should like very much to have you here but your Father thinks it is no place for you. I suppose he is afraid you will be led astray, he has his hands full to keep me straight."[49] Although domesticity in a general sense shaped the way Megquier understood her role in life, female reformers did not find in her a fellow crusader.

Women often valued domestic work in California not strictly from a sense of spiritual calling but because they found that it paid very well. Particularly during the first few years of the gold rush, women performing "women's work" could earn more money than most men by contracting their services. Margaret Frink traveled West because she heard "rumors a woman could get $16 a week for cooking for one man." Many Euro-American women took in boarders, did laundry, and cooked for large numbers of single men, including one who estimated having baked $18,000 worth of pies in 1852 alone.[50] Jerusha Merrill and her husband ran a twenty-room boarding house in San Francisco, and Jerusha wrote back excitedly to her siblings in Newington, Connecticut, about her business. "Never was there a better field for making money than now presents itself in this place at this time," she enthused. "We are satisfied to dig our gold in San Francisco."[51]

Like Merrill, many women worked as partners in family businesses. Some women mined for gold alongside their spouses, performing the relatively domestic task of washing the gold in a pan or rocker. In the small town of Rough and Ready, Mary Ann Dunleavy and her husband, a Methodist minister, ran a ten-pin bowling alley and a saloon. According to the 1850 census, fifteen of the twenty-three women living in Nevada City worked in boarding houses or taverns connected to them.[52] Although most women retained traditional female roles or domesticated tasks to fit their own standards of propriety, women, like men, executed all manner of duties necessary to support themselves and their families.

Some women engaged in more speculative ventures, like many of their male counterparts. Prostitution, like gambling and gold mining, represented a tremendous but risky opportunity for women to become upwardly mobile and gain economic stability and independence. Although no firm statistics on prostitutes are available and few women within the profession left behind diaries or correspondence to illuminate our understanding of their lives, evidence indicates that poverty was the usual reason that women chose to join the ranks of the "fair but frail." Prostitutes congregated in cities, near the gambling halls and saloons. Foreign-born women constituted the majority, with the earliest arrivals comprising Hispanics, French, Australian, Chinese, and German women. Many were fleeing economic deprivation and even famine in other countries. For female entrepreneurs, unlike the situation for males, the migration generally improved their economic status. The gamble turned out to be worthwhile.[53]

The difference between male and female speculation during the gold rush was that for women, their economic status was connected directly to their moral status. Economic necessity by definition pushed women into "moral danger." Consequently, marriage was less frequently a matter of attachment and intimacy than it was a question of economic, and thus moral, survival. This is not to say that women did not at times marry for love. It does suggest that their outlook on the matter of matrimonial commitment within mining society differed markedly from that of many men, who often benefited financially from mobility and the lack of domestic ties.

The ease of falling into moral jeopardy also prompted those women living on the privileged side of the line to draw distinctions strictly. Middle-class evangelical women expressed almost obsessive disapproval of the behavior of other women. Sarah Royce criticized those who accepted fancy presents and lavish attentions from many suitors and who seemed to enjoy the male competition for their attentions: "I blushed to discover . . . that there were instances of women watching each other, jealously, each afraid the other would get more or richer presents than herself."[54] Clear boundaries served to distinguish Royce and others morally from female prostitutes, prospectors, saloon managers, and other women whose behavior threatened their social and religious identities. Evangelical women thus rejoiced in the public separation of ladies from other women and insisted that men uphold the same distinctions.

As was also true for men, church attendance and religious observations for Protestant women, particularly in larger towns, were transformed or limited by the social and economic circumstances of the mining frontier. Merrill's boarding house doubled as a meeting house for church services in the early months of the gold rush. Dame Shirley, however, despite her professed piety, expressed few misgivings about the lack of worship in the town of Rich Bar. To her sister she wrote: "As for churches, 'the groves were God's first temples'. . . . In good sooth I fancy that nature intended me for an Arab or some other Nomadic barbarian, and by mistake my soul got packed up in a christianized set of bones and muscles."[55] Carrie Williams, a young married woman from Wisconsin who lived with her husband and his parents in Gold Flat in the late 1850s, attempted to attend church occasionally but more often relied on private devotions. She and her mother-in-law read sermons and other inspirational texts together in their home, and Williams resolved, on 1 January 1859, to read three chapters of the Bible daily "and profit thereby." She continually urged her husband to attend services with her, but on the many Sundays when he refused, she would not go by herself. "I have never went without him," she wrote in her diary, "and I dislike to make a beginning."[56]

Chief among those immigrants ready to uphold the importance of proper female influence and activity were the wives of home missionaries.[57] These women were important not only because they left perhaps the most extensive written record of their experiences in the West, but also because they exemplify both the singular religious difficulties faced by all missionaries and the moral and spiritual dilemmas endured by many other Euro-American immigrant women.

Missionary wives played a crucial and growing role in the antebellum mission movement. Initially, home mission leaders in the East debated whether to send married men to the Pacific Coast field. In the Methodist tradition, the rule of sending only single men dated back to the first American bishop, Francis Asbury, who recommended that the constant movement and hardships of itinerant life made it preferable for clergy to remain single. Over the course of the nineteenth century, Methodist leaders softened on this issue; by 1860, most of the clergy were married.[58] Perhaps because of the more settled nature of the ministerial calling, leaders in other denominations had never conceived of the ministry as a vocation specifically suited for single men. Since the time of the Reformation, in fact, the minister's wife had become increasingly essential to her husband's duties, shifting from the role of obedient, subservient companion with little public visibility to the more active role of assistant and partner in ministry. In the antebellum era, it was increasingly common for missionaries fresh out of the seminary and ready to head for their assigned fields, to inquire at female colleges such as Mount Holyoke about prospective partners for their chosen work.[59]

California presented far more formidable obstacles for missionary families, as illustrated by the cautionary tone of the AHMS missionary who warned that the region was still "an undesirable place for a lady." Eastern recruiters considered the region to be unsettled and perhaps dangerous for women and children. Even more problematic and probably more persuasive was an organizational shortage of funds: because of the onerous expense of traveling to the West Coast, home mission societies could barely afford to send single clergy. Once there, the extremely high cost of living made it difficult to find affordable housing for entire families; single men could take rooms in hotels, rooming houses, or even rely on the good will and generosity of local Christians.

Almost immediately, however, evangelicals in the region recognized that the need for a woman's presence far outweighed the burdens of expense. This was true for missionaries as well as for other forty-niners. "Young man, do you want to get married?" wrote a resident of the mining camp of Rough and Ready to the *California Christian Advocate*. If so, he urged, "don't come *here for a wife*! And by all means don't come without one. . . . Call a 'woman's rights convention'—not of *those* who *have on* the *'pants' already*; but of such as *would like* to wear them."[60] Speaking more specifically to the need for missionary wives, the Reverend John W. Douglas reported from San Jose: "If all the world is coming here we must have more ministers—more of our own order. . . . My wish is that more be sent, and I would remark here, that it would be well for those that are sent hereafter to be *married men*. We stand greatly in need here of woman—refined, educated woman—her society and its humanizing influence."[61]

California missionaries keenly felt the need for wives. By the 1850s, the role of the minister's wife, in the words of one scholar, resembled "nothing so much as a career."[62] A clerical spouse was expected to be a homemaker, a keeper of the minister's own sacred hearth, and also a director of church-related activities.[63] The New England Methodist minister Herrick M. Eaton, himself a married preacher, published a guide for the wives of itinerants in 1851.[64] Although addressed specifically to the situation of mobile Wesleyans, Eaton's advice also indicates the multifaceted roles expected of all clerical wives. The role of an itinerant's wife, he noted, was a true vocation, "demanding special gifts and qualifications. . . . More is expected of her by the public than of other persons, and generally her words and actions are considered with less charity than are those of others." As if this news was not cheery enough, Eaton then listed the minimum requirements for the job: a thorough knowledge of the Bible and experiential piety, independent of the beliefs of her husband; the caretaking of husband and children (which, given the minister's schedule, would devolve completely upon the wife, rendering the father "only an occasional visitor in his own family"); care for members of the congregation; and the endurance to withstand the special trials of itineracy, including frequent moves and "fault-finding" congregations. Her rewards for this life of hardship, Eaton hastened to add, included "an approving conscience as to her duty," the hope of joining her Christian friends in the hereafter, and "meeting her savior in heaven."[65]

Expectations for ministers' wives, increasing generally in the nineteenth century and expanding into the public sphere, were further intensified in the mining regions of California. "A great deal is expected of a minister's wife in such a place as this," commented Silas Harmon from Sonora. Only time would teach him the profound truth of this statement. His own wife, he reported in July 1853, was "cheerful & happy . . . & has never uttered one regret that she left pleasant associations at home that she might come to California for the sake of dying men & the glory of the Redeemer."[66] By the fall of 1854, her own health was instead in jeopardy; Harmon wrote that she had taken a teaching job at a nearby school to earn enough money for a domestic helper. "The hire for domestic assistance was an absolute necessity," Harmon emphasized, for "she could not have continued much longer without permanent injury to her health."[67] In the summer of 1856, a fellow missionary commented on the spiritual example set by Mrs. Harmon, who once again was managing the household on her own: "Mrs. Harmon is a model wife for such a missionary. With four small children to sew for, & without domestic help which is often to provide for & wash for, she nearly supports herself & *them*; & her husband under his church embarassments, by a *school* which she teaches during 5 days of each week. Any wife & mother may judge of her industry morning & eve'g of every day, & all day on Saturday to be ready for the *Sabbath* of *rest.* "[68] Given this schedule, it is doubtful whether Sunday was ever a day of rest for Mrs. Harmon.

Minister's wives in California served several functions that were characteristic of gold rush society. First, a wife made it possible to expand the ministry by providing a surrogate home life for the many young single men in the region. Congregations were more likely to give money for the minister's house if he had a wife who could supervise the social functions of the church. Some missionary couples, to be sure, spent their entire tenure in rented rooms or houses. Yet whenever feasible, the ability of the wife to extend hospitality to members of the congregation added to her husband's work tremendously, since the simple meeting houses afforded no room for socializing. In Downieville in 1856, William C. Pond described the difference that having a home of his own made to his ministry: "We are now settled in this new home, and once more I am able to make my family comfortable, and 'use hospitality,' according to the apostolic injunction, and also, by extending social courtesies, by making those who are homeless in this country find with us something like a home, and especially by attention to study, to further the main design of my coming here."[69]

The labor of missionary wives also made the ministry economically viable. The ministerial salaries of $500–600 a year, while considerably higher than those of clergy in other western states, seemed pitifully small in a society where houses rented for $200–$300 a month and monthly wages for female servants averaged $50–$75.[70] By taking in boarders, teaching school, and overseeing the housework that in an eastern, middle-class home would have been reserved for a hired helper, ministers' wives made it possible for their husbands to devote their time and energy to saving souls. In addition to domestic responsibilities, women also assumed leadership roles in the church—a vocation that had emerged in eastern churches just as middle-class women were being freed from domestic chores by improved technology and an increased ability to afford servants. Although the socioeconomic circumstances in California differed dramatically from the eastern norm, the role expectations for missionary wives remained the same and were perhaps heightened by the scarcity of females.[71]

Two examples illustrate the complexity of the roles played by the minister's wife in western mining society. The wife of a Presbyterian minister, Mrs. L. P. Webber arrived with her husband in the mining town of Austin, Nevada, in the early 1860s. Although technically not part of the mother lode, Austin shared many social characteristics of gold rush towns, most noticeably the lack of women. The Webbers' house consisted of an old stockade containing a single room approximately twenty feet square and covered with earth, grass, and brush. As the reverend labored in the ministry, Mrs. Webber, because of the high cost of living and the consequent difficulty of hiring help, went about fulfilling the duties of a good missionary spouse on her own. She did all the housework, watched over her sickly infant, and took up melodeon lessons so that she would be able to lead the choir on Sunday mornings. Within several years, Mrs. Webber died on the frontier. A close friend, in what could be read as a dark commentary on the arduousness of this kind of life, remarked that she had visited Mrs. Webber a few days before her death: *"She was ready and waiting,"* her friend concluded.[72]

Mrs. George Burrowes, another Presbyterian missionary wife, experienced a different but no less trying side of frontier existence. Stationed in San Francisco in the late 1850s and early 1860s, Mrs. Burrowes enjoyed many of the comforts of urban life unavailable to Mrs. Webber. She taught classes in the City College, a small school run by her husband. The Burrowes, despite access to the luxury goods unavailable in smaller mining towns to the east, were nonetheless unable to afford a home of their own. They lived in a bedroom in the college building and took their meals at hotels and boarding houses. "We were never able, up to the last, to have a house, however humble, of our own," Burrowes later commented. This domestic deficiency had a bright side for his wife in that it freed her from many of the household duties that consumed the energies of other women. Instead, she devoted herself to a full-time position in the primary class of the college, worked as an unpaid laborer with her husband, and lived with him on the small sums of money left over after the other teachers had been paid.[73]

Notwithstanding their demonstrated commitment to the spread of evangelical Protestantism, missionary wives perceived their roles differently from their male counterparts and mates. Most often they had joined their spouses gladly in the call to a missionary field and looked forward with anticipation to the challenges of the western settlements. Like men and other women, however, they too missed the female company that they had enjoyed in their eastern communities. Although these migrant women found ways to manage their households with little outside help, most continued to associate home and domesticity not simply with the nuclear family and their marital relations, but also with closely knit networks of female friends and relatives on whom they could rely for support and companionship. For many women, the Pacific Coast community would not be home until more like-minded women arrived.

Unfortunately, the lack of female society had additional spiritual consequences for missionary wives. Most of their church-related tasks, and hence their sense of a religious vocation outside the confines of the home, involved work with other women in the congregation: in fund-raising suppers, sewing circles, and ladies' prayer groups, the wives of ministers organized and led the female constituency of the church. Without female membership, therefore, missionary wives found their leadership roles in the religious community severely curtailed. Their husbands could minister to men and women alike, but in most circumstances it was not considered seemly for women to lead or speak before male groups or "promiscuous" assemblies in the church. For wives with a sharply defined sense of their own vocation, then, the absence of other women restricted their religious activities in the Golden State.

The life of Mary Hedges Hunt, the wife of missionary Timothy Dwight Hunt, illustrates how the special social circumstances of California society could impinge upon traditional female religious roles and alter their shape. Raised in a Presbyterian home in Newark, New Jersey, Mary married Dwight in November 1843, shortly after his graduation from Auburn Seminary. Dwight had already received a commission from the American Board of Commissioners for Foreign Missions, the nondomestic counterpart to the AHMS, and the newly married couple departed for the Sandwich Islands less than a month after their wedding. After an adventurous eight-month journey by clipper ship around Cape Horn highlighted by visits to the Azores and Tahiti, the Hunts arrived in Honolulu in July 1844. They remained there for four years, teaching and ministering to the natives in Waiohinu, Lahainaluna, and Honolulu with a close-knit band of Protestant missionaries.[74]

Dwight found that the call that had brought him to the Pacific was not sustained by his daily labors among the Islanders. He soon grew frustrated with his lack of success, and by mid-1847 he was seeking a dignified form of escape. His change of heart left Mary in anguish. "My happiness *depends* on my husband's happiness and usefulness," she wrote to her father in November 1847. "Were I certain he would have no heart to the work there even my *precious* home would have few attractions for me." Mary expressed frustration at the constraints of her status as support and helpmate in the work that was, theoretically, her husband's. She was torn between her own sense of vocation and her growing love of the field, and her desire to promote the happiness of her spouse. Indeed, Dwight's indecisiveness seemed to weigh more heavily on her than it did on him, perhaps because her missionary status was the more contingent. "His present state of feeling has taken me by a surprise most painful. . . . I do not wish to blame my dear husband, I most sincerely pity him. Would that I could help bear the burden that weighs on his heart; but until I see more clearly that it will be right for us to return to Am.[erica] I cannot encourage the undertaking."[75]

Mary was not a passive recipient of the hand that fate had dealt her, however. Her correspondence indicates both the deep affection she felt for her husband and the personal sense of calling that undergirded her work with him. When Dwight left for the Pacific Coast in late 1848, Mary stayed behind until she could secure more comfortable passage for herself and her children. The separation was painful for them both, as she explained to her parents: "I am very desirous of going to the coast to be with Dwight." As much as she enjoyed the hospitality of her friends at the Honolulu mission, "I think of my dearest earthly friend as lonely in a strange land & I long to go to him."[76]

The Hunt marriage illustrates the emergence in the nineteenth century of a new model of marital relations, highly dependent on the ascendance of romantic love as a cultural ideal. This companionate model espoused the notion of a partnership based on mutuality, respect, and love, as opposed to the economic expedience that often had characterized conjugal relations in an earlier era. Ironically, this ideal prompted rising expectations about the emotional fulfillment of marriage, expectations that increasingly led to the divorce court.[77] For the Hunts, however, this close attachment enhanced intimacy and encouraged a sense that their ministry was a shared venture. Home life became more crucial to Dwight's sense of ministry, as he remarked to Mary's parents after ten years of marriage: "I am more & more dependent on her for home happiness. . . . Indeed I have never enjoyed my home so well. Mary wears like a *diamond.*"[78]

Mary's affection for Dwight also gave her confidence about her own sense of ministry. Her identity, to be sure, was tied up with her role as a missionary wife, and she saw her spiritual fulfillment coming within the confines of that role—Mary was no advocate of woman's rights—still, her obedience to that calling was not automatic. Her letters home indicate that she carefully weighed the challenge of the California mission before passing judgment. Dwight's letters to her in Honolulu, describing the social chaos of the gold rush and the hardships of life in the region, finally convinced her of the importance of the field. "In going from here [to] there, I feel that I am leaving a home for a missionary field," she confided to her parents. "Should I be permitted to assume the duties of a pastor's wife at San Francisco I shall feel that I bear far greater & more solemn responsibilities than I ever have here as a missionary. . . . Pray for me that I may have grace to be seperate [sic] from the world, & diligent in doing good."[79]

How did Mary conceive of these new duties, and what kinds of distinctions did she draw between a home and a missionary field? Like the wives of George Burrowes and L. P. Webber, her time was occupied by the conflicting demands of church and home. "If I thought I could give you any proper idea of the life of a family in this place, I would try, but I can't," she wrote to her mother. "It's a hard place for a woman compared with homes in the States & yet *I* do not suffer at all in mind or body."[80] Before leaving Honolulu, Mary arranged passage for a servant and contracted with him, knowing how difficult it would be to engage domestic help in California. As was often the case with newly arrived migrants, the man ran off to the mines shortly after their arrival, leaving Mary with the task of housekeeping for the family of four.[81]

Despite the domestic demands on her time, Mary managed to fulfill the official capacities of a pastor's wife at the First Congregational Church of San Francisco, one of the first houses of worship in the city. She was active in the sewing circle: "Your daughter the queen of the lot," Dwight reported to her parents; she attended regular Scripture meetings with the small group of ministers' wives in town; and she organized the church fair that grossed over $4,500 (nearly five times her husband's annual salary).[82] As was often the case in western communities, the scarcity of women in the church meant that the onus of female organization fell on Mary's shoulders. Dwight, in fact, viewed the sewing circle as one of the church's most successful missionary activities, presumably because it was a sure means of attracting women to the congregation; he expressed great joy when six women showed up for choir practice one day in 1851.[83]

Sewing circles and church fairs may have created a semblance of normality for Protestant missionaries to the state, but the Hunts were also keenly aware that life on the edge of a mining frontier wrought its share of chaos on the ideals of the evangelical home. In turn, this upsetting of domestic order affected their ministry. Living, as Dwight later put it, on a salary "altogether too small" for their comfortable support, the Hunts necessarily shared the household tasks. "I regret that I cannot make things as comfortable for Mary as I could wish," he lamented: "To be sure I do what I can. I get up in the morning & go down & kindle a fire in the stove & put the tea-kettle on. I then draw the water for the day & cut the wood. This done I go up & relieve Mary who by this time has dressed the *bairnies* & finished her morning toilet." After completing family worship and breakfast, Hunt took the children into his study while Mary cleaned the kitchen. His struggle to write sermons and conduct business in the presence of rambunctious children presented an unintentionally comic picture. "Of course I have the children to look after & I tell you that while they are very agreeable themselves considered, yet they are not just the companions I like in my study. Perhaps I shall get used to it, but the truth is I do not fancy this kind of life."[84]

Mary articulated her sense of upheaval in more guarded and ultimately more self-deprecating ways. Even as Dwight rightly placed the blame for his diminished effectiveness on the topsy-turvy circumstances of California domesticity, Mary interpreted hers as a personal failing. The discrepancy between expectations of her role and social reality took their toll on her self-confidence. By nature, Mary was a shy woman, more comfortable with work behind the scenes than on center stage. In a letter to her father, offering advice about the education of her younger sisters, she obliquely described herself in the guise of "one sort of ministers' wife," comparing herself to other women: "One with all her goodness & consistency; home bred, quiet, not fond of making acquaintances, nor free to converse with any; nor yet conversant enough with the etiquette of society to mingle properly in it *even from a sense of duty*; not able either, for want of self confidence to originate or carry out plans for associations even in her own church, nor able enough with her pen to write a report for a benevolent society."[85]

As already discussed, the ideal of evangelical womanhood, and by extension of the ministers' wife as the crowning example of female virtue, was given greater weight in California because of the scarcity of women. Yet the social realities of labor in the western domestic economy—most notably the lack of household help and the absence of female support networks—made the ideal even harder to attain. The material circumstances that gave rise to the concept of evangelical womanhood in the East, including the growth of a middle-class endowed with disposable income and increasing amounts of leisure time, simply did not exist in the chaotic pattern of Pacific Coast life. Because one aspect of the evangelical ideology was its universalism, that is, its lack of dependence upon any particular socioeconomic circumstances to fulfill its promises, evangelicals refused to recognize the complexity of applying these standards to another culture. Inevitably, this chasm between ideology and reality meant that women would fall short. "I am now feeling very weary of the part I have so long been obliged to take in society, choir, etc. and am looking forward to a rest when we get into the new church," Mary confided to her mother. "I'm not sad though, only weary of other's thoughts about the church, the minister, the minister's wife, everything; you know I never like to be observed, scanned, judged."[86]

Mary also revealed that the chaotic social milieu affected her religious faith. In early 1853 her brother, Henry, experienced some sort of spiritual crisis, a situation that prompted sisterly advice. By way of counsel, Mary told him about her own faith and the path it had taken over the past few years. She was wary of confiding in him, perhaps out of a sense of her own failings: "Now dear brother I'll tell you how it is & long has been with me & if you think I am in error pray for me, but do not blame." Mary admitted that, like the men to whom Dwight ministered, life in El Dorado had dimmed the formerly sharp outlines of her faith; her forced concentration on temporal duties made the things of the next world increasingly indistinct. "My religion has long since lost what might be called its form. The twilight hour that was once to me so sacred, the care of little ones has occupied, & the early morning hour has not as once found me alone. . . . If my God had been a God afar off, surely He would long since have forsaken me," she mused. Yet these changes had not extinguished her commitment to her faith, as they did for many miners. Instead, Mary advised that Henry learn to view religion in a different light: "What religion I have enjoyed dear brother, has been in *action,* in the performance of daily duties with a right spirit; and not in meditation about things spiritual, nor anticipations of a life & world to come."[87] Perhaps these admissions were merely the spiritual growing pains of a busy woman with a family to care for; but certainly the demands Mary faced in California removed her even further from the religious world out of which she had come.

Did California ever become a home for Mary Hunt? Did *home* mean for her, as it did for her male counterparts, the presence of family and children? Emotionally and financially, the move to California made the Hunts and many

other missionary couples even more dependent on the support of their relatives in the East. Dwight's salary in San Francisco covered fewer of their
expenses than his earnings had in the Sandwich Islands, and the deficit was
often made up by the couple's parents. Highly symbolic of the continuing
equation of home with eastern relations was the fact that on their arrival in
San Francisco, Mary's parents shipped them a house. "Never before have we
more valued the love & kindness of our dear earthly parents & friends," Mary
wrote. "We were never before as dependent as now. But for the house you
have sent us, it seems as if we must have left the country. The *hope* of getting
into it, has enabled us to live along as we could from hand to mouth."[88]

As much as she relied on the support of family, what Mary missed most in
California was the presence of other women; this was the salient feature of
home for which she pined. During her years in Honolulu, Mary wrote letters
in which she imagined family scenes. In her renderings, female companionship played a prominent role. To her younger sisters she composed one such
reverie: "Sometimes I try to think how you look with your little pink frocks
and clean aprons on, doing your task of sewing, or reading and spelling to
Mama; or towards night when it is shady in front of the house, playing among
the flowers by the swing while Mama is sewing, and, perhaps Aunty Carter or
one of the other dear neighbors is talking with her."[89] This was the world in
which Mary felt most at home, one inhabited by girls in feminine frocks and
aprons engaged in domestic pursuits, and women confiding in one another
in the cool stillness of a summer evening. These were the ties of affection
that supported and sustained the kind of work that Mary had chosen and that
in an important sense gave it meaning.

In the Sandwich Islands Mary had found a circle of female companionship
that turned the field into a home. In California, the multiple tasks of a missionary wife and the dearth of women left her feeling isolated. "Papa speaks
of my being dependent on a 'few lady acquaintances,'" she wrote to her
mother. "Indeed I should rejoice might I *depend* on them. But each one as a
general thing has enough to do to get along herself." Even when women
found the time to socialize, the winter rains rendered even the streets of San
Francisco impassable for several months out of the year. In January 1850,
Mary noted that "for the last 2 months the mud has been *so* deep no woman
dare venture in the street. Ab't 6 weeks ago I made a desperate effort, and
with Julia went to call on Mrs. DeWitt. She had hardly seen a lady for 3
months."[90] In the towns of the mother lode, the choking dust, extreme summer heat, and snowy winters made female visiting even more difficult.

Mary did maintain friendships. She was particularly fond of Sarah
Blakeslee, the wife of another home missionary with whom she met occa-

sionally for Bible reading and prayer and of whom Mary wrote home often: "She is a real help to me. I love her much."[91] Yet in her moments of reflection Mary, like many other California women, expressed the conviction that female companionship was the missing feature of community that would someday transform El Dorado into a home. She revealed her own deepest fears of isolation when she described Mrs. DeWitt's reaction to an illness: "The sickness & loneliness had made her quite homesick, for she said she felt that she might have died, and no lady would have known it."[92]

Mary Hunt's confusion and isolation and the crises of confidence that she articulated suggest that missionary wives lost more than sympathetic company in their removal to the mines. More significantly, they lost the sphere of women that made sense of their roles in the family and in the church. As twentieth-century readers, we often underestimate the importance of female ties in the lives of antebellum women and fail to recognize that these eastern, middle-class, Protestant women inhabited a world bounded by home, church, and female companionship. Long-lived, intimate, and loving friendships were a common feature of most women's lives; in large measure, women defined themselves by these connections, and men "made but a shadowy appearance" in their affective experiences.[93] For missionary wives, the intensity and endurance of these relations were mitigated by the intimacy that frequent moves and a common sense of purpose often engendered between husbands and wives, as was certainly the case with Mary and Dwight Hunt. Mary's letters reveal that, in spite of her obvious affection for her husband, the ties that she had to other women—ties of shared labor, shared circumstances, and shared sensibilities—were deep and lasting. The absence of other women who could value her work and her support called into question her sense of identity and purpose.

For women without a deeply etched sense of religious vocation or strong intimacy with their husbands, the domestic world of California could be even more trying. Loneliness and isolation exacerbated the already debilitating headaches and depression of Sarah Walsworth, a young missionary wife from Avon, New York. She and her husband, the Presbyterian, AHMS appointee Edward Walsworth, were stationed in Marysville in 1853. Like the Hunts, the couple undertook the voyage around the Horn during the winter of 1852 with a youthful mixture of exhilaration and trepidation. Sailing on the *Trade Wind* in the company of seven other Pacific Coast missionaries and their families, Sarah gloried in the constant society and plentiful activities of life on board a ship. Indeed, the contained world of the clipper, captained by a "humble, simple-hearted, devoted Christian," punctuated by daily worship services, an informal debating society, and the publication of a weekly newspaper (for which Sarah, a lively and aspiring writer, served on the editorial staff), created in microcosm the ordered, evangelical world that the missionaries hoped to replicate in California.[94]

Arriving in San Francisco in early 1853, the Walsworths missed the earliest and most chaotic days of the gold rush. The port city itself was beginning to settle into a relatively stable if still somewhat disorderly network of cultural and economic relations.[95] It was here that the couple separated from their shipmates, traveled to the inland community of Marysville, and began their ministry. For Sarah, the transition to a secluded mining town was stressful. Hampered in her activities by the spring rains that flooded the streets, the intolerable summer heat, and the swirling dusts of autumn, she suffered frequently from headaches and homesickness. Typical of her state of mind was a diary entry from 14 May 1853: "Done nothing all day—I have at times to day felt that we did wrong to come to California at all."[96]

Unlike Mary Hunt, Sarah did not express a particular sense of vocation with respect to the ministry. References to her husband in her correspondence tend to be formal and distant; even less frequently does she refer to her work within the church community. We can only speculate that Sarah's lesser involvement in the missionary work of her husband made the deprivations of life in Marysville harder to endure. This interpretation is reinforced by the fact that, during the hottest part of the summer, Edward insisted that Sarah leave the small town and visit friends nearer to the ocean. In July 1853, shortly after their arrival, when the internal temperature of their boarding house room shot up over one hundred degrees, Sarah left Marysville for Oakland. She seemed pleased at the prospect and happily anticipated an extended visit with the wife of another *Trade Wind* missionary, Mrs. Samuel Bell. Indeed, her feeling of relief was palpable as she described her new location: Oakland "is so delightful & healthy a place. . . . I never saw finer vegetables than are raised about here & the few gardens I have seen are very good and handsome."[97]

Sarah also expressed the longing for female companionship articulated by other women. "There are many things in Marysville I like," she conceded to her parents. "There are several pleasant ladies there—there is a noisy activity & industry that I admire." More often, she ached for female friends and relatives: "Oh how I wish I could have visited Cousin Frank with you! how delightful a home she must have. . . . It is hard to be separate from you all to know I *cannot* see you at all—perhaps never more," she told her mother. "Oh! Eliza," she exclaimed on another occasion, "if I could only have you in my lap, with your dear head on my arms in the rocking-chair again & listen to your sweet laugh how happy, happy I would be!—come & live with *me always,* won't you?"[98]

Sarah's loneliness and feelings of isolation were clearly connected to her lack of proximity to a woman's world. They also manifested themselves psychosomatically in painful and debilitating ways. Indeed, it is possible to trace the intensity and duration of her headaches to her relations with women, revealing the interrelations between her physical and emotional well-being. Sarah was the most despondent and listless when she was home in Marysville; her physical condition improved dramatically whenever she was able to visit San Francisco or other communities with larger numbers of women. While staying with the Bells, Sarah attended a meeting with missionary wives across the bay: "I went with Mrs. Willey to the 2nd meeting of a society of S.F. Ladies at the [Pine Street Baptist Church] which is to be called the 'S.F. Ladies' Protection & Relief Soc.' There were some 80 or perhaps 100 of the first ladies in all the churches in town. Oh! what a beautiful sight—it did me much good."[99] Although she never explicitly made the connection between her illness and her isolation, she nonetheless couched her description of this visit to the Bay Area in terms of its restorative effects on her spirits.

The combination of her natural tendencies toward depression, her dependence on female society for a sense of worth and purpose, and the lack of a personal religious calling that might otherwise have sustained her, made life in gold rush California a trial for Sarah. Mary Hunt, in her darkest moments, could seek solace from her knowledge that she was struggling in the arms of a watchful God. Sarah rarely mentioned the state of her soul or her personal faith; her identity thus seemed even more dependent on external factors. This lack of internal guidance also left her particularly susceptible to the contradictory expectations of evangelical womanhood. The ordered world that boosted Sarah's spirits—the world of the *Trade Wind* and of Avon, New York—was a far cry from the frenzied community of Marysville. "I do little good & get little good now—I seem to be living for nothing—to be doing nothing—" she wrote one fall day in 1853. The next night she continued in the same vein, "Sad all the evening—Oh, how unworthy—how insufficient I am—how poor a minister's wife."[100]

The inability to recreate traditional gender roles in California—because of both a shortage of women and a lack of an effective support network for those women who did come West—had complex and wide-ranging effects on the missionary effort to evangelize the mining communities. Both men and women, for different reasons, needed women's presence to fulfill their religious duties and obligations. Women, it appears, suffered most keenly from the deficiency: they confronted rising male expectations for their innately religious influence and effectiveness in inverse proportion to their ability or desire to perform such tasks. Some women, like men, came West precisely to escape the expectations of proper behavior connected with families and institutions in the East and to seek new opportunities. In California, these women met both the condemnation and admiration of men, and they generally lacked the female support that many needed to develop a traditional evangelical identity.

Male missionaries felt nearly as frustrated in their attempts to preach a domestic religious ethic to a male audience. Evangelical religion by the mid-nineteenth century was a creature of a stable, middle-class, eastern, and familial culture. When transplanted to the world of the mining frontier, it resembled a rare and fragile species struggling in the midst of a harsh and uncompromising climate. California missionaries, in tacit recognition of their dilemma, attempted to alter the message, to adapt it to a new environment. In doing so, they inevitably upset the delicate balance of religious experience, doctrine, and social institutions that formed antebellum evangelicalism. Although they often excoriated miners for their lack of religious devotion, it may well have been the limits of their own strategies and, most notably, their theoretical attachment to a feminized faith, that made it so difficult for ordinary men and women to express their spiritual yearnings within the confines of the churches.

Chapter 7

A Marketplace
of Morals

A life by the cabin fire,
  A home in the northern mines;
We'll make a pile and retire,
  Won't that be charming and fine?
—*Old Put's Original California Songster*

Bayard Taylor was one of the first observers to describe the dramatic transformation of California from a chaotic frontier to an established western region. Yet he had missed the gradual internal changes that brought about the metamorphosis. Some of the most striking modifications took place in 1869–70, when a series of events signaled the decisive movement of California toward a more settled way of life. The 1869 completion of the transcontinental railway not only decreased the psychological distance between the Pacific and Atlantic coasts, its establishment also dramatically altered the nature of westward migration. With California just a short and relatively comfortable ride away from other populated regions, its potential as a vacation spot and its attraction to families increased, and Euro-American settlers subsequently undertook the journey in much greater numbers than before.[1] After nearly two decades of upheaval, moreover, the mining stampedes that had continuously depleted California's population and sent tens of thousands of migrants to Idaho, Nevada, Colorado, and British Columbia came to an end in 1870.[2] Finally, the settlement of Mexican land claims by the end of the 1860s cleared the way for agricultural development in California's fertile valleys. As a result, the state settled slowly into fixed economic and social patterns, based increasingly on wage labor in mining companies, the expanding agricultural industry, and the mercantile and banking businesses of San Francisco. The urban and rural landscapes became increasingly distinct as a professional class of merchants and wealthy landholders transformed San Francisco into a cosmopolitan center.[3]

Yet just when many of the impediments to missionary progress were being cleared away, eastern sponsors turned their attentions elsewhere. In 1861, the New School Presbyterians withdrew from the AHMS, leaving its California clergy to fend for themselves. The outbreak of the Civil War that same year further diverted eastern energies and resources to help support the Union. Protestant leaders gradually stopped apologizing for their lack of support for the West. After the war's end, home mission societies channeled most of their funds into educational and religious work among the 4 million ex-slaves in the South, opening another region to the civilizing influences of northeastern evangelicalism.

The brief duration of the religious worlds of the gold rush tempt us to see them, as did many of the participants, as a cultural aberration, just as scholars themselves have treated the American West as an historical anomaly. Yet people's beliefs and actions during this twenty-two-year period reveal a great deal about the subsequent religious development of California, religiosity in antebellum America, and the institutions and guiding principles of Protestant evangelicalism itself. My hope is that this study, rather than providing definitive answers, instead raises questions that prompt further research into the importance of western history for the study of American religion and culture.

Evangelical ministers ultimately did exert some control over the landscape, but religiosity in California still evinced numerous contradictions. Although Methodists, Baptists, Presbyterians, and Congregationalists, along with other Protestant denominations, eventually established stable congregations and other religious institutions in northern California, Protestant patterns there remained different from those in the Northeast and agricultural areas of the West. Religious leaders continued to complain about the relative irreligiosity of the population. Stephen Hilton, editor of the *Evangel* in 1869, admitted that it was a widely known fact that churches on the Pacific Coast were weak and feeble. Methodist leaders in the state, as late as 1875, still called publicly for the spiritual quickening that would turn around the religious fortunes of the state. Yet in this singular religious world, the 1860 census listed California as one of the states with the highest average church values in the country.[4]

The privatized and syncretistic patterns of spirituality that emerged during the years of the gold rush remained an important feature of religion in the state. As of 1890, the number of church communicants as a percentage of the total population stood at just over 23 percent, still well below that of most eastern states.[5] Increasingly, settlers looked for community, but they did not necessarily remain within the bounds of the Protestant churches. By the end of the century, California had become a new burnt-over district, boasting more communitarian experiments than any other state, including Theosophical colonies, an Icarian community, and the Kaweah Cooperative Commonwealth. It would not be until the twentieth century that California gained a reputation for its relatively orthodox spiritual strength, and even when it did, those Americans to the east deemed its patterns of belief and behavior highly suspect.[6]

The frontier experience of Protestants in California also raises intriguing questions about the vitality and potency of evangelicalism itself. Although Daniel Woods and others believed California to be a land of enchantment, it seems clear enough that moral and religious tendencies came West with the immigrants but were often sloughed off or transformed in the rush for wealth. We are left, then, like western missionaries, with nagging questions about the kinds of commitments that ordinary believers felt toward religious institutions, beliefs, and practices. Perhaps for too long, scholars have taken the evangelical ideology of Charles Finney and other clergy as a rendering of psychological and spiritual reality, particularly their pronouncements on conversion as the focus for Christian life, and the religious community as flowing naturally out of that experience. Neither of these notions explains the behavior and attitudes of California immigrants, many of whom nonetheless thought of themselves as pious Christians. The fact of El Dorado also calls into question the propensities of recent scholars to attribute many features of antebellum culture to some monolithic entity called "evangelicalism." It should be clear that not only were there many different interpretations of evangelicalism, but that ordinary believers often combined Protestant values with other kinds of beliefs and practices in exceedingly creative ways, well into the nineteenth century.

Highlighting the gold rush experience also suggests the need for scholarly reconsideration of the subsequent development of American Protestantism on the national level. Although the Civil War has often been used as a convenient watershed to separate the quaint piety of antebellum Protestants from the modern ways of their postbellum descendants, seeing California (and western states generally) instead as the first in a succession of domestic mission fields challenges current interpretations of religious reform in the late nineteenth century. Ideas and strategies for northeastern, urban missions did not simply arise from the battlefields of Gettysburg; they had already been developed and employed in other parts of the country for several decades. Typically urban problems were an early and important feature of California life, in the cities as well as the mining towns. Unprotected by the financial, social, and political legacies of a Protestant establishment, evangelical religion on the Pacific Coast in the 1850s and 1860s bore the full impact of an array of social and intellectual crises that increasingly plagued the country as a whole. By 1868, the state already manifested vast disparities between the wealth of the city and the poverty of the countryside.[7] In an important sense, the missionary activities undertaken during the California gold rush served as a dress rehearsal for the national urban revivals and institutional reforms of the 1880s and 1890s when ministers sought ways to appeal to young, unchurched workers flocking to eastern cities. Transiency and cultural heterogeneity were the key features of both of these eras.

The new moral challenges of a capitalist economy faced by the nation as a whole from the 1880s on also had a western dress rehearsal during, and after, the gold rush. Indeed, the frenzied pursuit of fortune and opportunity concentrated in the two decades of the California frontier stand as a metaphor for westward movement as a whole, from Jamestown to the Silicon Valley. The spiritual meaning of wealth, its proper acquisition, and its just distribution, were fundamentally called into question by the discovery of gold at Sutter's Mill. Ministers and miners both groped to understand how this economic revolution, this change in the ways of acquiring wealth, could be accepted within the traditional Protestant ethical framework. Once the mineral frenzy had subsided, the legal obstacles to family land ownership, followed by widespread agricultural speculation, prompted further concerns about the justice of property ownership and the laissez-faire attitudes of state and federal governments. Henry George was only the most famous observer to puzzle over the morality of a small minority of a community monopolizing the vast majority of land. In California, these issues were thrown into deeper relief at an earlier date by the speed of economic transition. In contrast, the growth of a marketplace economy in the East, and even the emergence of the stock market (which bore strong resemblances to gold mining and gambling in terms of the way wealth was acquired), took place gradually within a considerably more stable economic context. It was much easier, on the Atlantic Coast, to convince oneself that nothing much had changed.

The early emergence of a modern culture in California effected religious and intellectual changes as well. Most notably, a discernible theological rift developed between those who would later be identified as modernists and conservatives. Although it would be misleading and anachronistic to label religious leaders of the 1850s and 1860s with either term, it is clear that the disruptions of California life almost immediately began to disturb the antebellum evangelical understanding of the relation between nature and grace.

As Sandra Sizer Frankiel has pointed out, Protestant liberalism existed in California from the early days of statehood, giving rise to a wide variety of alternatives to traditional evangelical piety.[8] Although the circumstances surrounding the development of theological liberalism are complicated, we have seen how the difficulties of imposing a sacred order in the hearts of settlers and on the landscape itself may have predisposed some ministers—particularly Congregationalists and Presbyterians—to reassess issues of grace, conversion, and communal coherence in light of their experiences. These shifting theological formulations foreshadowed the eastern clerical dilemma in the urban environment, where a cohesive community could no longer be assumed and where liberal ministers such as Washington Gladden and Walter Rauschenbusch explained God's grace as working through the processes of social salvation. Like these later advocates of the Social Gospel, California ministers increasingly looked for common moral ground where they could find it: in educational endeavors, missions to Chinese prostitutes, and even in the sporadic uprisings of self-ordained vigilantes.

It is, finally, important to recognize the cultural effects that the California gold rush had on the development of other western societies. Rodman Paul sees the encounter with El Dorado as only the first and most consequential occurrence in a long line of events that created mining cultures throughout the western United States. Subsequent mineral rushes from the Pacific to the Rockies catalyzed many of the same religious and cultural dislocations and reconstitutions as did the discovery at Sutter's Mill. The later events were, moreover, indebted to some of the same Euro-American men and women who initially populated California: Paul relates that "old Californians" were a ubiquitous feature of nineteenth-century mining towns, men who spent their lives roaming the western landscape in search of fortune. Involving perhaps hundreds of thousands of men and women over a period of several decades, these movements had enormous and far-reaching implications for the development of religion in particular and western societies in general, as migrants, in John Hittell's words, attempted "to outrun old Time himself."[9]

If these stories were not enough for one volume, we should remind ourselves that the Euro-American narrative of religion during the gold rush is only one among the many tales of this era that bear repetition. Many cultures intersected in frontier California, and stories of their confrontation would undoubtedly reveal a great deal more about the assumptions and ideals of the various peoples that sought El Dorado, as well as the culture of a region still often seen as lacking in this most valued and unstable commodity.

Abbreviations

ABCFM	American Board of Commissioners for Foreign Missions
ABHMS	American Baptist Home Missionary Society
AHMS	American Home Missionary Society
HMR	*Home Mission Record*
PSR	Pacific School of Religion, Berkeley, California
PHS	Presbyterian Historical Society, Philadelphia
SFTS	San Francisco Theological Seminary, San Anselmo, California

Notes

INTRODUCTION

1. Taylor, *At Home and Abroad*, 37–39.
2. Royce, *California*, 297.
3. Woods, *Sixteen Months*, 47; on Bushnell in California, see Chrystal, "'A Beautiful Aceldama.'"
4. Hays, *To the Land of Gold and Wickedness*, 230.
5. See *The Life of the Mind in America*, 36–72, for Miller's analysis of the significance of the Revival to nineteenth-century evangelicals.
6. Statistics are from *The Population of the United States in 1860; compiled from the Original Returns of the Eighth Census (Washington: Government Printing Office, 1864);* and Frankiel, *California's Spiritual Frontiers*, xi. The total number of churches and ministers includes all Christian denominations.
7. Sweet, *Religion on the American Frontier*; Wright, *Culture on the Moving Frontier*. Several older studies of the home mission movement provide some useful data, although their conceptual frameworks are problematic: Joseph Bourne Clark, *Leavening the Nation: The Story of American Home Missions* (New York: Baker and Taylor, 1903); Goodykoontz, *Home Missions on the American Frontier*. A few more recent studies are expanding our knowledge of the contours of religion in the West: Kramer, ed., *The American West*; Guarnari and Alvarez, *Religion and Society in the American West*; Miyakawa, *Protestants and Pioneers*.
8. On denominational growth in California, see Anthony, *Fifty Years of Methodism*; Crompton, *Unitarianism on the Pacific Coast*; Ferrier, *Congregationalism's Place in California History*; Fleming, *God's Gold*; Harland Edwin Hogue, *The Long Arm of New England Devotion: One Hundred Years of Congregationalism in Northern California* (San Francisco: Northern California Congregational Conference, 1956); Leonidas Latimer Loofbourow, *In Search of God's Gold* (San Francisco: Methodist Church, 1951); John C. Simmon, *The History of Southern Methodism on the Pacific Coast* (Nashville: Southern Methodist Publishing House, 1886); Wicher, *The Presbyterian Church*.

9. Engh, *Frontier Faiths;* Frankiel, *California's Spiritual Frontiers*; Starr, *Americans and the California Dream.*

10. See Thomas Luckmann's theories as discussed in Sobel, *The World They Made Together,* ch. 1.

11. Although I prefer the term *popularization* to *democratization,* this study owes much to the recent work of Hatch, *The Democratization of American Christianity,* particularly his emphasis on the spiritual empowerment of the evangelical laity in the antebellum era.

CHAPTER 1: REPUBLICAN VIRTUES AND WESTERN DREAMS

1. Chapin, *A Discourse,* 4, 6.

2. Hickock, "A Discourse before the Presbytery of Rochester, New York," *Home Missionary* 21(8) (Dec. 1848).

3. Ibid.

4. On the founding of home mission societies, see Goodykoontz, *Home Missions on the American Frontier*; and Latourette, *The Great Century.*

5. Sweet, *The Congregationalists,* vol. 3, *Religion on the American Frontier,* 44–45.

6. On the vast literature of revivalism and antebellum social reform, see Cross, *The Burned-Over District;* Barnes, *The Anti-Slavery Impulse;* Thomas, "Romantic Reform in America"; Johnson, *A Shopkeeper's Millennium;* Ryan, *Cradle of the Middle Class.*

7. On the theology of revivalism, see McLoughlin, *Modern Revivalism;* and Ahlstrom, *A Religious History,* ch. 26. On the growing similarities between Presbyterians/ Congregationalists and Methodists/Baptists after the Finney revivals, see Sweet, *Revivalism in America,* 139.

8. *New Englander* 2(1) (Jan. 1844).

9. Smith, *Virgin Land,* 9, 15–18. Smith termed Jefferson the "intellectual father" of the American advance to the Pacific.

10. Paul Boyer points out that after the 1820s, the westward movement emerged as an issue that caused profound and increasing anxiety for evangelical reformers. In his study of America's moral response to the rise of the city in the nineteenth century, Boyer identifies urbanization and westward movement as two facets of a single concern: "The burgeoning interior and the burgeoning cities both represented massive challenges to the established social order, and fears about the menace of the city were reinforced and intensified by the parallel menace of the wilderness" (*Urban Masses,* 6).

11. On manifest destiny, see Merk, *Manifest Destiny*; and Weinburg, *Manifest Destiny.* The policy of manifest destiny tended to be more closely associated with Jacksonian Democratic politics, a fact that leaves unanswered the question of how northern evangelicals, closely allied to the Whig party, conceived of westward expansion.

12. For more on the connections between northern evangelicals and the Whig party, see Howe, *The American Whigs.*

13. This fear of decline was pervasive in American society by the 1830s and 1840s. Fred Somkin points out that the genre of catastrophic fiction grew markedly during this period and observes that "the essential fragility of civilization and its liability to instantaneous and utter destruction were themes constantly reiterated." See *Unquiet Eagle,* 38–49.

14. *Home Mission Record* 1(1) (Sept. 1849). *HMR* published correspondence and reports from missionaries commissioned by the ABHMS; its editor was the correspondence secretary for the society.

15. Chapin, *Discourse,* 4.

16. AHMS Executive Committee, *Our Country,* 10.

17. Hutchison, *Errand to the World,* 45.

18. *Home Missionary* 19(3) (July 1846).

19. Hickock, "Discourse before Presbytery," *Home Missionary* 21(8) (Dec. 1848).

20. *Home Missionary* 18(8) (Dec. 1845).

21. Ibid.

22. A genre of American history has grown out of the theme of New England passing along its cultural inheritance to western regions. See, e.g., Bridgman, *New England;* and Mathews, *Expansion.*

23. Hickock, "Discourse before Presbytery," *Home Missionary* 21(8) (Dec. 1848).

24. Wadsworth, *America's Mission in the World,* 6, 8.

25. Ibid., 5.

26. For more on the social theories of Puritanism and Republicanism, see Miller, *The New England Mind,* ch. 14; and Wood, *The Creation of the American Republic,* ch. 2.

27. Stout, "Rhetoric and Reality in the Early Republic," 62–76.

28. For an insightful and eloquent analysis of the evangelical balance of individual self-control and enthusiastic communal outpouring, see Isaac, *The Transformation of Virginia,* 169–72, 315–17.

29. Chapin, *Discourse,* 10.

30. *Home Missionary* 29(6) (Oct. 1856).

31. AHMS, *Our Country,* 59.

32. On the theocratic social model of Presbyterians and Congregationalists planned for western settlements, see Janzen, "The Transformation of the New England Religious Tradition," 1–28.

33. On the "New Haven Theology" and Taylor's contributions to it, see Haroutunian, *Piety versus Moralism;* and Mead, *Nathaniel William Taylor.*

34. On the shifting ideology of social reform in this era, see Thomas, "Romantic Reform in America."

35. For more on Leonard Woods and the "Andover School" of theology, see Williams, *The Andover Liberals,* ch. 1; and Foster, *A Genetic History.*

36. AHMS, *Our Country,* 16, emphasis in original.

37. On the relation between identities of descent and consent in American history, see Sollors, *Beyond Ethnicity,* 3–39.

38. For differing interpretations of the democratic implications of revivalism, see

Butler, *Awash in a Sea of Faith;* and Hatch, *Democratization.* These studies have largely superseded previous work in the field, although they are still indebted to the groundbreaking work of William Warren Sweet and Perry Miller. See esp. Sweet, *Religion in American Culture;* and Miller, *The Life of the Mind.*

39. *Home Mission Record* 1(2) (Oct. 1849).

40. AHMS, *Our Country*, 22–23.

41. Eastern images of western settlements, in this respect, directly reflected conceptions of masculinity prevalent in nineteenth-century America. On views of manhood during this period, see Rotundo, "Learning about Manhood," 35–51.

42. Wheeler, "Report of the Committee on the 'Far West,'" 1854, Excerpts from the *Home Mission Record*, Bancroft Library, Berkeley (hereafter *HMR* Excerpts), 40.

43. *Home Missionary* 19(12) (April 1847).

44. Ibid., 19(1) (May 1846).

45. Horsman, *Race and Manifest Destiny*, 5, 177–84. Albert Weinburg also points out that by the 1840s, this sense of racial superiority was a primary motivation for the policy of manifest destiny: "The philosophy of American nationalism developed a belief incongruous with the equalitarianism of democracy—the belief that, however equal men might be at birth, Americans had become subsequently a super-people" (*Manifest Destiny*, 126).

46. *America's Mission*, 10.

47. Ibid.

48. Imprecision about the meaning of the term continued throughout the nineteenth century, particularly among Anglo-Saxonist evangelicals committed to the principles of social Darwinism. Josiah Strong, in his influential and alarmist study of the state of the nation, devoted an entire chapter to "The Anglo-Saxon in World History." The term, in Strong's parlance, could be taken to include almost anyone who had learned to speak English, irrespective of their background. See *Our Country: Its Possible Future and Its Present Crisis* (1885, rev. ed., New York: Baker and Taylor, 1891), ch. 14.

49. Barnes, *Home Missionary* 19(1) (May 1846).

50. *Home Missionary* 17(5) (May 1844).

51. On the concept of reformers as stewards, see Griffin, *Their Brothers' Keepers.*

52. *Home Missionary* 19(6) (Oct. 1846).

53. On Whitman's millennial vision, see Smith, *Virgin Land*, 48.

54. *Home Missionary* 19(1) (May 1846).

55. Henry Nash Smith identifies the "myth of the garden" as one of the controlling themes of nineteenth-century American thought. Made manifest in the agrarian ideals of Benjamin Franklin and Thomas Jefferson, it was linked logically to the political ideal of a population of freeholding yeoman citizens. See *Virgin Land*, 124–33; and Nash, *Wilderness and the American Mind.*

56. On the "historyless" stereotype of America, see Cronon, *Changes in the Land*; and Davis, "Marlboro Country," in *From Homicide to Slavery*. In discussing the recurring theme of the West as a region of innocence, Davis emphasizes that "the notion

that the primitive West can somehow redeem the sins of our civilization has remained one of our most potent myths" (p. 109).

57. This understanding of the West is closely tied to Frederick Jackson Turner's frontier thesis, with its emphasis on the frontier as a region where the American experiment is constantly renewed by the democratizing tendencies of western life. See his *Frontier in American History* (New York: Henry Holt, 1920) and *The Significance of Sections in American History* (1932, rep. ed., Gloucester: Peter Smith, 1959) for a full exposition of his theories. Prior to Turner's formulation, however, some proponents of westward expansion and internal reform had emphasized the frontier as a "safety valve," an area that could forestall labor competition in the eastern states by providing a continuing job supply for immigrants. See Wilentz, *Chants Democratic*, 335–43.

58. William Hutchison characterizes the foreign mission movement as "profoundly historical," and the same can be said for the home mission movement, with its belief in the literal unfolding of providential history. Many scholars of evangelicalism have wrongly equated historical consciousness with regressive social theories. See Hutchison, *Errand*, 46.

59. *Home Mission Record* 1(1) (Sept. 1849).

60. Samuel W. Fisher, "Address delivered at the Twentieth Anniversary of the American Home Missionary Society," *Home Missionary* 19(3) (July 1846).

61. *Home Missionary* 22(2) (June 1849). See also *Home Missionary* 24(7) (Nov. 1851).

62. *Home Mission Record* 1(1) (Sept. 1849), emphasis in original.

63. In Whig ideology, the glorification of technological progress did not necessarily conflict with views of the western wilderness as naturally redemptive. Whigs envisioned an America industrialized but not urbanized, a republic in which small-town morality still held sway. Daniel Walker Howe describes the new sense of wonder over technological achievements and industrialization in the nineteenth century; economic progress was thought to provide a basis for all other forms of progress, and commerce was not opposed to virtue but instead nourished it. Economists such as Henry Carey even saw industrialization as a means of human redemption. See Howe, *The American Whigs*, ch. 5. Still the most subtle analysis of these themes of expansion and the relation between civilization and nature is found in the work of Perry Miller. See, esp., "Nature and the National Ego" in *Errand into the Wilderness*.

64. AHMS, *Our Country*, 7, 8.

65. J. W. Scott, "The Great West," *Debow's Review* 15 (July 1853): 51.

66. Ibid., 50.

67. Ibid.

68. *Home Missionary* 17(2) (June 1844).

69. Ibid., 18(8) (Dec. 1845).

70. Timothy Dwight, *Travels in New-England and New-York*, 4 vols. (New Haven, 1821–22), 2, 441, quoted in Nash, *Wilderness and the American Mind*, 30.

71. Nash, *Wilderness and the American Mind*, 24.

72. Edwards, *Home Missionary* 18 (8) (Dec. 1845).

73. Thomas Jefferson, a supporter of expansion, vigorously supported the opposing view, i.e., that a large country could still retain its virtue and in fact could profit from its ability to provide land for farmers. James Madison, in his classic argument for a tightly controlled federal government, disagreed. See Wood, *The Creation of the American Republic*, 499–506.

74. Lyman Beecher, "The Gospel the Only Security for Eminent and Abiding National Prosperity," *The American National Preacher* 3 (March 1829), 147, cited in Somkin, *Unquiet Eagle*, 18.

75. Brierly, "Address Before the ABHMS," *Home Missionary* 20 (9) (Jan. 1848).

76. Billington, "Anti-Catholic Propaganda," 362.

77. Ibid., 363; Billington, *The Protestant Crusade,* 119–21.

78. Beecher, *A Plea for the West*, 12.

79. Billington, *The Protestant Crusade,* 119.

80. Ibid., 239.

81. *Home Missionary* 20 (4) (Aug. 1847).

82. Ibid.

83. Billington points out that this new spirit of accommodation was present by the 1850s, but I see indications of it much earlier than he suggests, leaving open the question of how generalized the hatred of Catholics actually was among home mission theorists. Certainly, as he notes, by the 1850s evangelicals "pictured themselves as actors in a new Reformation in which the United States was to play the leading role." Yet this strand was also evident throughout the 1840s. See Billington, *Protestant Crusade*, 280.

84. Wadsworth, "America's Mission," 18.

85. Bushnell, *Barbarism the First Danger,* 1, 5.

86. Ibid., 6.

87. Ibid., 17.

88. Ibid., 25.

89. Ibid., 32.

90. Ibid., 19.

91. The desire to keep slavery out of western territories did not imply that northern evangelicals supported the immigration of free blacks. Indeed, free soil advocates were just as inhospitable to blacks as to white southerners. On free soil ideology, see Foner, *Free Soil, Free Labor, Free Men*.

92. "Some Themes of Counter-Subversion: Anti-Masonic, Anti-Catholic, and Anti-Mormon Literature," in *From Homicide to Slavery*.

93. AHMS, *Our Country,* 16.

94. Beecher, *A Plea for the West*, 31.

95. Yi-Fu Tuan's insightful analysis of the meanings attached to space points out the ambiguity of our symbolism of space: "Space is a common symbol of freedom in the Western world. Space lies open; it suggests the future and invites action. On the negative side, space and freedom are a threat. . . . To be open and free is to be

exposed and vulnerable. Open space has no trodden paths and signposts. It has no fixed pattern of established human meaning; it is like a blank sheet upon which meaning may be imposed" (*Space and Place,* 54). As I have indicated, the American West *did* have fixed patterns of human meaning already attached to it by a variety of indigenous peoples, previous Spanish, French, and Russian settlers, etc., but Americans largely ignored evidence of previous colonizations.

96. Rev. J. J. Miter, "Address delivered at the Twentieth Anniversary of the American Home Missionary Society," *Home Missionary* 19(3) (July 1846).

97. *Home Missionary* 28(6) (Oct. 1855).

98. Loewenberg, *Equality on the Oregon Frontier,* 35.

99. The large numbers of German Catholics that settled in the upper Midwest presaged the greater diversity of California; missionaries reporting from these areas commented extensively on their encounters with these groups. See Incoming Correspondence for Wisconsin and Minnesota, in Papers of the American Home Missionary Society.

100. For more on early missionary activity in Missouri, see Goodykoontz, *Home Missions on the American Frontier.* Flint wrote several books drawing on his experiences as a missionary, including *Recollections* (1826) and *Memoir of Daniel Boone* (1833).

CHAPTER 2: A GILDED OPPORTUNITY

1. Pomeroy, *The Pacific Slope,* 32, 36; Cook, "Historical Mythmaking," 109.

2. According to the Nineteenth Annual Report of the AHMS (1845), 239 missionaries were stationed in the New England states of Maine (82), New Hampshire (45), Vermont (39), Massachusetts (66), and Rhode Island (7); fifteen labored in Maryland (1), Virginia (1), Kentucky (7), Tennessee (3), Alabama (2), and Arkansas (1); 387 occupied fields in Ohio (99), Indiana (46), Illinois (95), Michigan (65), Missouri (20), Wisconsin (34), and Iowa (28). Additionally, the board reported one missionary each in Washington, D.C., and Texas, and six in Canada (Report presented by the Executive Committee at the Anniversary Meeting, May 7, 1845 [New York: William Osborn, 1845], 69).

3. On the Methodist mission to Oregon see Loewenberg, *Equality.* Loewenberg points out that this mission, like other early efforts in the Pacific Northwest, began as a mission to the Indian populations. With the influx of Anglo settlers to the Willamette River Valley, the Methodists gradually diverted some of their efforts to the evangelization of Euro-American settlers.

4. Ogden, "New England Traders," 400, 401, 408; Holbrook, *The Yankee Exodus,* 144–46; Billington, *Westward Expansion,* 553–54, 560. See also Starr, *Americans,* ch. 1, on early Yankee settlers in California.

5. On the ABCFM and its early mission to the Pacific world, see Hutchison, *Errand,* 46.

6. Horsman, *Race and Manifest Destiny,* 90.

7. Graebner, *Empire on the Pacific,* 7.

8. Hietala, *Manifest Design*, 57.
9. Billington, *Westward*, 562–63; Cook, "Historical Mythmaking," 106–8. Cook also argues that eastern "boosters," fearing that Dana's *Two Years Before the Mast* could be construed as depicting California in a less than ideal light, sought to bury the negative connotations of his work under a barrage of positive press.

   It is important, of course, that political and economic aspirations were not easily or neatly separated, either with respect to the theme of Pacific Basin dominance, or continental expansion. President James K. Polk, in his third annual message to Congress on 7 Dec. 1847, demonstrated the interconnections when he justified the conquest of California: "The bay of San Francisco and other harbors along the Californian coast," he asserted, "would afford shelter for our navy, for our numerous whale ships, and other merchant vessels employed in the Pacific Ocean" (James D. Richardson, ed., *A Compilation of the Messages and Papers of the Presidents*, vol. 5 [Washington, D.C.: Government Printing Office, 1897], 2390. Cited in Hietala, *Manifest Design*, 89).
10. Much of the following discussion draws upon Merk, *Manifest Destiny*; and Billington, *The Far Western Frontier*.
11. On religious opposition to the Mexican War, see Schroeder, *Mr. Polk's War*, ch. 7; and Johannsen, *To the Halls of the Montezumas*, 273–79.
12. Hart, *The Mexican War*, 3–6.
13. *New Englander* 4(3) (July 1846): 430, 432. See also 5(4) (Oct. 1847): 612.
14. Ellsworth, "American Churches," 304–5.
15. Johannsen, *To the Halls*, 277.
16. *New Englander* 5(1) (Jan. 1847): 141.
17. *Home Missionary* 21(12) (April 1849).
18. The Northern Methodist *Christian Advocate and Journal*, published in New York, voiced repeated expressions of alarm in the mid-1840s about the lack of funding for and the increasing public apathy toward the mission movement. The noticeable diminution of financial support prompted an editorial in 1845 that politely confronted the issue: "It might, perhaps, be of some importance to inquire whether the Methodists are tired of their missionary operations? Or whether any thing has happened to lessen the obligation to sustain and enlarge them?" (19[26] [12 Feb. 1845]).
19. On the Evangelical United Front, see Foster, *Errand of Mercy;* and Marsden, *The Evangelical Mind*, 117.
20. Lamar, "Jason Lee," in *Reader's Encyclopedia*, 661; see also Loewenberg, *Equality*.
21. *New York Christian Advocate* 19(26) (12 Feb. 1845).
22. Lamar, "Marcus Whitman," *Reader's Encyclopedia*, 1263; see also Drury, *Marcus and Narcissa Whitman*.
23. This characterization of California Indians as naturally peaceful, a legacy of the Spanish missions, has been challenged by the groundbreaking work of Albert Hurtado on the California Indian populations. Hurtado shows that Indian reactions to Euro-American encroachment in California during the 1850s varied considerably

by region, depending on how much experience a particular tribe had in dealing with Anglos. Violence occurred frequently between Anglo settlers and American Indians, quite often because whites instigated it. Mutual distrust made conflict inevitable, as white immigrants quickly destroyed the economic and cultural foundations of Indian ways of life. See his *Indian Survival.*

24. Letter, "M. E. W." to editor, *California Christian Advocate* 1(22) (15 April 1852).

25. Wheeler, "Our Mission in California," 31, *HMR* Excerpts.

26. *Home Missionary* 21(6) (Oct. 1848); and 21(7) (Nov. 1848); Fleming, *God's Gold,* 8.

27. J. Emery to *New York Christian Advocate* 22(42) (20 Oct. 1847); Anthony, *Fifty Years of Methodism,* 13–14. Ecclesiastical differences, both in the way Methodists understood themselves fundamentally as a missionary church and also in the way they organized their efforts, make it difficult to draw direct parallels with Baptist, Presbyterian, and Congregational efforts in California. Nonetheless, the Methodist Episcopal Church began to devote resources to the new territory at roughly the same time as did the ABHMS and AHMS, indicating that waxing interest among the various denominations followed a parallel pattern.

28. Bieber, "California Gold Mania," 7–23; Holliday, *The World Rushed In,* 33–35; Bancroft, *History of California,* vol. 6, 115–17.

29. Bieber, "Gold Mania," 23; quoted in Holliday, *World Rushed,* 50.

30. *Home Missionary* 21(11) (March 1849).

31. J. W. Douglas to AHMS, *Home Missionary* 21(11) (March 1849).

32. Worcester, *California,* 6.

33. Newell, *The Glories of a Dawning Age,* 10.

34. Shepard, *Addresses,* 4–5.

35. Badger, "Address delivered at the ordination service of California missionary J. H. Warren, Broadway Tabernacle, New York, September 8, 1850," *Home Missionary* 23(6) (Oct. 1850).

36. *Home Missionary* 22(2) (June 1849); see also Worcester, *California,* 5–6.

37. Beecher, *Address at Tremont Temple,* 23–24.

38. "The Hand of God in the Gold Region," *New Englander* 16 (Feb. 1850).

39. Beecher, *Address,* 33.

40. Worcester, *California,* 6.

41. Beecher, *Address,* 26.

42. *Home Missionary* 21(9) (Jan. 1849).

43. Ibid., 25(9) (Jan. 1853). An interesting comparison can be made between the missionary interpretation of Chinese immigration to California and the story of the Nez Perce Indians who traveled from the Oregon Territory to Missouri, purportedly in order to request Christian instruction for their tribe. This latter story was used to justify some of the early missionary efforts in the Pacific Northwest, the claim being that natives themselves had requested Euro-American assistance.

44. *California Christian Advocate* 1(3) (13 Nov. 1851).

45. Ibid., 1(28) (27 May 1852).

46. Shepard, *Addresses,* 5.

47. Beecher, *Address*, 24–25.

48. *Home Missionary* 23(1) (May 1850).

49. Ibid., 21(11) (March 1849).

50. "California, Its Characteristics and Prospects," *New Englander* 16 (1858), 168–69.

51. "Hand of God," 86.

52. In Shepard, *Addresses*, 6.

53. Cleaveland, *Hasting to be Rich*, 15–16.

54. Excerpt from an article in *Harper's Monthly Magazine*, reprinted in the *California Christian Advocate* 1(9) (31 Dec. 1851).

55. *Home Mission Record* 1(7) (March 1850).

56. Shipps, *Mormonism*, 51–61.

57. Wadsworth, *America's Mission*, 27.

58. Coates, "The Golden Future," 141.

59. Burgess, *The Gospel*, 18.

60. Brigham, *Address*, 5.

61. Bushnell, *Prosperity Our Duty*, 3–6, 12.

62. Ibid., 15, 17; Wyllie, *The Self-Made Man*, 62–64, 71–72.

63. Bushnell, *Prosperity our Duty*, 12.

64. Rogers, *The Work Ethic*, 14–15, 28. See also Wilentz, *Chants Democratic*, 146–150, on the economic ethics of the working classes.

   Workers had good reason to be suspicious. Edward Pessen points out that in the 1830s and 1840s, the distribution of wealth in the United States became increasingly unequal. He argues that despite American disdain for European aristocratic traditions, the wealthiest Americans had just as much money—and in some instances more—than their European cousins. See Pessen, *Riches*, 25, 41.

65. Cawelti, *Apostles*, 46–51.

66. Social Gospel leaders such as Washington Gladden, Richard Ely, and Walter Rauschenbusch worried about the ethical consequences of an industrial economy; their liberal optimism, however, prevented them from challenging the essential justice of the economic system. Few Protestant leaders in America, in any period, have seriously questioned the morality of industrial capitalism. For more on the Social Gospel, see Abell, *The Urban Impact;* Hopkins, *The Rise of the Social Gospel;* May, *Protestant Churches*.

67. Note that, in effect, laissez-faire economics already dictated that enlightened self-interest should govern the marketplace. In this sense, the business culture was already an amoral sphere, not governed by the ethics of Christian virtue. Yet religious leaders throughout the antebellum era refused to acknowledge the extent to which capitalism could not be pulled under the sway of religious values; sermons such as Bushnell's were far more prescriptive than descriptive.

68. Frothingham, *Gold*, 9–10, 13.

69. Thayer, *The Price of Gold*, 7–11.

70. Shepard, *Addresses*, 5; Avery, *The Land of Ophir*, 9; Brigham, *Address*, 1.

71. Farley, *The Moral Aspect*, 7, 9–11.

72. Lunt, *The Net*, 8.

73. Johnson, *California*, 6, 8.

74. Cawelti argues that the myth of the self-made man was actually a synthesis of several conflicting beliefs and aspirations. Two of these were the middle-class Protestant ethic, stressing piety, frugality, and diligence; and the ethic of individual advancement that encouraged competitive and aggressive risk-taking in the economic sphere. Both of these strands were present in the advice of the evangelical clergy (*Apostles*, 4–5).

75. Brigham, *Address*, 3.

76. Shepard, *Addresses*, 7.

77. Curtiss, *Lines to New Englanders*.

78. Boutelle, *Sermon*, 10.

79. Foster, *The Uncertainty of Life*, 9, 13.

80. Shepard, *Addresses*, 5.

81. Avery, *Land of Ophir*, 4, 5, 10.

CHAPTER 3: TAMING THE PHYSICAL LANDSCAPE

1. Willey, *Decade Sermons*, 35.

2. *Home Missionary* 18(4) (Aug. 1845).

3. *Home Mission Record* 2(12) (Aug. 1851).

4. Wheeler, *Early Baptist History*, 19.

5. This estimate is based primarily on the comments of missionaries about their numbers, on lists of clergy contained in the minutes of the annual conference of the Methodist Episcopal church in California, on the scrapbook of pioneer Congregational ministers in California housed at the Pacific School of Religion, and on the correspondence of ministers to the American Home Missionary Society. These official lists, however, undoubtedly underestimate the numbers of clergy in the region between 1848 and 1870.

6. *Pacific* 9(27) (5 July 1860). The editors reported that to date there were 3 Congregationalist ministers in San Francisco, 3 in Oakland, 2 in Sacramento, and a dozen spread throughout the mining regions. These numbers are somewhat deceptive, given the fact that New School Presbyterian and Congregationalist ministers were employed interchangeably in some places. Timothy Dwight Hunt, for example, was a Presbyterian by background and training, but he conducted most of his pastoral labors while in California in Congregational churches, including the First Congregational Church of San Francisco.

7. Ibid. In 1860, the *Pacific* related that 15 New School ministers labored in California: 1 in San Francisco, 3 in Oakland, and the rest scattered in mining towns. There were also 18 Old School Presbyterians in the state: 6 in San Francisco, 1 in Sacramento, and 11 in the agricultural and mining districts.

8. The Baptist *Evangel* reported in 1864 that California contained 77 northern Methodist churches, 101 Sabbath Schools, and 85 traveling preachers (7[1] [7 Jan. 1864]).

9. Handy, *History of Union Seminary,* 16–17. Union Seminary had a special connection to the AHMS: the president of the school, Knowles Taylor, had served as a treasurer of the missionary organization; another member of Union's board, Absalom Peters, was a founder and secretary of the AHMS.

10. Henry M. Scudder to Society of Missionary Inquiry, Auburn Theological Seminary, 7 Aug. 1845, Presbyterian Historical Society, Philadelphia (hereafter PHS). Scudder wrote from his post in Madras, India, to encourage other young seminarians to become foreign missionaries. Still one of the best overviews of the foreign missions effort in the nineteenth century is Latourette, *The Great Century.*

11. John D. Paris to E. B. Walsworth, 3 June 1851, E. B. Walsworth Papers, Huntington Library, San Marino, Calif. Walsworth apparently discussed the possibility of going to California with his former schoolmate and friend, James Pierpont, another missionary to the state, demonstrating the importance of educational networks and peer groups in the fostering of missionary interest. See letter from James Pierpont to E. B. Walsworth, 13 Sept. 1852, Walsworth Papers.

12. Drury, "Samuel Hopkins Willey: California's Pioneer Missionary and Educator," typescript copy in Uncatalogued Records and Papers of Clifford M. Drury, San Francisco Theological Seminary, San Anselmo, Calif. (hereafter SFTS).

13. *Home Missionary* 21(7) (Nov. 1848). Editors of the Baptist *Home Mission Record* also published endless statistics quantifying the promise of the region.

14. Ibid., 21(9) (Jan. 1849).

15. Andrew, *Rebuilding,* 46–49.

16. Allmendinger, *Paupers and Scholars,* 12–18.

17. Maclay, *Journal* 6, 12 May 1850, cited in Hodges, "Charles Maclay," pt. 1, 136.

18. Pond to Brother Nash, undated, in Sermons of William Chauncey Pond, Pacific School of Religion, Berkeley, Calif. (hereafter PSR); Clark, *History of Bangor Seminary,* 130.

19. Pond, *Gospel Pioneering,* 15.

20. Burrowes, *My Early Labors,* 1–9, PHS.

21. W. C. Anderson to unnamed friend, 23 June 1846, Correspondence and Papers of W. C. Anderson, PHS.

22. See Hunt to Henry Hedges, 23 Oct. 1847, Diaries, Letters, and Papers of Timothy Dwight and Mary Hedges Hunt (hereafter Hunt Papers), SFTS.

23. Ibid.

24. Hunt to Rufus Anderson, 8 Nov. 1847, Hunt Papers.

25. Ibid., 18 Nov. 1847.

26. Hunt to father, 13 Nov. 1847, Hunt Papers.

27. Ibid.

28. Mary Hedges Hunt to her father, 12 Nov. 1847, Hunt Papers.

29. Hunt to parents of Mary Hedges Hunt, 12 March 1848, Hunt Papers .

30. Ibid., 26 Feb. 1850. To his wife, still back in the Islands while he searched for a place for them to live, Hunt reiterated: "Let it be borne in mind that for the first time in my ministerial life have I found *my place"* (Hunt to Mary Hedges Hunt, 14 Aug. 1850, Hunt Papers).

31. Hunt to Henry Hedges, 7 April 1851, Hunt Papers.
32. Hunt to parents of Mary Hedges Hunt, 29 Jan. 1852, Hunt Papers. Given Hunt's Presbyterian background, it is intriguing that he continually identified his own work with the Congregational heritage of his ancestors.
33. Willey to AHMS, 11 April 1849, Correspondence and Papers of Samuel H. Willey, 1848–1874 (hereafter Willey papers), Bancroft Library, Berkeley, Calif.
34. *Home Missionary* 23(4) (Aug. 1850).
35. Anthony, *Fifty Years*, 159–60.
36. Cool, "Biographical Sketch of Peter Cool," Huntington Library, San Marino, Calif.
37. Anthony, *Fifty Years*, 19–20.
38. King to E. B. Walsworth, 22 Nov. 1860, Walsworth Family Papers, Bancroft. Kevin Starr maintains that King took the California post because of the status it offered and the rejection he had encountered among the Boston Unitarian elite. Sandra Sizer Frankiel argues that King remained in California because he felt more needed there than he had in the East. While both are right to point to these factors, the financial motivation to immigrate certainly was great; recognizing its power also reinforces the fact that the educated clergy were not "above" their Baptist and Methodist counterparts, nor were they motivated solely by intellectual or social considerations (Starr, *Americans and the California Dream,* 97–105; Frankiel, *California's Spiritual Frontiers,* 20). For more on King's career, see Crompton, *Apostle of Liberty;* and Wendte, *Thomas Starr King.*
39. Briggs to R. Burr, Jr., 27 Sept. 1849, Correspondence and Papers of Martin C. Briggs, Bancroft.
40. Willey, "Personal Memoranda," 4, SFTS.
41. Pond, *Gospel Pioneering,* 68.
42. Willey to AHMS, 1 Aug. 1853, Willey Papers.
43. Richard C. Wade, introduction to Lotchin, *San Francisco,* vii. On the growth of an urban frontier, see Wade, *The Urban Frontier;* and Barth, *Instant Cities.*
44. Harmon to AHMS, 2 Aug. 1856, California Correspondence, Papers of the American Home Missionary Society, 1816–1936, Yale Divinity School Library (hereafter AHMS Papers).
45. Willey, *Quarter-Century Discourse.* See also Lotchin, *San Francisco,* ch. 5.
46. See Johnson, *Shopkeeper's Millennium,* on the communal effects of in-migration. Sean Wilentz carefully describes the social consequences of the influx of Irish to New York City, beginning in the 1830s, in *Chants Democratic,* 266–69.
47. My discussion of the early socioeconomic circumstances of California is based largely on Brown, *Hard-Rock Miners;* Mann, *After the Gold Rush;* and Paul, *California Gold.* See esp. Paul, xii–xiii, 82, 122; and Mann, 17, 213, 230.
48. *Home Missionary* 22(7) (Nov. 1849).
49. Holliday, *The World Rushed In*, 307–8.
50. Wheeler, "Our Mission in California," 1 June 1849, *HMR* Excerpts.
51. *Home Missionary* 27(3) (July 1854).
52. Willey to New York *Evangelist,* 28 June 1849, transcribed by Drury, Uncatalogued

Records and Papers of Clifford M. Drury, SFTS.

53. Brier to AHMS, 11 Jan. 1851, AHMS Papers.

54. *Home Missionary* 30(1) (May 1857).

55. Ibid., 27(3) (July 1854).

56. Ibid., 27(7) (Nov. 1854). The construction costs of new churches in the 1850s averaged $4,000–5,000.

57. Bell to AHMS, 1853? AHMS Papers.

58. Fleming, *God's Gold,* 130.

59. Bell to AHMS, 19 Aug. 1856, AHMS Papers.

60. Bartlett to AHMS, 27 April 1860, AHMS Papers.

61. Gates, *The Farmer's Age,* 387–90; Heizer and Almquist, *The Other Californians,* 149–50; Pitt, *Decline of the Californios,* 86.

62. "Doctor" to *California Christian Advocate* 2(18) (6 April 1853).

63. Willey to AHMS, 4 Sept. 1857 and 17 July 1859, AHMS Papers.

64. *Home Missionary* 31(9) (Jan. 1859).

65. Anthony, *Fifty Years,* 47.

66. *Home Missionary* 24(7) (Nov. 1851) and 27(4) (Aug. 1854).

67. Harmon to AHMS, 13 Oct. 1853, AHMS Papers.

68. *California Christian Advocate* 2(4) (30 Dec. 1852). Conversely, Silas Harmon reported in 1854 that a drought had halted the mining industry in Sonora, "and money, tho' we literally tread on gold, is very scarce" (Harmon to AHMS, 7 Jan. 1854, AHMS Papers).

69. See ch. 1 for a discussion of the theme of a moral wilderness in the West.

70. The European idea of ownership being attached to "improvement" of the land has a long history in encounters between European settlers and indigenous American peoples. See Cronon, *Changes in the Land,* for an insightful analysis of this theme.

71. Eliade, *Sacred and Profane,* 20–22.

72. Eliade notes the crucial symbolism of the sign in designating sacred territory: "In such cases the *sign,* fraught with religious meaning, introduces an absolute element and puts an end to relativity and confusion. *Something* that does not belong in this world has manifested itself apodictically and in so doing has indicated an orientation or determined a course of conduct" *(Sacred and Profane,* 27).

73. *California Christian Advocate* 1(32) (24 June 1852). This statement gains all the more force from its source: Methodists, generally, were more apt to wage their battles against the internalized spiritual enemy of human sinfulness. But they, too, recognized the need for sacralized space.

74. Methodists also were more likely than their evangelical colleagues to remain in the streets; in keeping with the itinerant tradition, fiery preachers like William Taylor made a profession as well as a virtue out of speaking on Portsmouth Plaza in San Francisco, or other public places. See, e.g., Taylor, *Seven Years.*

75. *Home Missionary* 24(12) (April 1852).

76. Ibid., 23(12) (April 1851).

77. Ibid., 24(7) (Nov. 1851).

78. *Seven Years,* 52–53.
79. Cutler, *A Thanksgiving Sermon,* 6.
80. On Sabbatarian and other Protestant reform causes in early California, see Hanchett, "The Blue Law Gospel"; Hanchett, "The Question of Religion"; and Luckingham, "Benevolence."
81. Bell to AHMS, 19 May 1853, AHMS Papers.
82. *Home Missionary* 26(7) (Nov. 1853).
83. Ibid., 24(12) (April 1852). The Reverend Edward S. Lacy in Crescent City was more innovative and blew a large horn on Sunday mornings to arouse his congregation: "This horn we find an excellent substitute for a bell, being made large for the especial purpose, and the only one of the kind in town (I think it far more *scriptural* than a bell)" (*Home Missionary* 27[6] [Oct. 1854]).
84. Ibid., 27(12) (April 1855).
85. Wheeler, *Our Present Danger,* 15.
86. *California Christian Advocate* 1(1) (10 Oct. 1851).
87. Ibid.
88. The natural environment affected other observers in equally profound ways. California scientists in the late nineteenth century developed a special way of understanding the place of science in the natural order as a result of their encounter with the beauty of the state. See Smith, *Pacific Visions.*
89. Sermon copied in Hale to AHMS, 24 Oct. 1853, AHMS Papers.

CHAPTER 4: MAPPING THE MORAL LANDSCAPE

1. Willey, *Thirty Years,* 42.
2. Willey, "Personal Memoranda," 23–25.
3. *Home Mission Record* 1(5) (Jan. 1850).
4. *New York Christian Advocate* 25(16) (18 April 1850).
5. "Our Mountain Strength," *Pacific* 1(2) (29 Aug. 1851).
6. *Home Missionary* 28(12) (April 1856).
7. Wheeler, Sept. 1849, to New York *Recorder* 5 (28 Nov. 1849), cited in Fleming, "Selected Letters," no. 2, pp. 124–25.
8. *Home Missionary* 29(6) (Oct. 1856).
9. "An Eighth Anniversary Record of California," *Pacific* 6(33) (6 Aug. 1857).
10. *Recorder* 5 (19 Sept. 1849), cited in Fleming, "Selected Letters of Wheeler," no. 1, p. 16.
11. *Home Missionary* 29(7) (Nov. 1856).
12. Ibid., 28(2) (June 1855).
13. Ibid., 30(10) (Feb. 1858).
14. Baker to AHMS, 1 April 1856, AHMS Papers.
15. *Home Missionary* 26(9) (Jan. 1854).
16. David Deal, *Diary for 1880,* PSR. The frequent absurdity of the discrepancy between institutions and membership is demonstrated by the situation of John G. Hale,

minister of an AHMS church in Grass Valley. In early 1855, Hale wrote to the AHMS to announce that the church was finally paid for ($4,600), after being $1,000 in debt the year before. Dampening his enthusiasm, however, was the fact that the church had only nine members! (*Home Missionary* 27[11] [March 1855]).

17. Hunt to AHMS, 17 Jan. 1856, AHMS Papers. Another AHMS missionary, W. L. Jones, grew resentful because he felt that Californians were giving him money out of pity: "They are willing to give occasionally, & then bless themselves for their great benevolence, just as they would give to a respectable pauper, or as they would feed some poor creature that has strayed away & has been so unfortunate as to come into their enclosure" (Jones to AHMS, 11 Dec. 1856, AHMS Papers).

18. Walsworth to Maria Walsworth Kinney, 1 Dec. 1853, Walsworth Family Papers.

19. Hamilton to AHMS, 17 March 1856, AHMS Papers.

20. New York *Recorder* 5 (28 Nov. 1849), 138, cited in Fleming, "Selected Letters," no. 2, p. 124.

21. Brayton to AHMS, 13 Jan. 1851, AHMS Papers.

22. *New York Christian Advocate* 27(2) (8 Jan. 1852).

23. Baker to AHMS, 17 Dec. 1855, AHMS Papers.

24. Hunt to AHMS, 5 June 1856, AHMS Papers.

25. Prevaux to parents, 4 Nov. 1856, Prevaux Papers, Bancroft.

26. Wheeler observed that gold fever affected "the religious interests of the place very unfavorably: and yet there is a peculiar sort of interest in religion very prevalent." Letter of 1 June 1849 to *Home Mission Record* 1(1) (Sept. 1849).

27. Taylor, *Seven Years,* 342.

28. Brier to AHMS, 1 Sept. 1860, AHMS Papers.

29. The significance of racist ideology in the missionary movement is a fascinating and complex subject; such ideology had ramifications significantly different for home and foreign missions fields. For more on racial theories and their role in the politics of manifest destiny in the antebellum era, see Horsman, *Race and Manifest Destiny.*

30. Douglas to AHMS, 29 June 1849, AHMS Papers.

31. *Home Missionary* 28(9) (Jan. 1856).

32. Douglas to AHMS, 29 June 1849, AHMS Papers.

33. *Home Missionary* 28(7) (Nov. 1855).

34. Ibid., 24(12) (April 1852).

35. Ibid., 28(12) (April 1856).

36. *Evangel* 3(15) (1 Nov. 1860).

37. Brayton to AHMS, 20 April 1858, AHMS Papers; Fleming, *God's Gold,* 143.

38. Brier to AHMS, 18 May 1857, AHMS Papers.

39. Prevaux to parents, 19 June 1858, Prevaux Papers.

40. *Minutes of the Annual California Conference of the Methodist Episcopal Church,* vol. 1, 39.

41. Pond, *Gospel Pioneering,* 62.

42. Hunt to AHMS, 15 June 1855, AHMS Papers.

43. Pond, *Gospel Pioneering,* 67–68. As of 1867, Pond reported that 55 Baptist churches

in the state had become "extinct," along with 13 Presbyterian and 4 Congregational.

44. *Home Missionary* 32(10) (Feb. 1860).
45. Ibid., 31(4) (Aug. 1859).
46. Taylor, *California Life,* 287.
47. Jones to AHMS, 31 Oct. 1856, AHMS Papers.
48. Willey, *Thirty Years,* 42.
49. Willey to AHMS, June 1849, Willey Papers.
50. Douglas to AHMS, 29 June 1849, AHMS Papers.
51. Letter to AHMS quoted in Pond, *Gospel Pioneering,* 39–40.
52. Capen, 30 April 1851, "Report of the Committee on the Far West," 18, *HMR* Excerpts.
53. Willey to AHMS, 8 Jan. 1855, AHMS Papers.
54. Griffin, *Their Brothers' Keepers,* 65.
55. Ibid., 203.
56. Harmon to AHMS, 1 July 1853, AHMS Papers.
57. Taylor, *California Life,* 30–31.
58. Brier to AHMS, 2 Feb. 1857, AHMS Papers.
59. Brayton to AHMS, 3 June 1857, AHMS Papers.
60. *Home Missionary* 28(1) (May 1855).
61. Prevaux to parents, 1[?] Jan. 1851, Prevaux Papers.
62. Prevaux to Sarah Ann Moulton, 17 June 1857, Prevaux Papers.
63. *Home Missionary* 28(1) (May 1855).
64. The subject of the editing of missionary letters for publication is a fascinating one, and could well take up a chapter of its own. Virtually all of the original incoming correspondence to the AHMS contains in it the editorial marks of the Secretary for Correspondence, detailing what was to be printed and what omitted. A careful correlation of these letters to what was actually printed in the *Home Missionary* could offer important insights into the intentions of the Board and its relationship to the missionaries in the field.
65. Willey to AHMS, June 1849, Willey Papers.
66. Hunt to AHMS, 5 June 1856, AHMS Papers.
67. *Home Missionary* 30(12) (April 1858).
68. Ibid., 30(5) (Sept. 1857).
69. Brayton to AHMS, 19 June 1857, AHMS Papers.
70. Benton to AHMS, 30 Jan. 1850, Willey Papers. This letter was written by Benton on Willey's behalf, presumably in the form of dictation, when Willey was taken ill.
71. Bushnell, "California," 142–82.
72. Willey to AHMS, 4 Sept. 1857, AHMS Papers.
73. Rev. Samuel Roosevelt Johnson, the rector of St. John's Church in Brooklyn, New York, emphasized how much more effectively the East could use the material gains of California, given its "more favored" cultural status: "Time may show that they [the inhabitants of California] distribute their gathered stores and golden treasures throughout this mother region, enriching it far more than their own less favored coast. But eternity will make mention, that we have given them the infi-

nitely greater treasure of the two, a treasure for earth—a treasure for heaven" (*California*, 19).

74. Typical of the early optimism of mission societies was the comment of Milton Badger of the AHMS in a letter to Samuel Willey. Badger promised that as soon as Willey sent back more definite reports about the needs of the field, the society would "set immediately about gathering & sending to your help all the reinforcements you may think can advantageously be employed. . . . I have no doubt we shall be able to obtain the right kind of men in sufficient numbers." Somewhat ominously, he then added that the one candidate already designated had died before he could depart for the West! (Badger to Willey, 14 March 1849, Willey Papers).

75. *Home Mission Record* 1(3) (Nov. 1849), cited in Fleming, *God's Gold*, 47–53.

76. Wheeler, "Our Weakness in California," 6, *HMR* Excerpts.

77. Fleming, *God's Gold*, 79, 81.

78. In 1852 the endeavor was suspended briefly owing to monetary difficulties. Explained the editor of the *Home Mission Record*, "It has been deemed unadvisable to increase our liabilities in that direction until our resources would more clearly justify it" (3[5] [Jan. 1852]).

79. *Home Missionary* 23(4) (Aug. 1850), emphasis in original.

80. Ibid., 22(9) (Jan. 1850).

81. Ibid., 27(1) (May 1854).

82. *Evangel* 6(13) (9 July 1863).

83. Willey to AHMS, 3 April 1857, AHMS Papers.

84. Blakeslee to AHMS, 19 July 1858, AHMS Papers.

85. Brier to AHMS, 11 Jan. 1851; Eli Corwin, Willey, and others, to AHMS, 30 Oct. 1854; Hunt to AHMS, 15 Aug. 1855; all in AHMS Papers. The substance of these suggestions, for obvious reasons, was not printed in the *Home Missionary*.

86. Willey to AHMS, Dec. 1857, AHMS Papers.

87. Kellogg to AHMS, 10 Nov. 1858, AHMS Papers.

88. "G. N." to *California Christian Advocate* 24(35) (2 Sept. 1875).

89. Kellogg to AHMS, 18 May 1858, AHMS Papers.

90. *Home Missionary* 31(2) (June 1859).

91. *Evangel* 4(21) (7 Nov. 1861).

92. *California Christian Advocate* 1(3) (13 Nov. 1851).

CHAPTER 5: THE MORAL WORLD OF THE CALIFORNIA MINER

1. Shirley, *The Shirley Letters*, 34–35. Like many Anglos in California, Dame Shirley was quick to equate drunkenness with the behavior of foreign immigrants—in this case, some of the many Chilean immigrants in the camps.

2. Bancroft, *History of California*, vol. 6, 52, 56.

3. Royce, *California*, 175.

4. Butler, "Magic, Astrology," 318; see also Butler, *Awash in a Sea of Faith*, ch. 3.

5. Ginzburg, *Cheese and Worms*, xvii.

6. The Anglo perspective, obviously, is not the only vantage point from which to view this society. It is, however, the best-documented one, given the self-consciousness with which Americans flocked to the mines and recorded their impressions. Miners, like ministers, recognized that they were participating in a significant historical event (probably because so many eastern promoters told them so). Euro-Protestant miners left hundreds of diaries and collections of letters, fully documenting their experiences of westward migration and settlement. Several important European and Hispanic Catholic diaries have also survived, and these sources have been cited when their impressions seem to correspond closely to those of their Euro-American counterparts. In contrast, only two journals by African-American writers have been identified. Clearly, much more work needs to be done to locate and analyze non-European accounts of life in the mines. For the purposes of this study, given the importance that missionaries attached to the evangelization of Euro-Americans and the subsequent tensions that resulted from these clerical expectations, their viewpoint will be my focus.

7. Paul, *Mining Frontiers,* 15–17.

8. Newman to James R. De Long, 10 Jan. 1854, in Carl I. Wheat, ed., "'California's Bantam Cock,' The Journals of Charles E. De Long, 1854–1863," *California Historical Society Quarterly* 11 (March 1932), 58; cited in Paul, *Mining Frontiers,* 34.

9. Because the earlier tallies were thought to be unreliable, the 1850 census statistics for California were amended in 1852 by an act of Congress.

10. Pitt, *The Decline of the Californios,* 52; Woo, "Protestant Work," 2; Mann, *After the Gold Rush,* 18; Paul, *California Gold,* 25–27; Lapp, *Blacks in Gold Rush California,* 22; Hurtado, *Indian Survival,* 1. Pitt bases his estimates on the work of Doris M. Wright, who compiled figures from the questionable aggregate census statistics of 1850. Comparing the estimates of the various sources proves to be an exercise in frustration: neither Wright nor the census takers counted the American Indian population at all, and many discrepancies exist between sources as to the remaining figures (How does one count a population that will not sit still?). Pitt's very rounded numbers, then, should be taken as educated guesses, in conjunction with Wright ("The Making of Cosmopolitan California").

11. My understanding of regional variations and its connections to the mining economy comes from the work of Susan Johnson on gender and ethnicity in the southern mines: "Scratching"; see also Beilharz and Lopez, *We Were Forty-Niners!* xvii; and Pitt, *Decline,* 48–68.

12. On vigilance committees, see Brown, *Strain of Violence.*

13. Missionaries were not without their explanations for vigilante actions. After the Vigilance Committee of 1856 formed in San Francisco, local ministers preached a rash of sermons on the subject. Most praised vigilantism as a necessary antidote to a corrupt legal system.

14. Doten, *The Journals of Alfred Doten,* 103.

15. Mrs. Lee Whipple-Haslam, *Early Days in California* (Jamestown, Calif.: Mother Lode Magnet, 1925); cited in Moynihan, Armitage, and Dichamp, eds., *So Much to be Done,* 30.

16. Doten, *Journals,* 107, 110, 115.

17. Perkins, *Gold Rush Diary,* 151.

18. Taylor, *Eldorado: or, Adventures in the Path of Empire* (New York: G. P. Putnam's Sons, 1865), 55–61, 99–103; cited in Davis, *Antebellum American Culture,* 125.

19. Decker, *The Diaries of Peter Decker,* 155.

20. Doten, *Journals,* 106.

21. Ferguson, *Experiences of a Forty-Niner,* 141–42.

22. Steele, *In Camp and Cabin,* 20.

23. Perlot, *Gold Seeker,* 87.

24. Hutchings, *Seeking the Elephant,* 201.

25. Perkins to B. Gates, Esq., 27 Dec. 1850, in Perkins, *Gold Rush Diary,* 195.

26. On the development of religious life in Los Angeles, see Engh, *Frontier Faiths.*

27. Willey to AHMS, 1[?] December 1849, Personal Memoranda, SFTS.

28. Mulford, *Prentice Mulford's Story,* 163.

29. Doten, *Journals,* 225.

30. Hill, *Journal,* 1849, vol. 2, p. 3, Alonzo A. Hill Papers, Beinecke Library, Yale University.

31. Woods, *Sixteen Months,* 35, 37. These events must have puzzled observers familiar with Protestant depictions of Catholicism as an authoritarian tradition, run by tyrannical priests, that allowed no voice for the individual believer. For more on anti-Catholic propaganda in the antebellum era, see Davis, "Some Themes of Counter-Subversion." Note also that reports of Hispanic Catholicism and even American Indian rituals undoubtedly were shaped by romanticized literary depictions of exotic travel, e.g., Melville's renderings of the South Seas. Nonetheless, it seems important that intercultural contact, regardless of how it was characterized, had an effect on Euro-Americans that distinguished their experiences from those of their eastern relatives who had only read about distant lands.

32. Hurtado, *Indian Survival,* 11, 101–24. As with the Anglo population, generalizations about California Indians are usually misleading in their simplicity. Hurtado cautions that relations between mining society and Indians differed greatly by region, depending on what tribes were involved, how the region developed economically, and how miners responded to their presence. The Indian begging criticized by many Anglos resulted from the disruptions to native ways of life caused by the presence of so many immigrants.

33. Doten, *Journals,* 240.

34. "Madeline" to *California Christian Advocate* 1(3) (13 Nov. 1851).

35. John Doble carefully observed the skill with which a young male Indian washed his clothes with a soap plant "which washes nearly as well as soap" (*Journal,* 58). Indian women were nearly universally admired for their unstintingly hard labors (as opposed to the Anglo perception of Indian men as lazy). Doten noted that during the Digger medical festival, "No civilized lady and her daughter ever worked harder, or made more bustle on such occasions, than do the Digger ladies of fashion in the preparation of their acorn, grubworm, grasshopper and other delectable delicacies" (ibid., 242).

36. Doten, *Journals*, 181.

37. In an intriguing study of the development of a unique Afro-Baptist faith in the New World, Mechal Sobel posits a direct link between the acquisition of new linguistic forms and the internalization of religious values. Drawing on the work of Thomas Luckmann, Sobel observes that "socialization can be viewed as the unconscious internalization of [a] system of meaning, accomplished by means of an integrally related style of thinking as objectified in symbols, movement, and, most crucially, language" (*Trabelin' On*, 3). The use of Spanish by some miners, then, may well have indicated the unconscious adoption of new forms of meaning.

38. This estimate is based on a sampling of the lists of three New England mining companies: the Bay State Company (Massachusetts), the Connecticut Mining and Trading Company, and the Hartford Union Mining and Trading Company. They represent a total of 238 men. Of this number, over 50 percent listed their occupation as skilled craftsman; approximately 20 percent were farmers; merchants and clerks accounted for 7 percent each; 6 percent were manufacturers; 3 percent were professionals; 2 percent were unskilled laborers. This sample is impressionistic rather than statistically significant. Additionally, the majority of men changed jobs upon arrival in California (approximately 76 percent of the men responding to the 1850 census listed their occupation as "miner"). For occupational lists of these mining companies, see Hall, *Around the Horn in '49*, 6; Lyman, *Journal of a Voyage*, 7; Hill, *Journal for 1849*, vol. 1, Hill Papers.

39. The literature on the relation between Protestantism and ascetic self-discipline in the early years of the industrial revolution is vast. For a classic statement of this theme, see Thompson, *The Making of the English Working Class*, 350–400. The relation between evangelical revivalism and work patterns in upstate New York is treated in Johnson, *Shopkeeper's Millennium*, 95–115. For the authoritative theoretical treatment of the relation between Calvinism and the Protestant work ethic, see Weber, *The Protestant Ethic;* and "The Social Psychology of the World Religions," in *From Max Weber*, 267–301.

40. Decker, *Diaries*, 211.

41. Findlay, *People of Chance*, 4.

42. Cleaveland, *Hasting*, 6, 15, 17. Although more tolerant of the specific vices of drinking, gambling, and card playing, Catholic priests also feared for the souls of miners who were exposed to the temptations of easy wealth. Pedro Isidoro Combet, a Chilean miner recently arrived in the state, attended mass in San Jose and expressed amazement at the nature of the service: "Nothing could have been more impressive and picturesque than this gathering of the faithful of all Catholic nations," he remarked. The priest was practical and down to earth, and "talked of love for religion in clear and simple terms." From the Catholic perspective, not surprisingly, the problems of gold rush California arose from the temptations and seductions introduced by the arrival of Americans and Protestantism. The priest consequently advised a devotion to hard work as "the true source of wealth" (Beilharz and Lopez, *We Were Forty-Niners!* 164).

43. Shirley, *Shirley Letters,* 12.

44. Fabian, "'Rascals and Gentlemen,'" 23; Findlay, *People of Chance,* 4.

45. Kenaga to parents, 4 Sept. 1860, Kenaga Family Papers, Beinecke.

46. Delano to his wife, 12 June 1851, Delano Letters, Beinecke.

47. Paul, *Mining Frontiers,* 28–34.

48. Woods, *Sixteen Months,* 100.

49. Davis to his wife, 20 May 1853, Charles Davis Letters, Beinecke.

50. Woods, *Sixteen Months,* 72.

51. Hill to Washington Hill, 29 April 1854, and Hill to family, 20 May 1857, Hill Papers.

52. Steele, *In Camp,* 6–8.

53. Fabian, "Rascals and Gentlemen," 310.

54. Findlay, *People of Chance,* 80.

55. Beilharz and Lopez, *We Were Forty-Niners!* 196.

56. Decker, *Diaries,* 252.

57. Beilharz and Lopez, *We Were Forty-Niners!* 196.

58. Steele, *In Camp,* 6.

59. Haskins, *The Argonauts of California,* 172. Fabian, in her study of American gambling in the nineteenth century, finds that the general ambivalence Americans felt about such practices led to a dichotomy in the way professional gamblers were perceived; many people could not decide whether they were sporting gentlemen or thieving rascals. See Fabian, "Rascals and Gentlemen," introduction.

60. Thomas, *Religion and the Decline of Magic,* 243, 664.

61. Haskins, *Argonauts,* 133, 140, 141.

62. On the relation between occult and magical practices and the origins of Mormonism, see Shipps, *Mormonism,* 6–12; and Quinn, *Mormonism.*

63. This explanation is in accord with the reasons Jon Butler gives for the decline of occult practices in eighteenth-century America. He suggests, among other things, that the greater difficulty of acquiring books on occultism from England, combined with the growing strength of an evangelical faith dedicated to extinguishing such practices, contributed to the decline of these activities. But he also notes that one of the communities in which these behaviors survived was among the German-speaking populations in Pennsylvania, indicating that German occult traditions may have been more resistant to changes. See Butler, "Magic," 339–46.

64. Haskins, *Argonauts,* 139, 141.

65. Holliday, *The World Rushed In,* 364.

66. Steele, *In Camp,* 64.

67. Shirley, *Shirley Letters,* 27.

68. Clifford Geertz asserts that it is precisely in the rituals of religious observance that religious conviction or certainty is attained. Given the importance of bodily acts, it is understandable that miners would have fallen back on familiar ceremonies as a way of symbolically reasserting moral order in their lives. See Geertz, "Religion as a Cultural System," 112–14.

69. Welles, *Three Years' Wandering,* 284. Missionaries undoubtedly would have taken

exception to the statement that their pay was ever bountiful.

70. "Philo" to his sister, 10 Nov. 1850, "Philo" Letters, Beinecke. The dangers of mining life added to the mortality rates: accidents, snowslides, fires, storms, and flash floods took high tolls.

71. Brown, *Hardrock Miners*, 15–19, 40–44.

72. Moxley to his sisters, 16 Dec. 1849, Charles Moxley Papers, Beinecke.

73. Chase to Jane Chase, 7 Aug. 1852 (typescript copy), Nathan Chase Letters, Beinecke.

74. Perkins, *Gold Rush Diary*, 152.

75. Ver Mehr, *A Checkered Life*, 342–43.

76. Kenaga to Benjamin Kenaga, 8 Sept. 1860, Kenaga Family Papers, Beinecke.

77. Paul, *California Gold*, 80–83.

78. Bell, *Home Missionary* 29(7) (Nov. 1856).

79. Doten, *Journals*, 97.

80. Decker, *Diaries*, 205.

81. Doten, *Journals*, 142.

82. Decker, *Diaries*, 53, 66, 113–14.

83. Ibid., 75.

84. Ibid., 159–60.

85. Ibid., 234, 236.

86. Doten, *Journals*, 198, 81.

87. Perkins, *Gold Rush Diary*, 153.

88. Fabian, *Card Sharps*, 112.

89. Butler, *Awash in a Sea of Faith*; Hall, *Worlds of Wonder;* Quinn, *Mormonism*. Quinn cites a number of instances of clergy in the Northeast in the 1820s and 1830s using divining rods to locate buried treasure (*Mormonism*, 22–25).

90. Unruh, *The Plains Across*, 93–96.

91. Geertz, "Religion as a Cultural System." Geertz's functional description of religion does not necessarily imply that religious beliefs function solely in an explanatory capacity; beliefs are not like items of clothing that we try on until we find one that fits. Although beliefs can and do function in this manner, they also, in turn, shape the way we perceive reality.

92. *Home Missionary* 27(7) (Nov. 1854).

93. Sobel, *The World They Made Together*, 9.

94. Kevin Starr maintains that most miners saw California in this light, as an atemporal, ahistorical moment, where the "bottom dropped out of the nineteenth century." For some men, this characterization is certainly true, but it may overstate the extent to which men felt themselves to be living in a time out of time. See Starr, *Americans and the California Dream*.

95. *The Seventh Census of the United States: 1850* (Washington, D.C.: Robert Armstrong, 1853), 966–67.

96. Ferguson, *Experiences of a Forty-Niner*, 9.

97. Welles, *Three Years*, 15, 264, 344.

98. Ibid., 328–29.

99. *Home Missionary* 24(6) (Oct. 1851).

100. Davis to his wife, 13 May 1850, Davis Letters.

101. Like many Anglo miners, Doten invariably equated Latinas and prostitution; see Mann, *After,* 50. This was another way of morally "protecting" the reputations of white women in the community.

102. Information on Doten's background comes from the introduction to Doten's journals by Walter Van Tilburg Clark, ed., *Journals.*

103. Doten, *Journals,* 232.

104. Ibid., 215.

105. Ibid., 190.

106. Turner, "Betwixt and Between," 340, 342.

107. These views were in turn influenced by the publication of various accounts of travel and adventure in the West, encouraging the notion that this was a suitable pursuit for a young man perched on the edge of adulthood. Two of the most popular were Dana, *Two Years before the Mast*; and Edwin Bryant, *What I Saw.*

108. Mulford, *Prentice Mulford's Story,* 15.

109. *Sunday Dispatch,* Columbus, Ohio, 2 Oct. 1849, cited in Unruh, *The Plains Across,* 96.

110. Chase to Jane Chase, 5 March 1852, and 7 Aug. 1852, Chase Letters.

111. Davis to his wife, 12 Aug. 1850, Davis Letters.

112. Woods, *Sixteen Months,* 70–71.

113. Background information on Doble comes from the introduction to his journal by Charles L. Camp, ed., *John Doble's Journal,* xiii–xiv.

114. Doble, *Journal,* 1, 2–4.

115. Ibid., 20, 121.

116. Ibid., 29, 32, 40.

117. Ibid., 85.

118. Ibid., 71, 83.

119. Ibid., 40.

120. Daniel Woods corroborated Doble's description of the intensity of male competition for women in mining society when he reported on a woman he knew whose husband had recently passed away. Within a week of his death, she received three marriage proposals (*Sixteen Months,* 76).

121. Doble to Lucas, 4 March 1864, *Doble's Journal,* 277.

122. Ibid., 9 Nov. 1862, *Doble's Journal,* 267.

123. Ibid., 29 Nov. 1860, *Doble's Journal,* 226.

124. Ibid., 22 Feb. 1862, *Doble's Journal,* 244.

125. Ibid., 24 Oct. 1861, *Doble's Journal,* 238.

126. Ibid., 29 Nov. 1860, *Doble's Journal,* 226.

127. Ibid., 11 June 1860, *Doble's Journal,* 221.

128. Brigham, *Address,* 5.

129. Ibid., 3.

130. Doble to Lucas, 24 Oct. 1861, *Doble's Journal,* 239.

131. Doble, *Journal,* 120–21.

132. Ibid., 54.

133. Ibid., 149, 83.

134. Ibid., 163. Doble was impressed by the large number of attendees at the meeting, but he complained that "they dont seem to be any verry thorough going men among them."

135. Ibid., 245.

136. Ibid., 179, 140–44.

137. Ibid., 180–81.

138. Ibid., 57.

139. Doten, *Journals,* 178.

140. Paul, *California Gold,* 118, 120, 177–78; Mann, *After the Gold Rush,* 71, 73.

141. Hittell, *Mining in the Pacific States of North America* (San Francisco, 1861), 35, cited in Paul, *Mining Frontiers,* 44.

CHAPTER 6: THE "WONDROUS EFFICACY" OF WOMANHOOD

1. Soule, Gihon, and Nisbet, *The Annals of San Francisco,* 666–68; cited in Barnhart, *The Fair But Frail,* 29–30.

2. Royce, *A Frontier Lady,* 113–14.

3. McDannell, *The Christian Home in Victorian America,* 19. The literature on the ideology of domesticity, evangelical religion, and the theory of woman's sphere is extensive. Along with McDannell's work, my interpretation is based primarily on the following studies: Cott, *The Bonds of Womanhood;* Epstein, *The Politics of Domesticity;* Ryan, *Cradle;* Sklar, *Catherine Beecher.*

4. *Seventh Census,* 966–67; *Population of the United States in 1860, Compiled from the Original Returns of the Eighth Census* (Washington, D.C.: Government Printing Office, 1864), 25; Jeffrey, *Frontier Women,* 56; Jensen and Miller, "The Gentle Tamers Revisited," 189; Paul, *California Gold,* 82.

5. For a detailed and suggestive study of settlement patterns common in agricultural regions such as the Old Northwest, see Faragher, *Sugar Creek.*

6. Paul, *California Gold,* 27, 82. Urban areas such as San Francisco and Sacramento did have larger populations of women and children; still, it is significant that even ministers in these cities lamented the lack of female influence into the 1860s.

7. *Home Missionary* 22(7) (Nov. 1849).

8. Several recent studies document "women's work for women" in the late nineteenth century. See Deutsch, *No Separate Refuge;* Pascoe, *Relations of Rescue;* and Yohn, "Religion, Pluralism, and the Limits of Progressive Reform." On women foreign missionaries in the late nineteenth century, see Hill, *The World Their Household;* and Hunter, *The Gospel of Gentility.*

9. *Home Missionary* 23(11) (March 1851).

10. Ryan, *Cradle,* 76–83, 110, 116–23; Charles Foster points out that benevolent activity

was the only acceptable way for antebellum American women to be involved in public affairs (*Errand of Mercy,* 128).

11. Williams, *A Pioneer Pastorate and Times,* 106; Hale to AHMS, 24 Oct. 1853, AHMS Papers; Hale, *Home Missionary* 26(10) (Feb. 1854).

12. "Haste to Be Rich," *Pacific* 1(1) (1 Aug. 1851).

13. Ibid.

14. *California Christian Advocate* 3(13) (24 March 1854).

15. Ibid., 1(1) (10 Oct. 1851).

16. Benton, *California as She Was,* 10.

17. "Do They Miss Me? . . . Yes, We've Missed Thee," by "Lusanah," *California Christian Advocate* 1(41) (26 Aug. 1852). The same poem was also printed in the *Pacific* 1(12) (7 Nov. 1851). This kind of appeal was not unique to gold rush California. The temperance movement, for example, made use of all manner of sentimental songs to convince men that drinking destroyed family life.

18. Wadsworth, *A Mother's Sorrow,* 5, 10–12, 17, 19.

19. Douglas to AHMS, 29 June 1849, AHMS Papers.

20. *California Christian Advocate* 3(46) (10 Nov. 1854).

21. Willey, *Thirty Years,* 47.

22. See Hutchison, *Errand,* on the history of Protestant missionary debates about christianization and civilization.

23. Letter to the editor from "O.C.T.," *California Christian Advocate* 3(14) (31 March 1854).

24. "Influence of Woman in California," *Pacific* 1(11) (31 Oct. 1851).

25. Steele, *In Camp,* 65–66.

26. Washburn, *Philip Thaxter,* 124.

27. Ibid., 243.

28. Ferguson, *Experiences of a Forty-Niner,* 149.

29. Ibid., 151.

30. *Home Missionary* 29(7) (Nov. 1856).

31. Westover to Betsey Westover, 10 Nov. 1852, Charles Westover Letters, Beinecke.

32. Post to Winslow, 5 Jan. 1853, Beinecke.

33. *Sixteen Months,* 98.

34. "Philo" to sister, 10 Nov. 1850, "Philo" Letters, Beinecke.

35. Woods, *Sixteen Months,* 119.

36. Jaqueline Baker Barnhart argues that, during the first few years of the gold rush, prostitution was accepted quite openly; prostitutes were "not viewed as deviants from the norm, because there was no norm" (*The Fair But Frail,* 1). Protestant ministers, of course, attempted to impose a set of communal norms with respect to women's behavior, but they were only partially successful. The same patterns prevailed in other mining regions with similarly skewed sex ratios. John Milleain, convicted of killing a prostitute in the Comstock Lode of Nevada in the late 1860s, addressed his last words to the ladies present: "'In Virginia City it is different,' he explained, "the public women are more respected than ladies'" (*Territorial Enter-*

prise, 26 April 1868, cited in Goldman, *Gold Diggers and Silver Miners,* 142).

37. Taylor, *California Life Illustrated,* 177, 178.
38. For detailed descriptions of gambling halls in western towns and cities, see Findlay, *People of Chance,* 80.
39. Hale to AHMS, 24 Oct. 1853, AHMS Papers.
40. *California Christian Advocate* 3(43) (20 Oct. 1854); E. S. Lacy, *Home Missionary* 27(6) (Oct. 1854).
41. Griswold, "Anglo Women," 22–26.
42. Jeffrey, *Frontier Women,* 118.
43. Myres, *Westering Women,* 165–66. Scholars have long debated what effects the westering experience had on women's roles. For more on this theme, see Faragher, *Men and Women,* and Jeffrey, *Frontier Women.*
44. Schlissel, *Women's Diaries,* 150.
45. In 1852–53, hundreds of French prostitutes sailed to the Pacific Coast. Their passage was paid by a national lottery system, ordered by Louis Napoleon, who hoped to rid the country of "revolutionaries" and "criminals." Ironically, once in California, French prostitutes were in high demand, and were desired by men as the most elegant and fashionable of companions. See Goldman, *Gold Diggers,* 69; and Barnhart, *Fair But Frail,* 52.
46. On statistics for men, see ch. 5.
47. Schlissel, *Women's Diaries,* 150.
48. Megquier to Milton Benjamin, 18 Feb. 1849, in *Apron Full of Gold,* 5.
49. Megquier to Milton Benjamin, 11 Nov. 1849; to her mother, 28 April 1850; to her daughter, 14 Nov.(?) 1849, *Apron,* 30, 40, 32.
50. Schlissel, *Women's Diaries,* 62–64; Levy, *They Saw the Elephant,* 92–94.
51. Moynihan et al., *So Much to Be Done,* 8–9.
52. Levy, *They Saw the Elephant,* 101, 112, 122.
53. Goldman, *Gold Diggers,* 67, 70; Barnhart, *Fair But Frail,* 40–45.
54. Royce, *A Frontier Lady,* 115.
55. Moynihan, *So Much to Be Done,* 13; Shirley, *Shirley Letters,* 54–55.
56. Moynihan, *So Much to Be Done,* 74, 77, 97.
57. The evangelical terminology with respect to these women is neither satisfactory nor consistent. Occasionally, home mission boards referred to these women as missionaries, but technically speaking they had not been commissioned by the societies. These women were in the West by virtue of being married to male missionaries since no female home missionaries existed at this date. Most women, however, saw what they did as a special religious vocation in its own right. I therefore use the term *missionary wives* to refer to them, while acknowledging its inadequacy to convey the scope of their activities.
58. Gifford, *The Nineteenth-Century,* introduction.
59. Sweet, *The Minister's Wife.* Friends could also be a convenient source of references for appropriately pious young women. Mary Orne Tucker, the wife of a Methodist circuit-rider in New England, related that she had met her husband through some

216	Notes to Pages 168–74

mutual acquaintances who had recommended her to him as a "suitable person for a minister's wife." During their first meeting, Mr. Tucker asked her whether she liked to travel, and soon after he proposed (*Itinerant Preaching in the Early Days of Methodism* [Boston: B. B. Russell, 1872], 34–35), reprinted in Gifford, *Nineteenth-Century*.

60. *California Christian Advocate* 1(10) (7 Jan. 1852).
61. *Home Missionary* 22(4) (Aug. 1849).
62. Gifford, *Nineteenth-Century*, n.p.
63. Boyd, "Presbyterian Ministers' Wives," 3–17.
64. Eaton, *The Itinerant's Wife: Her Qualifications, Duties, Trials, and Rewards* (1851), reprinted in Gifford, *Nineteenth-Century*.
65. Ibid., 8, 9–10, 45.
66. Harmon to AHMS, 1 July 1853, AHMS Papers.
67. *Home Missionary* 27(7) (Nov. 1854).
68. Hunt to AHMS, 18 June 1856, AHMS Papers.
69. *Home Missionary* 29(8) (Dec. 1856).
70. Soule, *Annals*, 504–5. These figures are from early 1854. Ministers in San Francisco were able to command much higher salaries for their work; by the late 1850s, congregations in the city were attracting well-known eastern clergy to their churches by offering highly inflated sums of money. Other clergy in the city were alarmed when word leaked out in 1854 that Dr. William Anderson Scott, a famous Presbyterian cleric from New Orleans, had been induced to take a church in San Francisco for the annual salary of $10,000—about ten times what many local ministers earned.
71. Jeffrey suggests that in California towns, ministers' wives became the center of female influence, despite the other demands on their time (*Frontier Women*, 100).
72. Jackson, *Scrapbook, 1870–1883*, 14–15, PHS.
73. Burrowes, *Early Labors*, 132–33, SFTS.
74. On foreign missionary efforts in Hawaii, see Hutchison, *Errand*, 69–77; and Andrew, *Rebuilding the Christian Commonwealth*. On missionary wives in particular, see Grimshaw, *Paths of Duty*.
75. Mary Hedges Hunt to her father, 12 Nov. 1847, Hunt Papers.
76. Mary Hedges Hunt to her parents, 2 March 1849, Hunt Papers.
77. Degler, *At Odds*, 5; Griswold, *Family and Divorce*. Griswold examines the effects of the "divorce crisis" in late nineteenth-century California, attributing it in part to the flowering of the companionate ideal of marriage.
78. Hunt to Hedges, 15 Sept. 1853, Hunt Papers.
79. Mary Hedges Hunt to her parents, 2 March 1849, Hunt Papers.
80. Mary Hedges Hunt to her mother, 10 Jan. 1850, Hunt Papers.
81. Hunt to his parents, 29 June 1849, Hunt Papers.
82. Hunt to Hedges family, 30 Aug. 1851, and Mary Hedges Hunt to her father, 4 May 1852, Hunt Papers.
83. Hunt to Hedges family, 31 Aug. 1850, Hunt Papers.

84. Hunt to his parents, 29 June 1849, Hunt Papers. The Reverend James Woods described the first Presbytery meeting (Old School) held in California in the spring of 1850. It was held in Woods's small house, and was attended by Albert Williams and Sylvester Woodbridge. "While the Presbytery was transacting its business," Woods relates, "my wife was preparing dinner for us in the same room; and I was rocking the cradle with my foot while handling presbyterial papers" (Woods, *Recollections,* 31–32).

85. Mary Hedges Hunt to her father, 13 Jan. 1853, Hunt Papers.

86. Mary Hedges Hunt to her mother, 4 June 1852, Hunt Papers.

87. Mary Hedges Hunt to Henry Hedges, 29 April 1853, Hunt Papers.

88. Mary Hedges Hunt to her mother, 10 Jan. 1850, Hunt Papers.

89. Mary Hedges Hunt to her sisters, 8 Aug. 1845, Hunt Papers.

90. Mary Hedges Hunt to her mother, 10 Jan. 1850, Hunt Papers.

91. Mary Hedges Hunt to her mother, 4 June 1852, Hunt Papers.

92. Mary Hedges Hunt to her mother, 10 Jan. 1850, Hunt Papers.

93. This interpretation draws upon the work of Carroll Smith-Rosenberg in her groundbreaking essay "The Female World of Love and Ritual," in *Disorderly Conduct,* 53, 60–61; and Cott, *Bonds of Womanhood,* 163–68.

94. Walsworth, Journal, 13 Nov. 1852; Diary for Sarah Walsworth, 1852, vol. 1; Walsworth Family Papers.

95. See Lotchin, *San Francisco,* for more on the early development of the city.

96. Walsworth, Diary for 1853, Walsworth Family Papers.

97. Walsworth to her parents, 14 July 1853, Walsworth Family Papers.

98. Ibid.; Walsworth to her mother, 13 Oct. 1853; Walsworth to her parents, 28 Dec. 1853; Walsworth Family Papers.

99. Walsworth, Diary for 1853, 27 July 1853, Walsworth Family Papers.

100. Ibid., 11, 12 Oct. 1853, Walsworth Family Papers.

CHAPTER 7: A MARKETPLACE OF MORALS

1. Takaki, *Iron Cages,* 173.

2. Paul, *Mining Frontiers,* 41.

3. San Francisco still retained a distinctive ethos, despite its economic growth. See Starr, *Americans,* 239–87.

4. *Evangel* 11(2) (14 Jan. 1869); *Statistics of the United States (Including Mortality, Property, &c.) in 1860* (Washington, D.C.: Government Printing Office, 1864), 502. The census indicates that the average value of each church in California was $6,325.

5. *Abstract of the Eleventh Census: 1890,* 2d ed. (Washington, D.C.: Government Printing Office, 1896), 259. Eastern states did not have percentages as high as one might think: New York tallied 36 percent, Ohio 33 percent, and most of the southeastern states also stood in the thirties. No settled states in the West measured higher than 27 percent.

6. On regional variations in contemporary Protestantism, see Hammond, *Religion and Personal Autonomy*.

7. Paul, *Mining Frontiers*, 51.

8. Frankiel, *California's Spiritual Frontiers*, xiii.

9. Paul, *Mining Frontiers*, 36–46.

Select Bibliography

MANUSCRIPT SOURCES

Berkeley, California. Bancroft Library, University of California
  Briggs, Martin C. Correspondence and Papers, 1848–1890
  Excerpts from the *Home Mission Record*. Typescript
  King, Thomas Starr. Letters and Papers, 1839–1863
  Pamphlets on churches in California
  Pamphlets by California authors on religion
  Prevaux, Francis E., and Lydia Prevaux. Family Correspondence, 1846–1859
  Walsworth, E. B., and Sarah Walsworth. Walsworth Family Papers, 1842–1906
  Willey, Samuel H. Correspondence and Papers, 1848–1874

Berkeley, California. Pacific School of Religion Archives
  Benton, Joseph A. Papers
  Congregational Association of Northern California. *Minutes of Annual Meetings, 1857–1889*
  Deal, David. Diary for 1880
  Dwinell, Israel E. Papers, Sermons, Letters, 1849–1860
  Fish, Isaac B. Miscellaneous Account Books and Sermon Notes
  Owen, Isaac. Correspondence and Papers, 1830–1868
  Pond, William Chauncey. Sermons
  Ross, John W. Diaries and Notebooks, 1852–1879
  Sheldon, Henry B. Diary, 1 January 1851–5 February 1854
  Warren, James H. Album of all the Congregational Ministers who labored as pastors, acting pastors, stated supplies, educators, editors, etc., in California during the first twenty-five years, 1849–1874
  Willey, Samuel H. Correspondence and Reports, 1846–1907

San Anselmo, California. San Francisco Theological Seminary
  Burrowes, George. Diaries and Papers, 1811–1882
  Drury, Clifford M. Uncatalogued Records and Papers
  ———. Index to References to Churches, Clergymen, and Religious Subjects Mainly

on the Pacific Coast, in the *Pacific,* Organ of the Northern California Congregational Conference, 1851–1868

Hunt, Timothy Dwight, and Mary Hedges Hunt. Diaries, Letters, and Papers,
1843–1860

Pamphlets on religion in early California. Microfilm

Willey, Samuel H. Personal Memoranda on California, 1848–1849

San Marino, California. Huntington Library

Cool, Sarah Mahala. Biographical Sketch of Peter Cool

Walsworth, E. B. Walsworth Papers, 1840–1859

New Haven, Connecticut. Beinecke Library, Yale University

Chase, Nathan. Letters

Davis, Charles. Letters

Delano, Ephraim. Letters

Hill, Alonzo. Papers

Kenaga, Levi. Kenaga Family Papers

Moxley, Charles. Papers

"Philo." Letters

Post, J. H. Letter to Reverend Winslow, 5 January 1853

Westover, Charles. Letters

New Haven, Connecticut, Yale Divinity School Library

Papers of the American Home Missionary Society, 1816–1936. Microfilm

Philadelphia, Pennsylvania. Presbyterian Historical Society

Anderson, William C. Correspondence and Papers

Biographical files of Presbyterian ministers in California

Burrowes, George. Journal: *My Early Labors in San Francisco*

Jackson, Sheldon. Scrapbook, 1870–1883

Scudder, Henry M. Letter to the Society of Missionary Inquiry, Auburn Theological
Seminary, 7 August 1845

Webber, L. P. Diary

NEWSPAPERS AND PERIODICALS

California Christian Advocate. 1851–1880.

Domestic Missionary Chronicle. 1845–1855

The Evangel. 1858–1875

The Home Missionary. 1826–1860

Home Mission Record. 1849–1867

New York Christian Advocate and Journal. 1844–1852

The New Englander. 1840–1865

The Pacific. 1851–1865

PRIMARY SOURCES

American Home Missionary Society Executive Committee. *Our Country, Its Capabilities, Its Perils, and Its Hope, being a plea for the early establishment of Gospel institutions in the destitute portions of the United States*. New York: Executive Committee of the American Home Missionary Society, 1842.

Anderson, William C. *The Ocean Telegraph, A discourse delivered in the First Presbyterian Church, San Francisco*. San Francisco: Towne and Bacon, 1858.

Avery, J. H. *The Land of Ophir, Ideal and Real, A Discourse delivered at Austinburg, Ohio, before a company about proceeding to California*. New York: E. O. Jenkins, 1853.

Beecher, Edward. *Address at Tremont Temple to the New England and California Trading and Mining Association, January 25, 1849*. Boston: The Company, 1849.

Beecher, Lyman. *A Plea for the West*. Cincinnati: Truman and Smith, 1835.

Beilharz, Edwin A., and Carlos U. Lopez, trans. and eds. *We Were Forty-Niners! Chilean Accounts of the California Gold Rush*. Pasadena: Ward Richie Press, 1976.

Benton, Joseph A. *The California Pilgrim*. Sacramento: Solomon Alter, 1853.

———. *California As She Was, As She Is, As She Is To Be, Discourse delivered at the First Church of Christ, Sacramento City, November 30, 1850*. Sacramento: Placer Times Press, 1850.

———. *Some of the Problems of Empire*. San Francisco: Bacon, 1868.

———. *Sermon preached at Sacramento, May 18, 1856, in the Congregational Church on Sixth Street*. [Sacramento? 1856?]

Boutelle, A. *Sermon occasioned by the death of Newell Marsh, at Shasta City, California, November, 1852: Delivered at Peacham, VT., January, 1853*. Concord, N.H.: McFarland and Jenks, [1853].

Brier, William W. *The Opening Sermon before the Synod of Alta California, October 3, 1860*. San Francisco: Towne and Bacon, 1860.

Brierly, Benjamin. *Thoughts for the Crisis, a discourse delivered in the Washington Street Baptist Church, San Francisco, on the Sabbath following the assassination of James King of William*. San Francisco: Eureka Book and Job Office, 1856.

Brigham, Charles. *An Address delivered to the companies of California adventurers of Taunton*. Taunton, Mass., 1849.

Bristol, Sherlock. *The Pioneer Preacher; Incidents of Interest and Experiences in the Author's Life*. New York: Fleming H. Revell, 1887.

Bryant, Edwin. *What I Saw in California*. New York: D. Appleton, 1848.

Burgess, George. *The Gospel in its Progress Westward, Sermon preached in Trinity Church, New York City, October 28, 1853, at the consecration of Rev. W. Ingraham Kip as Missionary Bishop of California*. Albany: Joel Munsell, 1853.

Bushnell, Horace. *Barbarism the First Danger, A Discourse for Home Missions*. New York: Printed for the American Home Missionary Society, 1847.

———. "California, Its Characteristics and Prospects." *New Englander* 16 (1858).

———. *Prosperity Our Duty, A Discourse delivered at the North Church, Hartford, January 31, 1847*. Hartford: Case, Tiffany and Burnham, 1847.

———. *Society and Religion, A Sermon for California, delivered Sunday, July 6, 1856 at the installation of the Reverend E. S. Lacy, pastor of the First Congregational Church, San Francisco*. San Francisco: Sterett, 1856.

California Conference of the Methodist Episcopal Church. *Minutes of the Annual California Conference of the Methodist Episcopal Church, 1855–1887*. 2 vols. San Francisco: Methodist Episcopal Church, 1887.

Chapin, Steven. *A Discourse before the American Baptist Home Missionary Society*. [Baltimore? 1841?]

Cleaveland, Elisha Lord. *Hasting to be Rich, A Sermon preached in New Haven and Bridgeport, January and February, 1849*. New Haven: J. H. Benham, 1849.

Coates, Reynell. "The Golden Future, or, Our Empire of the West." *Sartain's Magazine* 7 (Sept. 1850): 133–41.

Curtiss, N. P. B. *Lines Addressed to New Englanders in California*. Words by "Eliza." Boston: J. Prentiss, 1850. Song sheet.

Cutler, Rufus. *A Thanksgiving Sermon, delivered at the First Unitarian Church, Stockton Street, San Francisco, on November 22, 1856*. San Francisco: Commercial Book and Job Steam Printing Establishment, 1856.

Dana, C. W. *The Garden of the World, or, the Great West*. Boston: Wentworth, 1856.

Dana, Richard Henry, Jr. *Two Years Before the Mast. A Personal Narrative of Life at Sea*. New York: Harper and Brothers, 1840.

Decker, Peter. *The Diaries of Peter Decker: Overland to California in 1849 and Life in the Mines, 1850-1851*. Ed., with an introduction by Helen S. Giffen. Georgetown, Calif.: Talisman Press, 1966.

Doble, John. *John Doble's Journal and Letters from the Mines: Mokelumne Hill, Jackson, Volcano and San Francisco, 1851–1865*. Ed., with an introduction by Charles L. Camp. Denver: Old West Publishing, 1962.

Doten, Alfred. *The Journals of Alfred Doten, 1849–1903*. Vol. 1. Ed., with an introduction by Walter Van Tilburg Clark. Reno: University of Nevada Press, 1973.

Dwinell, Israel E. *The Higher Reaches of the Great Continental Railway, a Highway for our God*. Sacramento: H. S. Crocker, 1869.

Eno, Henry. *Twenty Years on the Pacific Slope: Letters, 1848–1871*. New Haven: Yale University Press, 1965.

Ferguson, Charles D. *The Experiences of a Forty-Niner in California*. Ed. Frederick T. Wallace. 1888. New York: Arno Press, 1973.

Foster, Joseph C. *The Uncertainty of Life, a sermon occasioned by the death of Mr. Henry L. Bemis, at Stockton, California*. Brattleboro: J. B. Miner, 1849.

Frothingham, Nathaniel L. *Gold, A Sermon preached to the First Church on Sunday, December 17, 1848*. Boston: John Wilson, 1849.

Hall, Linville John. *Around the Horn in '49. Journal of the Hartford Union Mining and Trading Company*. 1849. Wethersfield, Conn.: L. J. Hall, 1898.

"The Hand of God in the Gold Region." *New Englander* 16 (Feb. 1850).

Hart, Burdett. *The Mexican War, A Discourse delivered at the Congregational Church in Fair Haven, on the Annual Fast of 1847*. New Haven: Peck and Stafford, Printers, 1847.

Haskins, C. W. *The Argonauts of California: Being the Reminiscences of Scenes and Incidents that Occurred in California in Early Mining Days*. New York: Fords, Howard and Hulbert, 1890.

Hays, Lorena L. *To the Land of Gold and Wickedness: The 1848–1859 Diary of Lorena L. Hays*. Ed. Jeanne Hamilton Watson. St. Louis: Patrice Press, 1988.

Howe, Octavius Thorndike. *The Argonauts of '49: History and Adventures of the Emigrant Companies from Massachusetts, 1849–1850*. Cambridge: Harvard University Press, 1923.

Hunt, Timothy D. *Address delivered before the New England Society of San Francisco, December 22, 1852*. San Francisco: Cooke, Kenny, 1853.

———. *Sermon suggested by the execution of Jenkins, on the plaza, by "the people" of San Francisco during the night of the tenth of June, 1851*. San Francisco: Marvin and Hitchcock, 1851.

———. *The Past and Present of the Sandwich Islands*. San Francisco: Whitton, Towne, 1853.

Hutchings, James Mason. *Seeking the Elephant, 1849: James Mason Hutchings' Journal of His Overland Trek to California*. Ed. Shirley Sargent. Glendale, Calif.: Arthur H. Clark, 1980.

Johnson, Samuel Roosevelt. *California: A Sermon preached in St. John's Church, Brooklyn, New York, on Sunday, February 11, 1849*. New York: Stanford and Swords, 1849.

Kip, William I. *A California Pilgrimage*. Fresno: Privately published, 1921.

———. *Characteristics of the Age: a charge to the clergy of the diocese of California, at the opening of the twenty-sixth annual convention in Trinity Church*. San Francisco: Cubery, 1876.

———. *The Early Days of My Episcopate*. New York: Thomas Whittaker, 1892.

Lunt, William P. *The Net that Gathered of Every Kind, A Discourse delivered Sunday, October 21, 1849, to the First Congregational Church of Quincy, Massachusetts*. Boston: Dutton and Wentworth, 1849.

Lyman, Albert. *Journal of a Voyage to California and Life in the Gold Diggings. And Also of a Voyage from California to the Sandwich Islands*. Hartford: E. T. Pease, 1852.

Megquier, Mary Jane. *Apron Full of Gold: The Letters of Mary Jane Megquier from San Francisco, 1849–1856*. Ed. Robert Glass Cleland. San Marino: Huntington Library, 1949

Moynihan, Ruth B., Susan Armitage, and Christiane Fischer Dichamp, eds. *So Much to be Done: Women Settlers on the Mining and Ranching Frontier*. Lincoln: University of Nebraska Press, 1990.

Mulford, Prentice. *Prentice Mulford's Story: Life by Land and Sea*. New York: F. J. Needham, 1889.

Newell, W. W. *The Glories of a Dawning Age, A discourse delivered at Liverpool, N. Y. . . . at the ordination of Mr. Samuel B. Bell, together with a farewell address to missionaries about to sail for California*. Syracuse: Thomas S. Truair, 1853.

Perkins, Elisha Douglass. *Gold Rush Diary: Being the Journal of Elisha Douglass Perkins on the Overland Trail in the Spring and Summer of 1849*. Ed. Thomas D. Clark. Lexington: University of Kentucky Press, 1967.

Perkins, George William. *An Address to the "Pacific Pioneers," on the eve of their departure for California, March 22, 1849*. West Meriden, Conn.: E. Hinman, 1849.

Perlot, Jean-Nicholas. *Gold Seeker: Adventures of a Belgian Argonaut during the Gold Rush Years*. Trans. Helen Harding Bretnor and ed. Howard R. Lamar. New Haven: Yale University Press, 1985.

Pond, William Chauncey. *Gospel Pioneering: Early Congregationalism in California, 1833-1920*. Oberlin: News Printing, 1921.

Royce, Josiah. *California, From the Conquest in 1846 to the Second Vigilance Committee in San Francisco: A Study in American Character*. 1886. New York: Alfred A. Knopf, 1948.

Royce, Sarah. *A Frontier Lady: Recollections of the Gold Rush and Early California*. Ed. Ralph Henry Gabriel. New Haven: Yale University Press, 1932.

Scott, J. W. "The Great West." *Debow's Review* 15 (July 1853).

Shepard, George, and S. L. Caldwell. *Addresses of the Reverends Professor George Shepard and S. L. Caldwell to the California Pilgrims from Bangor, Maine*. Bangor: Smith and Sayward, 1849.

Shirley, Dame [Louise Amelia Knapp Smith Clappe]. *The Shirley Letters: Being Letters written in 1851–1852 from the California Mines*. Published serially in *The Pioneer* magazine, 1854–55. Santa Barbara: Peregrine Smith, 1970.

Soule, Frank, John Gihon, M.D., and James Nisbet. *The Annals of San Francisco*. 1855. Comp. Dorothy H. Huggins. Palo Alto: Lewis Osborne, 1966.

Steele, John. *In Camp and Cabin: Mining Life and Adventure in California During 1850 and Later*. Lodi, Wis.: J. Steele, 1901.

Sweet, William Warren. *The Baptists, 1783–1830: A Collection of Source Materials*. Vol. 1 of *Religion on the American Frontier*. New York: H. Holt, 1931.

———. *The Presbyterians, 1783–1840: A Collection of Source Materials*. Vol. 2 of *Religion on the American Frontier*. Chicago: University of Chicago Press, 1936.

———. *The Congregationalists: A Collection of Source Materials*. Vol. 3 of *Religion on the American Frontier*. 1939. New York: Cooper Square Publishers, 1964.

———. *The Methodists: A Collection of Source Materials*. Vol. 4 of *Religion on the American Frontier*. Chicago: University of Chicago Press, 1946.

Taylor, Bayard. *At Home and Abroad, A Sketch-Book of Life, Scenery and Men*. 2d ser. New York: G. P. Putnam's Sons, 1862.

———. *Eldorado: or, Adventures in the Path of Empire*. New York: G. P. Putnam's Sons, 1865.

Taylor, William. *California Life Illustrated*. 1858. New York: Carlton and Porter, 1867.

———. *Seven Years Street Preaching in San Francisco, California: Embracing Incidents, Triumphant Death Scenes, Etc*. New York: Carlton and Porter, 1857.

Thayer, William Makepeace. *The Price of Gold, A Sermon occasioned by the death of*

Henry Martyn Allard . . . preached at Ashland, Massachusetts, August 22, 1852. Boston: J. B. Chisholm, 1852.

Townsend, Huddart R. *Appeal on Behalf of the Church in California.* New York: W. van Norden, 1849.

Ver Mehr, Jean Leonard. *Checkered Life: In the Old and New World.* San Francisco: A. L. Bancroft, 1877.

Wadsworth, Charles. *America's Mission in the World, a Sermon preached in the Arch Street Presbyterian Church, Philadelphia, November 22, 1855.* Philadelphia: T. B. Peterson, 1855.

————. *A Mother's Sorrow, A Sermon preached before the Y.M.C.A. of San Francisco.* San Francisco: Rooms of the Association, 1864.

Washburn, Charles A. *Philip Thaxter, A Novel.* New York: Rudd and Carleton, 1861.

Waugh, Lorenzo. *Autobiography of Lorenzo Waugh.* Oakland: Pacific Press, 1883.

Welles, C. M. *Three Years' Wanderings of a Connecticut Yankee, in South America, Africa, Australia, and California.* New York: American Subscription Publishing House, 1859.

Wheeler, Osgood Church. "Selected Letters of O. C. Wheeler." Pts. 1–4. Ed. Sandford Fleming. *California Historical Society Quarterly* 27 (1948).

————. *The Story of Early Baptist History in California.* [Sacramento?]: 1889.

Willey, Samuel H. *Decade Sermons.* San Francisco: Towne and Bacon, 1859.

————. *Thirty Years in California, A Contribution to the History of the State, from 1849 to 1879.* San Francisco: A. L. Bancroft, 1879.

————. *Quarter-Century Discourse; open questions in California in 1849, and the answers given by them in twenty-five years.* Santa Cruz: Santa Cruz Enterprise, 1874.

————. *Farewell Discourse.* San Francisco: Towne and Bacon, 1862.

Williams, Albert. *A Pioneer Pastorate and Times.* San Francisco: Wallace and Hassett, 1879.

Woods, Daniel B. *Sixteen Months at the Gold Diggings.* New York: Harper and Brothers, 1851.

Woods, James. *A Sermon on the Dedication of the Presbyterian Church of Stockton, California, May 5, 1850.* Barre: Patriot Press, 1851.

————. *Recollections of Pioneer Work in California.* San Francisco: Joseph Winterburn, 1878.

Worcester, Samuel M. *California, An Address delivered before the Naumkeag Mutual Trading and Mining Company, Tabernacle Church, Salem, Massachusetts, January 14, 1849.* [Salem?]: 1849.

Wyman, Walker, ed. *California Emigrant Letters.* New York: Bookman Associates, 1952.

SECONDARY SOURCES

Books

Abell, Aaron I. *The Urban Impact on American Protestantism, 1865–1900.* Cambridge: Harvard University Press, 1943.

Ahlstrom, Sydney E. *A Religious History of the American People*. New Haven: Yale University Press, 1972.

Allmendinger, David F., Jr. *Paupers and Scholars: The Transformation of Student Life in Nineteenth-Century New England*. New York: St. Martin's Press, 1975.

Andrew, John A. III. *Rebuilding the Christian Commonwealth: New England Congregationalists and Foreign Missions, 1800–1830*. Lexington: University Press of Kentucky, 1976.

Anthony, C. V. *Fifty Years of Methodism*. San Francisco: Methodist Book Concern, 1901.

Bancroft, Hubert Howe. *History of California, 1542–1890*. 7 vols. San Francisco: The History Company, 1890.

Baptist Home Missions in North America . . . 1832–1882. New York: Baptist Home Mission Rooms, 1883.

Barnes, Gilbert H. *The Anti-Slavery Impulse, 1830–1844*. 1933. New York: Harcourt, Brace and World, 1964.

Barnhart, Jaqueline Baker. *The Fair but Frail: Prostitution in San Francisco, 1849–1900*. Reno: University of Nevada Press, 1986.

Barth, Gunther. *Bitter Strength: A History of the Chinese in the United States, 1850–1870*. Cambridge: Harvard University Press, 1964.

———. *Instant Cities: Urbanization and the Rise of San Francisco and Denver*. New York: Oxford University Press, 1975.

Bercovitch, Sacvan. *The American Jeremiad*. Madison: University of Wisconsin Press, 1978.

Billington, Ray Allen. *The Protestant Crusade, 1800–1860: A Study of the Origins of American Nativism*. 1938. Chicago: Quadrangle Books, 1964.

———. *Westward Expansion: A History of the American Frontier*. 3d ed. New York: Macmillan, 1967.

———. *The Far Western Frontier, 1830–1860*. New York: Harper Torchbooks, 1956.

Boyer, Paul. *Urban Masses and Moral Order in America, 1820–1920*. Cambridge: Harvard University Press, 1978.

Bridgman, Howard Allen. *New England in the Life of the World*. Boston: Pilgrim Press, 1920.

Brown, Richard Maxwell. *Strain of Violence: Historical Studies of American Violence and Vigilantism*. New York: Oxford University Press, 1975.

Brown, Ronald C. *Hard-Rock Miners: The Intermountain West, 1860–1920*. College Station: Texas A & M University Press, 1979.

Burleson, Hugh Latimer. *The Conquest of the Continent*. Milwaukee: Young Churchman, 1917.

Butler, Jon. *Awash in a Sea of Faith: Christianizing the American People*. Cambridge: Harvard University Press, 1990.

Cawelti, John G. *Apostles of the Self-Made Man*. Chicago: University of Chicago Press, 1965.

Clark, Calvin Montague. *History of Bangor Theological Seminary*. Boston: Pilgrim Press, 1916.

Cochran, Alice Cowan. *Miners, Merchants, and Missionaries: The Roles of Missionaries and Pioneer Churches in the Colorado Gold Rush and Its Aftermath, 1858–1870*. Metuchen: Scarecrow Press and American Theological Library Association, 1980.

Cott, Nancy. *The Bonds of Womanhood: Woman's Sphere in New England, 1780–1835*. New Haven: Yale University Press, 1977.

Crompton, Arnold. *Apostle of Liberty: Starr King in California*. Boston: Beacon Press, 1950.

———. *Unitarianism on the Pacific Coast: The First Sixty Years*. Boston: Beacon Press, 1957.

Cronon, William. *Changes in the Land: Indians, Colonists, and the Ecology of New England*. New York: Hill and Wang, 1986.

Cross, Whitney. *The Burned-over District: A Social History of Enthusiastic Religion in Western New York, 1800–1850*. Ithaca: Cornell University Press, 1950.

Davis, David Brion. *From Homicide to Slavery: Studies in American Culture*. New York: Oxford University Press, 1986.

———. *Antebellum American Culture: An Interpretive Anthology*. Lexington: D. C. Heath, 1979.

Degler, Carl. *At Odds: Women and the Family in America from the Revolution to the Present*. New York: Oxford University Press, 1980.

Deutsch, Sarah. *No Separate Refuge: Culture, Class, and Gender on an Anglo-Hispanic Frontier in the American Southwest, 1880–1940*. New York: Oxford University Press, 1987.

Drury, Clifford M. *Marcus and Narcissa Whitman, and the Opening of old Oregon*. 2 vols. Glendale: A. H. Clark, 1973.

———. *California Imprints, 1846–1876: Pertaining to Social, Educational, and Religious Subjects*. Glendale: Privately printed for the author, 1970.

Eliade, Mircea. *The Sacred and the Profane: The Nature of Religion*. Trans. Willard R. Trask. San Diego: Harcourt Brace Jovanovich, 1959.

Engh, Michael E., S.J. *Frontier Faiths: Church, Temple and Synagogue in Los Angeles, 1846–1888*. Albuquerque: University of New Mexico Press, 1992.

Epstein, Barbara Leslie. *The Politics of Domesticity: Women, Evangelism, and Temperance in Nineteenth-Century America*. Middletown: Wesleyan University Press, 1981.

Fabian, Ann. *Card Sharps, Dream Books, and Bucket Shops: Gambling in Nineteenth-Century America*. Ithaca: Cornell University Press, 1990.

Faragher, John Mack. *Sugar Creek: Life on the Illinois Prairie*. New Haven: Yale University Press, 1986.

———. *Men and Women on the Overland Trail*. New Haven: Yale University Press, 1979.

Ferrier, William Warren. *Congregationalism's Place in California History*. Berkeley: 1943.

Findlay, John M. *People of Chance: Gambling in American Society from Jamestown to Las Vegas*. New York: Oxford University Press, 1986.

Fleming, Sandford. *God's Gold: The Story of Baptist beginnings in California, 1849–1860*. Philadelphia: Judson Press, 1949.

Foner, Eric. *Free Soil, Free Labor, Free Men: The Ideology of the Republican Party Before the Civil War*. London: Oxford University Press, 1970.

Foster, Charles. *Errand of Mercy: The Evangelical United Front, 1790–1837*. Chapel Hill: University of North Carolina Press, 1960.

Foster, Frank H. *A Genetic History of the New England Theology*. Chicago: University of Chicago Press, 1907.

Frankiel, Sandra Sizer. *California's Spiritual Frontiers: Religious Alternatives in Anglo-Protestantism*. Berkeley: University of California Press, 1988.

Gates, Paul. *The Farmer's Age: Agriculture, 1815–1860*. Vol. 3, *The Economic History of the United States*. New York: Holt, Rinehart and Winston, 1960.

Gifford, Carolyn De Swarte, ed. *The Nineteenth-Century American Methodist Itinerant Preacher's Wife*. New York: Garland Publishing, 1987.

Ginzburg, Carlo. *The Cheese and the Worms: The Cosmos of a Sixteenth-Century Miller*. Trans. John and Anne Tedeschi. New York: Penguin Books, 1982.

Goldman, Marion S. *Gold Diggers and Silver Miners: Prostitution and Social Life on the Comstock Lode*. Ann Arbor: University of Michigan Press, 1981.

Goodykoontz, Colin Brummitt. *Home Missions on the American Frontier, with Particular Reference to the American Home Missionary Society*. Caldwell, Idaho: Caxton Printers, 1939.

Graebner, Norman A. *Empire on the Pacific: A Study in American Continental Expansion*. New York: Ronald Press, 1955.

Griffin, Clifford S. *Their Brothers' Keepers: Moral Stewardship in the United States, 1800-1865*. New Brunswick, N.J.: Rutgers University Press, 1960.

Grimshaw, Patricia. *Paths of Duty: American Missionary Wives in Nineteenth-Century Hawaii*. Honolulu: University of Hawaii Press, 1989.

Griswold, Robert L. *Family and Divorce in California, 1850–1890: Victorian Illusions and Everyday Realities*. Albany: State University of New York Press, 1982.

Guarnari, Carl, and David Alvarez, eds. *Religion and Society in the American West: Historical Essays*. Lanham, Md.: University Press of America, 1987.

Hall, David D. *Worlds of Wonder, Days of Judgment: Popular Religious Belief in Early New England*. Cambridge: Harvard University Press, 1990.

Hammond, Phillip E. *Religion and Personal Autonomy: The Third Disestablishment in America*. Columbia: University of South Carolina Press, 1992.

Handy, Robert T. *A History of Union Theological Seminary in New York*. New York: Columbia University Press, 1987.

Harlow, Neal. *California Conquered: War and Peace on the Pacific, 1846–1850*. Berkeley: University of California Press, 1982.

Haroutunian, Joseph. *Piety Versus Moralism: The Passing of the New England Theology*. New York: Henry Holt, 1932.

Hatch, Nathan. *The Democratization of American Christianity*. New Haven: Yale University Press, 1989.

Heizer, Robert F., and Alan F. Almquist. *The Other Californians: Prejudice and Discrimination under Spain, Mexico, and the United States to 1920*. Berkeley: University of California Press, 1971.

Hietala, Thomas R. *Manifest Design: Anxious Aggrandizement in Late Jacksonian America*. Ithaca: Cornell University Press, 1985.

Hill, Patricia. *The World Their Household: The American Woman's Foreign Mission Movement and Cultural Transformation, 1870–1920*. Ann Arbor: University of Michigan Press, 1984.

Hine, Robert V. *California's Utopian Colonies*. New Haven: Yale University Press, 1966.

Holbrook, Stewart H. *The Yankee Exodus: An Account of Migration from New England*. New York: Macmillan, 1950.

Holliday, J. S. *The World Rushed In: The California Gold Rush Experience*. New York: Simon and Schuster, 1981.

Hopkins, Charles H. *The Rise of the Social Gospel in American Protestantism, 1865–1915*. New Haven: Yale University Press, 1940.

Horsman, Reginald. *Race and Manifest Destiny: The Origins of American Racial Anglo-Saxonism*. Cambridge: Harvard University Press, 1981.

Howe, Daniel Walker. *The Political Culture of the American Whigs*. Chicago: University of Chicago Press, 1979.

Hunter, Jane. *The Gospel of Gentility: American Women Missionaries in Turn-of-the-Century China*. New Haven: Yale University Press, 1984.

Hurtado, Albert. *Indian Survival on the California Frontier*. New Haven: Yale University Press, 1988.

Hutchison, William. *Errand to the World: American Protestant Thought and Foreign Missions*. Chicago: University of Chicago Press, 1987.

Isaac, Rhys. *The Transformation of Virginia, 1740–1790*. New York: W. W. Norton, 1988.

Jeffrey, Julie Roy. *Frontier Women: The Trans-Mississippi West, 1840–1880*. New York: Hill and Wang, 1979.

Johannsen, Robert W. *To the Halls of the Montezumas: The Mexican War in the American Imagination*. New York: Oxford University Press, 1985.

Johnson, Paul E. *A Shopkeeper's Millennium: Society and Revivals in Rochester, New York, 1815–1837*. New York: Hill and Wang, 1978.

Kramer, William E., ed. *The American West and the Religious Experience*. Los Angeles: Will Kramer, 1975.

Lamar, Howard, ed. *Reader's Encyclopedia of the American West*. New York: Thomas Y. Crowell, 1977.

Lapp, Rudolph M. *Blacks in Gold Rush California*. New Haven: Yale University Press, 1977.

Latourette, Kenneth. *The Great Century, A.D. 1800–A.D. 1914: Europe and the United States of America*. Vol. 4, *A History of the Expansion of Christianity*. New York: Harper and Brothers, 1941.

Levy, Jo Ann. *They Saw the Elephant: Women in the California Gold Rush*. Hamden, Conn.: Archon Books, 1990.

Loewenberg, Robert J. *Equality on the Oregon Frontier: Jason Lee and the Methodist Mission, 1834–1843*. Seattle: University of Washington Press, 1976.

Lotchin, Roger W. *San Francisco, 1846–1856: From Hamlet to City*. Lincoln: University of Nebraska Press, 1979.

McDannell, Colleen. *The Christian Home in Victorian America, 1840–1900*. Bloomington: University of Indiana Press, 1986.

McLoughlin, William G. *Modern Revivalism: From Charles Grandison Finney to Billy Graham*. New York: Ronald Press Company, 1959.

Mann, Ralph. *After the Gold Rush: Society in Grass Valley and Nevada City, California, 1849–1870*. Stanford: Stanford University Press, 1982.

Marsden, George. *The Evangelical Mind and the New School Presbyterian Experience: A Case Study of Thought and Theology in Nineteenth-Century America*. New Haven: Yale University Press, 1970.

Mathews, Lois Kimball. *The Expansion of New England*. Boston: Houghton Mifflin, 1909.

May, Henry. *Protestant Churches and Industrial America*. New York: Harper and Brothers, 1949.

Mead, Sidney E. *Nathaniel William Taylor, 1786–1858: A Connecticut Liberal*. Chicago: University of Chicago Press, 1942.

Merk, Frederick. *Manifest Destiny and Mission in American History: A Reinterpretation*. New York: Alfred A. Knopf, 1963.

Miller, Perry. *The Life of the Mind in America: From the Revolution to the Civil War*. New York: Harcourt, Brace and World, 1965.

———. *The New England Mind: The Seventeenth Century*. Cambridge: Harvard University Press, 1939.

Miyakawa, T. Scott. *Protestants and Pioneers: Individualism and Conformity on the American Frontier*. Chicago: University of Chicago Press, 1964.

Myres, Sandra L. *Westering Women and the Frontier Experience, 1800–1915*. Albuquerque: University of New Mexico Press, 1982.

Nash, Roderick. *Wilderness and the American Mind*. 3d ed. New Haven: Yale University Press, 1982.

Pascoe, Peggy. *Relations of Rescue: The Search for Female Moral Authority in the American West, 1874–1939*. New York: Oxford University Press, 1990.

Paul, Rodman W. *California Gold: The Beginning of Mining in the Far West*. Lincoln: University of Nebraska Press, 1965.

———. *Mining Frontiers of the Far West, 1848–1880*. New York: Holt, Rinehart and Winston, 1963.

Pessen, Edward. *Riches, Class and Power before the Civil War*. Lexington: D. C. Heath, 1973.

Pitt, Leonard. *The Decline of the Californios: A Social History of Spanish-Speaking Californians, 1846–1890*. Berkeley: University of California Press, 1966.

Pomeroy, Earl. *The Pacific Slope: A History of California, Oregon, Washington, Idaho, Utah, and Nevada*. New York: Alfred A. Knopf, 1965.

Quinn, D. Michael. *Mormonism and the Magic World View*. Salt Lake City: Signature Books, 1987.

Rogers, Daniel T. *The Work Ethic in Industrial America, 1850–1920*. Chicago: University of Chicago Press, 1978.

Ryan, Mary P. *Cradle of the Middle Class: The Family in Oneida County, New York, 1790–1865*. Cambridge: Cambridge University Press, 1981.

Schlissel, Lillian. *Women's Diaries of the Westward Journey*. New York: Schocken Books, 1982.

Schroeder, John H. *Mr. Polk's War: American Opposition and Dissent, 1846–1848*. Madison: University of Wisconsin Press, 1973.

Shipps, Jan. *Mormonism: The Story of a New Religious Tradition*. Urbana: University of Illinois Press, 1985.

Sklar, Katherine Kish. *Catherine Beecher: A Study in American Domesticity*. New York: Norton, 1976.

Smith, Henry Nash. *Virgin Land: The American West as Symbol and Myth*. Cambridge: Harvard University Press, 1978.

Smith, Michael L. *Pacific Visions: California Scientists and the Environment, 1850–1915*. New Haven: Yale University Press, 1988.

Smith-Rosenberg, Carroll. *Disorderly Conduct: Visions of Gender in Victorian America*. New York: Alfred A. Knopf, 1985.

Sobel, Mechal. *Trabelin' On: The Slave Journey to an Afro-Baptist Faith*. Princeton: Princeton University Press, 1988.

———. *The World They Made Together: Black and White Values in Eighteenth-Century Virginia*. Princeton: Princeton University Press, 1987.

Sollors, Werner. *Beyond Ethnicity: Consent and Descent in American Culture*. New York: Oxford University Press, 1986.

Somkin, Fred. *Unquiet Eagle: Memory and Desire in the Idea of American Freedom, 1815–1860*. Ithaca: Cornell University Press, 1967.

Starr, Kevin. *Americans and the California Dream, 1850–1915*. New York: Oxford University Press, 1973.

Sweet, Leonard I. *The Ministers' Wife: Her Role in Nineteenth-Century American Evangelicalism*. Philadelphia: Temple University Press, 1983.

Sweet, William Warren. *Religion in the Development of American Culture, 1765–1840*. New York: Charles Scribner's Sons, 1952.

———. *Revivalism in America: Its Origin, Growth, and Decline*. Gloucester, Mass.: Peter Smith, 1965.

Thomas, Keith. *Religion and the Decline of Magic*. New York: Charles Scribner's Sons, 1971.

Thompson, E. P. *The Making of the English Working Class*. New York: Random House, 1966.

Tuan, Yi-Fu. *Space and Place: The Perspective of Experience*. Minneapolis: University of Minnesota Press, 1977.

Unruh, John D. *The Plains Across: The Overland Emigrants and the Trans-Mississippi*

West, 1840–1860. Urbana: University of Illinois Press, 1978.

Wade, Richard. *The Urban Frontier: The Rise of Western Cities, 1790–1830*. Cambridge: Harvard University Press, 1959.

Weber, Max. *The Protestant Ethic and the Spirit of Capitalism*. Trans. Talcott Parsons. New York: Charles Scribner's Sons, 1958.

————. *From Max Weber: Essays in Sociology*. Trans. and ed. H. H. Gerth and C. Wright Mills. 1946. New York: Oxford University Press, 1980.

Weinburg, Albert K. *Manifest Destiny: A Study of Nationalist Expansionism in American History*. Baltimore: Johns Hopkins Press, 1935.

Wendte, Charles W. *Thomas Starr King: Patriot and Preacher*. Boston: Beacon Press, 1921.

Wicher, Edward A. *The Presbyterian Church in California, 1849–1927*. New York: Frederick L. Hitchcock, 1927.

Wilentz, Sean. *Chants Democratic: New York City and the Rise of the American Working Class, 1788–1850*. New York: Oxford University Press, 1986.

Williams, Daniel Day. *The Andover Liberals: A Study in American Theology*. New York: King's Crown Press, 1941.

Wood, Gordon S. *The Creation of the American Republic, 1776–1787*. Chapel Hill: University of North Carolina Press, 1969.

Wright, Louis B. *Culture on the Moving Frontier*. Bloomington: Indiana University Press, 1955.

Wyllie, Irvin G. *The Self-Made Man in America: The Myth of Rags to Riches*. New Brunswick: Rutgers University Press, 1954.

Articles

Bieber, Ralph. "California Gold Mania." *Mississippi Valley Historical Review* 35 (June 1948): 3–28.

Billington, Ray Allen. "Anti-Catholic Propaganda and the Home Missionary Movement, 1800–1860." *Mississippi Valley Historical Review* 22 (1935): 361–84.

Boyd, Lois. "Presbyterian Ministers' Wives—A Nineteenth-Century Portrait." *Journal of Presbyterian History* 59 (Spring 1981): 3–17.

Butler, Jon. "Magic, Astrology, and the Early American Religious Heritage, 1600–1760." *American Historical Review* 84(2) (April 1979): 317–46.

Chrystal, William G. "'A Beautiful Aceldama': Horace Bushnell in California, 1856–1857." *New England Quarterly* 57 (Sept. 1984): 384–402.

Cook, Tony Stanley. "Historical Mythmaking: Richard Henry Dana and American Immigration to California, 1840–1850." *Southern California Quarterly* 68(2) (Summer 1986): 97–117.

Crampton, Charles G. "Gold Rushes and Their Significance in the History of the Trans-Mississippi West." In *Greater America: Essays in Honor of Herbert Eugene Bolton*. Berkeley: University of California Press, 1945.

Ellsworth, Clayton Sumner. "The American Churches and the Mexican War." *American Historical Review* 45(2) (Jan. 1940): 301–26.

Geertz, Clifford. "Religion as a Cultural System." In *The Interpretation of Cultures*. New York: Basic Books, 1973.

Griswold, Robert. "Anglo Women and Domestic Ideology in the American West in the Nineteenth and Early Twentieth Centuries." In *Western Women: Their Land, Their Lives,* ed. Lillian Schlissel, Vicki L. Ruiz, and Janice Monk. Albuquerque: University of New Mexico Press, 1988.

Hanchett, William. "The Blue Law Gospel in Gold Rush California." *Pacific Historical Review* 24 (1955): 361–68.

———. "The Question of Religion and the Taming of California, 1849–1854." Pts. 1–2. *California Historical Society Quarterly* 32 (March): 49–56; and 32 (June): 119–44.

Hansen, Klaus. "The Millennium, the West, and Race in the Antebellum Mind." *Western Historical Quarterly* 3 (Oct. 1972): 373–90.

Hinckley, Ted C. "American Anti-Catholicism during the Mexican War." *Pacific Historical Review* 31 (May 1962): 121–37.

Hodges, Hugh T. "Charles Maclay: California Missionary, San Fernando Valley Pioneer." Pts. 1–3. *Southern California Quarterly* 68 (Summer): 119—66; (Fall): 207–56; (Winter): 329–64.

Jensen, Joan M., and Darlis A. Miller. "The Gentle Tamers Revisited: New Approaches to the History of Women in the American West." *Pacific Historical Review* 49 (May 1980): 173–213.

Luckingham, Bradford. "Benevolence in Emergent San Francisco." *Southern California Quarterly* 55 (4) (1973): 431–43.

Miller, Perry. "Nature and the National Ego." In *Errand into the Wilderness*. Cambridge: Harvard University Press, 1956.

Ogden, Adele. "New England Traders in Spanish and Mexican California." In *Greater America: Essays in Honor of Herbert Eugene Bolton*. Berkeley: University of California Press, 1945.

Pomeroy, Earl. "Josiah Royce: Historian in Quest of Community." *Pacific Historical Review* 40 (Feb. 1971): 1–20.

Rotundo, E. Anthony. "Learning about Manhood: Gender Ideals and the Middle-Class Family in Nineteenth-Century America." In *Manliness and Morality: Middle-Class Masculinity in Britain and America, 1800–1940,* ed. J. A. Mangan and James Walvin. New York: St. Martin's Press, 1987.

Stout, Harry. "Rhetoric and Reality in the Early Republic: The Case of the Federalist Clergy." In *Religion and American Politics: From the Colonial Period to the Present,* ed. Mark A. Noll. New York: Oxford University Press, 1990.

Thomas, John L. "Romantic Reform in America, 1815–1860." *American Quarterly* 17 (Winter 1965): 656–81.

Thompson, E. P. "Time, Work-Discipline, and Industrial Capitalism." *Past and Present* 38 (1967): 56–97.

Turner, Victor W. "Betwixt and Between: The Liminal Period in *Rites de Passage*." In *Reader in Comparative Religion: An Anthropological Approach,* 3d ed., ed. William A. Lessa and Evon Z. Vogt. New York: Harper and Row, 1972.

Wentz, Richard. "Region and Religion in America." *Foundations* 24 (1981): 148–56.

Wright, Doris M. "The Making of Cosmopolitan California: An Analysis of Immigration, 1848–1870." Pts. 1–2. *California Historical Society Quarterly* 19 (Dec. 1940): 323–42; 20 (March 1941): 65–79.

Dissertations

Fabian, Ann Vincent. "Rascals and Gentlemen: The Meaning of American Gambling, 1820–1890." Ph.D. diss. Yale University, 1982.

Janzen, Kenneth L. "The Transformation of the New England Religious Tradition in California, 1849–1869." Ph.D. diss. Claremont Graduate School, 1964.

Johnson, Susan L. "Scratching the Surface and Digging In: Gender, Ethnicity, and Ideology in California's Southern Mines, 1848–1860." Ph.D. diss. Yale University, forthcoming.

Woo, Wesley Stephen. "Protestant Work among the Chinese in the San Francisco Bay Area, 1850–1920." Ph.D diss. Graduate Theological Union, 1984.

Yohn, Susan M. "Religion, Pluralism, and the Limits of Progressive Reform: Presbyterian Women Home Missionaries in New Mexico, 1870–1930." Ph.D. diss. New York University, 1987.

Index

ABCFM. *See* American Board of Commissioners for Foreign Missions (ABCFM)

ABHMS. *See* American Baptist Home Missionary Society (ABHMS)

African-Americans, 114, 182. *See also* Slavery

Agricultural regions, 39, 49, 78–79, 151

AHMS. *See* American Home Missionary Society (AHMS)

Alcohol, 82, 117, 125, 129, 134, 139–40, 151, 157, 158

American Baptist Home Missionary Society (ABHMS), 13, 14, 17, 31, 40, 44, 65, 69, 105, 106, 108

American Board of Commissioners for Foreign Missions (ABCFM), 43, 171

American Home Missionary Society (AHMS): and Brayton, 100, 102, 107; and California, 44, 64, 102; on Catholics, 32; and competing denominational obligations, 42; financial condition of, 108; founding of, 14; on homogeneity as goal, 23; and Hunt, 70; and Lacy, 96; missionaries' letters to, 91, 97, 98, 156; missionaries of, 39, 66, 81, 82; and paucity of missionaries in California, 106, 108; and Pond, 95; and salaries of missionaries, 99; and Willey, 86, 97, 104; withdrawal of New School Presbyterians from, 182. See also *Home Missionary*

American Indians, 42, 43, 115, 116, 118–19

Anderson, Rufus, 69

Anderson, William C., 68

Anglo immigrants. *See* Miners

Anthony, Charles V., 72

Anthony, Elihu, 72

Anti-Catholicism, 31–34

Antislavery. *See* Slavery

Asbury, Francis, 167

Avery, J. H., 62

Badger, Milton, 46–47, 86–87, 107

Baker, A. A., 90, 92, 94

Baker, O. C., 95

Bancroft, Hubert Howe, 111

Baptist church: in California, 3, 6, 24, 94, 109, 144, 182; in East and Midwest, 6; field agents in, 107; and home mission societies, 14, 22, 42; and millennial importance of western progress, 52; ministers in California, 64–65, 71–72, 78, 92; and paucity of missionaries to California, 105–6; regressive and progressive elements of, 28; salary of missionaries, 99; and self-discipline, 21

Barnes, Albert, 25, 27

Barrows, Rev. E. P., 26

Bartlett, Rev. William, 78

Beecher, Edward, 47–50

Beecher, Lyman, 30, 31, 32, 35, 47

Bell, Samuel B., 78, 82, 89

Beman, Rev. N. S. S., 24–25

Bemis, Henry, 61

Benton, Rev. Joseph A., 85, 89, 154

Benton, Thomas Hart, 40

Billington, Ray Allen, 31

Blacks. *See* African-Americans; Slavery

Blakeslee, Samuel, 107

Blakeslee, Sarah, 176–77

Boutelle, A., 61

Boyle, Charles Elisha, 135

Brayton, Rev. Isaac, 81, 91, 100, 102, 103

Brewster, William, 69
Brier, William W., 77, 93, 94, 100
Brierly, Rev. David, 31
Briggs, Martin Clock, 73, 84
Brigham, Charles, 6, 54, 57, 60
Bryant, Edwin, 40, 66
Buchanan, P. G., 49
Burgess, Rev. George, 54
Burial rites, 61, 126–27
Burrowes, George, 68, 173
Burrowes, Mrs. George, 170–71
Bushnell, Horace, 2, 33–34, 36, 54–56, 104, 156
Butler, Jon, 112, 129

Caldwell, Rev. George, 62
Caldwell, S. L., 51, 60
California: agricultural districts in, 78–79; as all-male culture, 150–51; after Civil War, 146–47, 181–85; creation of sacred landscape in, 80–85; easterners' perceptions of, 98–99, 101–4; economy of, 77–78, 95, 102–3, 113; erratic development of towns in, 76–77; evangelicals' interest in, before gold rush, 38–39, 43–44; failure of revivalism in, 78–79; frontier California as term, 11; growth and change of, 48–50, 74–77, 105, 146–47, 181–85; heterogeneity of, 48–51, 74–75, 96, 113–19, 130; moral diversity in, 86–109, 117–18, 123–25, 182–83; natural beauty of, 84–85, 109; natural disasters in, 79–80; population of, 39, 105, 113–14, 150–51; Protestant evangelicalism's significance in, 182–85; social fluidity in, 75–76; spiritual perils of, 57, 59–62, 84, 93–94, 120, 131; statistics on churches in, 5–6, 182–83; and trade, 39–40; travel literature on, 40, 66–67. See also Gold rush; San Francisco; Westward expansion California Christian Advocate, 48, 49, 81, 84, 107, 154, 168
Capen, Rev. James W., 65, 98–99, 105
Catholic church. See Roman Catholic church
Chapin, Rev. Steven, 13–14, 17, 21
Chase, Nathan, 136
Cheney, D. B., 94, 106–7, 108–9
Chinese immigrants, 48, 51, 74, 96, 114, 166

Christmas, 128–29
Church, Osgood, 44
Church attendance, 88, 90–91, 125, 144, 145, 160, 166
Church bells, 82–83
Church buildings, 78–82, 84, 92, 95, 133, 153
Churches. See Protestant evangelicalism; and specific denominations
Civil War, 182
Clark, William, 16
Cleaveland, Elisha Lord, 51, 120
Clergy. See Ministers
Coates, Reynell, 54
Congregational church: in California, 6, 182; and Calvinist understanding of human nature, 22; church attendance versus church membership, 90; church buildings in California, 81; in East and Midwest, 6; and home mission societies, 14, 15, 18; image of woman in, 153; laity's role in, 87; and Mexican War, 40–41; ministers in California, 65, 71, 72, 102, 185; organizational inflexibility of, 107; and paucity of ministers in California, 108; Puritan heritage of, 18, 19; and religious independence of miners, 91; women's contributions to, 153
Conversion, 111, 135, 144, 156–57, 185
Cool, Peter J., 72
Cutler, Rufus, 82

Dana, Richard Henry, Jr., 40
Davis, Andrew Jackson, 90
Davis, Charles, 121, 136
Davis, David Brion, 35
Deal, David, 84, 90
Decker, Peter, 115, 119, 122–23, 127–28
Delano, Ephraim, 120–21
Diehl, David, 80
Doble, Abner, 140
Doble, Catherine Huffman, 137
Doble, John, 137–46, 160
Doble, Margaret, 140
Doble, William, 137
Doten, Alfred, 114, 115, 117, 118, 119, 127, 128, 131, 134, 146
Douglas, Rev. John W., 44, 93, 97, 156, 168
Drunkenness. See Alcohol
Dunleavy, Mary Ann, 165
Dwight, Timothy, 30, 84

Earthquakes, 84
Eaton, Maj. Amos B., 156
Eaton, Herrick M., 168–69
Edwards, B. B., 18, 29, 30
Eliade, Mircea, 80–81, 83
Episcopal church, 3, 14, 54, 58–59, 105
Ethnic groups. *See* African-Americans;
    Chinese immigrants; Hispanics
Evangelical United Front, 42, 74
Evangelicalism. *See* Protestant evangeli-
    calism
Everbeck, Charles, 115

Fabian, Ann, 122, 129
Family, 135–37, 154–56, 160–61, 175–76
Farley, Rev. Charles, 58
Farnham, Thomas Jefferson, 40
Ferguson, Charles D., 115–16, 132, 146,
    159
Findlay, John, 119–20
Finney, Charles Grandison, 15, 183
Fires, 79, 84
First Great Awakening, 52
Fisher, Rev. Samuel W., 18, 27–28
Flint, Timothy, 37
Foster, Joseph C., 61
Frankiel, Sandra Sizer, 185
Franklin, Benjamin, 140
Fremont, Lt. Col. John C., 40, 67, 92
Frink, Margaret, 165
Frothingham, Nathaniel, 57
Funerals. *See* Burial rites
Fur trade, 39–40

Gambling, 82, 102, 122–23, 125, 127, 129,
    143–44, 151, 154, 161, 184
Geertz, Clifford, 130
Gender issues. *See* Women
George, Henry, 184
Giddings, Samuel, 37
Ginzburg, Carlo, 113
Gladden, Washington, 185
Gold rush: author's approach to, 9–10;
    beginning of, 44–45; discovery of gold
    as conversion experience, 111; growth
    of settlements due to, 48–50; and
    heterogeneous character of California
    immigrants, 48–51; and meaning and
    purpose of wealth, 54–62; Protestant
    evangelicals' view of, 1–3, 45–54, 81,
    87–88; Puritan connection to, 47–48;

reactions to gold discoveries in rest of
    U.S., 44–45; and slavery, 47–48; and
    values of wealth versus Christian piety,
    4–5, 46, 56–62, 184; wealth from,
    102–3. *See also* Miners; Mining
Grenell, Levi, 105
Griswold, Robert, 163

Hale, John G., 98, 153
Hall, David D., 129
Hamilton, Rev. Laurentine, 91, 160
Harmon, Mrs. Silas S., 169
Harmon, Silas S., 77, 80, 98, 100, 169
Hart, Rev. Burdett, 40–41
Haskins, C. W., 124
Hays, Lorena L., 2
Hickock, Rev. M. J., 14, 19
Hill, Alonzo A., 118, 121–22, 136
Hilton, Stephen, 182
Hispanics, 114, 115, 118, 119, 122, 166
Hittell, John, 185
Holiday celebrations, 128–29
Home mission societies: beginnings of, 3,
    14; and belief in innate superiority of
    American character, 23–26; after Civil
    War, 182; concerns about strategy of,
    97–109; contradictions in, 36–37, 59–62;
    in early nineteenth century, 14–16;
    ecumenical nature of, 15, 22, 36; in
    *1840*s, 41–44; and fear of heterogeneity,
    23–26; female religious influence on,
    152–67; financial support of, 152–53;
    and gold rush, 45–54, 87–88; interest in
    California before gold rush, 39, 43–44;
    and Mexican War, 40–41; in Midwest,
    48–49; and millennial importance of
    western progress, 26–31, 49–53; minis-
    ters' conflicts with eastern missionary
    boards, 97–109; in Pacific Northwest in
    *1840*s, 42–43; perceived threats to,
    31–36; and preservation of eastern
    culture, 35–36; Puritanism versus
    Republicanism in, 17–23; and sacred
    American destiny, 13–23; women's
    organizational skills in, 152–53. *See also*
    Ministers *Home Missionary,* 17, 26, 28,
    32, 36, 41, 44, 45, 50, 66, 67, 71, 77, 83,
    89, 96, 101, 102, 103, 131, 152
Horsman, Reginald, 25
Howe, Daniel Walker, 17
Hunt, Mary Hedges, 70, 71, 171–77, 179

Hunt, Timothy Dwight, 69–71, 90, 92–95, 102, 153–54, 171–74, 177
Hutchison, William, 18

Immigrants. *See* African-Americans; Chinese immigrants; Hispanics; Miners; Women
Indians. *See* American Indians
Iowa, 5–6, 39, 49, 98, 150

Jackson, Andrew, 17, 40
Jefferson, Thomas, 16
Johnson, Paul, 119
Johnson, Samuel Roosevelt, 58–59
Jones, Rev. W. L., 90, 97

Kalloch, Amariah, 105
Kellogg, Rev. Martin, 88–89, 108
Kenaga, Levi, 120, 126–27
King, Thomas Starr, 72
Kip, William Ingraham, 54

Lacy, Edward S., 96
Larkin, Thomas Oliver, 39, 40
Lee, Jason, 42, 43
Lewis, Meriwether, 16
Lucas, Lizzie, 140–42, 144, 160
Lunt, William, 58

McClure, Rev. David, 89
McDannell, Colleen, 150
MacKenna, Benjamin Vicuña, 122–23
Maclay, Charles, 67
Madison, James, 30
Manifest destiny. *See* Westward expansion
Marriage, 135–36, 156, 158–60, 166, 167–79
Marsden, George, 42
Marsh, Newell, 61
Marshall, James, 44
Masquerade balls, 148–49
Megquier, Mary Jane, 164
Merrill, Jerusha, 165, 166
Methodist (Episcopal) church: in California, 3, 6, 9, 43, 44, 92, 95, 144, 145, 182; church attendance versus church membership of, 90; and distinctive nature of California, 107–8; in East and Midwest, 6; field agents in, 107; and home mission societies, 14, 22, 42; and land titles in California, 104; lay leader-

ship in, 87; married clergy in, 167, 168; and Mexican War, 41; and millennial importance of western progress, 52; ministers in California, 64–66, 67, 72, 73, 80, 82, 84, 88, 125, 156, 161; in Oregon, 39; and religious independence of miners, 91–92; salary of missionaries, 99; and self-discipline, 21
Mexican War, 40–41, 137, 146
Mexicans. *See* Hispanics
Millennialism, 26–31, 49–53
Miller, Perry, 3
Millerite adventism, 42, 53
Miners: age of, 74, 132, 134–35; alcohol use of, 117, 125, 129, 134, 139–40, 158; in all-male culture, 150–51; Anglos as, 119–20; and burial rites, 61, 126–27; church attendance of, 90–91, 125, 144, 145, 160; and decline of gold mining in California, 146–47; and divination and magical practices, 123–24; domestic activities of, 160–61; entertainment of, 127; ethics of, 110–13, 140–46; ethnic and racial diversity of, 48–51, 113–19, 130; failure of revivalism with, 92–96; financial condition of, 113, 146; gambling of, 122–23, 125, 127, 129, 143–44, 161; holiday celebrations of, 128–29; and images of evangelical womanhood, 158–63; inaccessibility of churches to, 107, 116–17; in-depth portrait of Doble, 137–46; ministers as, 71, 72, 100, 106; ministers' instructions to, 60–62, 120, 142; moral and religious diversity of, 86–113, 117–18, 123–25, 133–34, 140–46, 160, 183; reasons for coming to California, 74, 131–37; relations with ministers, 97, 133–34, 137, 144; risk-taking of, 120–22; Sabbath observation of, 82, 116–17, 127–29; strikes of, 77; suicide of, 121–22; trip as rite of passage for, 134–35
Mining: decline of, 146, 181; easterners' view of, 103, 121; risk involved in, 120–22; seasonal and sporadic character of, 76; service industries for, 113; in states other than California, 147, 181, 185; statistics on population engaged in, 113; types of, 75, 76, 121
Ministers: age of, 74; association of wilderness with spiritual chaos, 80–81;

author's use of term, 9; characteristics
of, 64–74; and church attendance
versus church membership, 90–91, 144;
conflicts with eastern missionary
boards, 97–109; and distinctiveness of
California, 92–93, 107–9; in East and
Midwest versus California, 6; establishment of Christian institutions by, 95–97,
98; and failure of revivalism, 92–96;
financial conditions of, in California, 72,
99–101, 170, 174; geographic origins of,
65–66; homes of, 169–71; and image of
evangelical womanhood, 152–67; and
infidelity of miners, 89–90; instructions
to miners on immigration to California,
60–62, 120, 142; and lay leadership, 87;
as miners, 71, 72, 100, 106; and moral
diversity in California, 86–109; obstacles
faced by, 74–80, 88–91, 130–31;
optimism on spiritual growth of
California, 86–88, 91–92, 109; paucity
of, 105–7; reasons for going to
California, 66–74; relations with miners,
97, 133–34, 137, 144; and religious independence of miners, 91–92; responsibilities of, 63–64; sacred order imposed
on physical landscape by, 80–85;
salaries of, 99, 170; and social fluidity in
California, 75–76; southern missionaries, 8–9; statistics on, in California, 65;
use of idioms of battle by, 62; wives of,
167–79
Missionaries. *See* Home mission societies;
Ministers
"Moral vacuum" theory, 33–35
Mormonism, 34, 38, 42, 53, 117, 124, 145
Motherhood, as symbol, 155
Moxley, Charles, 126
Mulford, Prentice, 135

Nativism, 31, 32, 116
Natural disasters, 79–80, 84
New School Presbyterians, 40, 42, 65, 66,
69, 182
New Years' Day, 129
New York, 5–6
Newell, Rev. W. W., 46
Newman, W. S., 113

Ohio, 5–6, 39, 49
Old School Presbyterians, 3, 14, 19, 155

Oregon, 37, 39, 42, 43, 76, 79, 150
Owen, Isaac, 71

Pacific Northwest, 42–43
Paul, Rodman, 147, 185
Perkins, Elisha Douglass, 115, 126
Perlot, Jean-Nicholas, 116
Peters, Rev. Absalom, 26–27
Pierpont, Mrs. James, 83
Pierpont, Rev. James, 76, 77, 79, 83
Pitt, Leonard, 113
Plan of Union of *1801*, 3, 65
Polk, James, 40, 41
Pond, Enoch, 67
Pond, Rev. William C., 67–68, 90, 95–96,
98, 169–70
Presbyterian church: in California, 3, 6,
182; and Calvinist understanding of
human nature, 22; church buildings in
California, 82; and divine mission of
America, 19; in East and Midwest, 6;
and heterogeneity of western popula-
tion, 25; and home mission societies,
14, 15; image of women in, 153, 155;
laity's role in, 87; and Mexican War, 40;
ministers in California, 65, 68–72, 76,
77, 90, 91, 156, 160, 170, 177, 185; organizational inflexibility of, 107; and paucity
of ministers in California, 108; and religious independence of miners, 91;
seminary of, 68; women's contributions
to, 153
Prevaux, Francis, 92, 94–95, 100–101, 105
Prosperity. *See* Wealth
Prostitution, 149, 154, 161–62, 166, 185
Protestant evangelicalism: and ambivalence toward western expansion,
29–30, 36, 51; and America's covenantal
relation with God, 13–14, 17–20; and
America's political genius, 19–21; and
Anglo-Saxon superiority, 25–26; and
belief in superiority of American character, 23–26; beliefs and values of, 4–5,
16–37, 119–20, 156–57, 184–85; after
Civil War, 182–85; and cultural homogenization, 23, 35; and fear of heterogeneity, 23–26, 50–51; and gender issues, 5,
149–80; and gold rush, 1–3, 45–54,
87–88; interest in California before
gold rush, 38–39, 43–44; and Mexican War, 40–41; and millennial

Protestant evangelicalism *(continued)*
  importance of western progress, 26–31,
  49–53; perceived threats to, 31–36; and
  preservation of eastern culture, 35–36;
  Puritan heritage of, 17–19, 20, 21–22;
  and Roman Catholic church, 31–33;
  and sacred American destiny, 13–23;
  significance of, in California, 182–85;
  southern evangelicals, 8–9; statistics,
  5–6, 182; and wealth, 46, 54–62; and
  Whig party, 17, 26; withdrawal of
  support for the West, 182–83. *See also*
  Home mission societies; Ministers; and
  specific denominations
Protestant liberalism, 184–85
Puritanism, 17–22, 33–34, 47, 48, 55–56

Quinn, D. Michael, 129

Racial groups. *See* African-Americans;
  Chinese immigrants; Hispanics
Rauschenbusch, Walter, 185
Republicanism, 19–21
Revivalism, 3, 8, 15, 23–24, 41, 52, 86,
  92–96, 156–57
Rite of passage, 134–35
Robinson, Alfred, 40
Rogers, Daniel T., 56
Rollinson, Rev. William, 78
Roman Catholic church, 6, 31–34, 38, 44,
  78, 88–89, 116–18, 144
Rousseau, Jean-Jacques, 36
Royce, Josiah, 1, 111–12
Royce, Sarah, 149, 166
Ryan, Mary, 153

Sabbath observation, 82, 116–17, 127–29,
  160
Sacramento: changes in, 99; churches in,
  78, 79; Dr. "Y" in, 158; honesty of inhabitants of, 115; Kalloch preaching in, 105;
  miners in off-season in, 76; as relative
  havens of stability, 77; river, 114; as stopping point for migrants, 75
San Francisco: after *1860*, 182; boarding
  houses in, 164–65; churches in, 78, 80,
  82, 90, 94–96, 100, 123, 149, 173–74;
  clergy's views of, 2; economy of, 95; in
  1845, 38; in *1859*, 1; in *1860*s, 74; fire in,
  80, 84; gambling and moral disorder in,
  77, 82, 102, 122–23; and gold discover-

ies, 44; hotel accommodations in, 75;
  masquerade balls in, 148–49; miners in
  off-season in, 76; ministers' salaries in,
  72; street preachers in, 82; women in,
  149, 164–65, 173–74
Scott, J. W., 28–29
Second Great Awakening, 3, 15, 37, 42
Self-discipline, 21, 119–20, 130, 131, 137,
  139–46
Seminaries, 22, 65, 66–69, 108
Shepard, Rev. George, 46, 49
Shipps, Jan, 53
Shirley, Dame, 110–12, 115, 120, 125, 142,
  166–67
Simonds, S. D., 84–85, 156
Slavery, 34–35, 41, 47–48, 92, 114, 155
Smith, Rev. A. D., 48
Smith, Joseph, Jr., 53
Sobel, Mechal, 131
Southern evangelicals, 8–9
Spiritualism, 89–90, 117, 123–24, 145
Starr, Kevin, 11
Steele, John, 116, 122, 123, 158
Stout, Harry, 20
Suicide, 121–22
Swain, William, 125
Sweet, William Warren, 6

Taylor, Bayard, 1, 115, 181
Taylor, Nathaniel William, 22–23
Taylor, Rev. William, 71, 82, 92–93, 96, 100,
  125, 161
Thanksgiving, 128
Thayer, William, 57
Thomas, Keith, 123
Thoreau, Henry, 84
Trade, 39–40
Travel literature, 40, 66–67
Turner, Victor, 134–35
Tyler, E. Royall, 41
Tyler, John, 40

Unitarian church, 58, 72, 82
Unruh, John D., Jr., 129

Ver Mehr, Rev. Jean Leonard, 126
Vigilanteeism, 114–16, 185

Wadsworth, Rev. Charles, 19, 25, 33, 53,
  155
Walsworth, Edward B., 66, 91, 177–78

Walsworth, Sarah, 90–91, 177–78
Warren, Rev. J. H., 81, 83, 102–3, 108, 133
Washburn, Charles, 158–59
Wealth, 46, 54–62, 102–3, 120, 184
Webber, L. P., 173
Webber, Mrs. L. P., 170
Welles, C. M., 125, 132, 133, 134
Westover, Charles, 160
Westward expansion: ambivalence toward, 29–30, 36, 51–52, 80–81; millennial importance of, 26–31, 49–53; and sacred American destiny, 13–23; selective process of migration, 129; and sex ratios, 150–51; and slavery, 34–35. *See also* California; Gold rush
Wheeler, Elizabeth Hamilton, 44
Wheeler, Osgood Church, 24, 65, 76, 84, 88, 91, 100, 105
Whig party, 17, 26, 50
Whipple-Haslam, Mrs. Lee, 115
Whitman, Marcus, 42, 43
Whitman, Narcissa, 43
Whitman, Walt, 27
Willey, Mrs. Samuel Hopkins, 179
Willey, Samuel Hopkins: and AHMS, 86–87, 97, 104; on California, 74, 76, 79, 97, 107, 117; correspondence of, 101–2; decision to become missionary, 66; on duties of minister, 63–64; on family, 156; geographic origins of, 65; on gold rush, 87–88; and lack of information about California, 73; on ministers as miners, 71; on easterners' views of California, 99, 103–4; San Francisco church of, 82; travel to California, 44, 66
Williams, Carrie, 167
Willing, M. E., 88, 92
Winthrop, John, 37
Wolcott, L. M., 116–17
Women: church attendance and religious observations of, 166–67, 175; church organizational and fund-raising activities of, 148–49, 152–53, 159–60, 173–74; difficulties of, in California, 173–79; employment of, 164–66; and female friends and relatives, 171, 176–79; idealization of evangelical womanhood, 5, 150, 152–67, 174–75; as ladies, 166; at masquerade balls in San Francisco, 148–49; and migration to agricultural regions, 151; ministers' image of, 152–67; as ministers' wives, 167–79; on morality in mining towns, 110–11, 112, 115; motherhood as symbol, 155–56; and prostitution, 149, 154, 161–62, 166; reasons for coming to the West, 163–63, 179; reform activities of, 163–64; salaries of, 165; and sex ratios in U.S. versus the West, 150–51; as spiritual caretakers of men, 156–58
Woods, Daniel B., 2, 118, 121, 160, 161, 183
Woods, Leonard, 22–23
Worcester, Samuel, 46, 48
Wright, Louis B., 6

Zelie, J. S., 88, 93